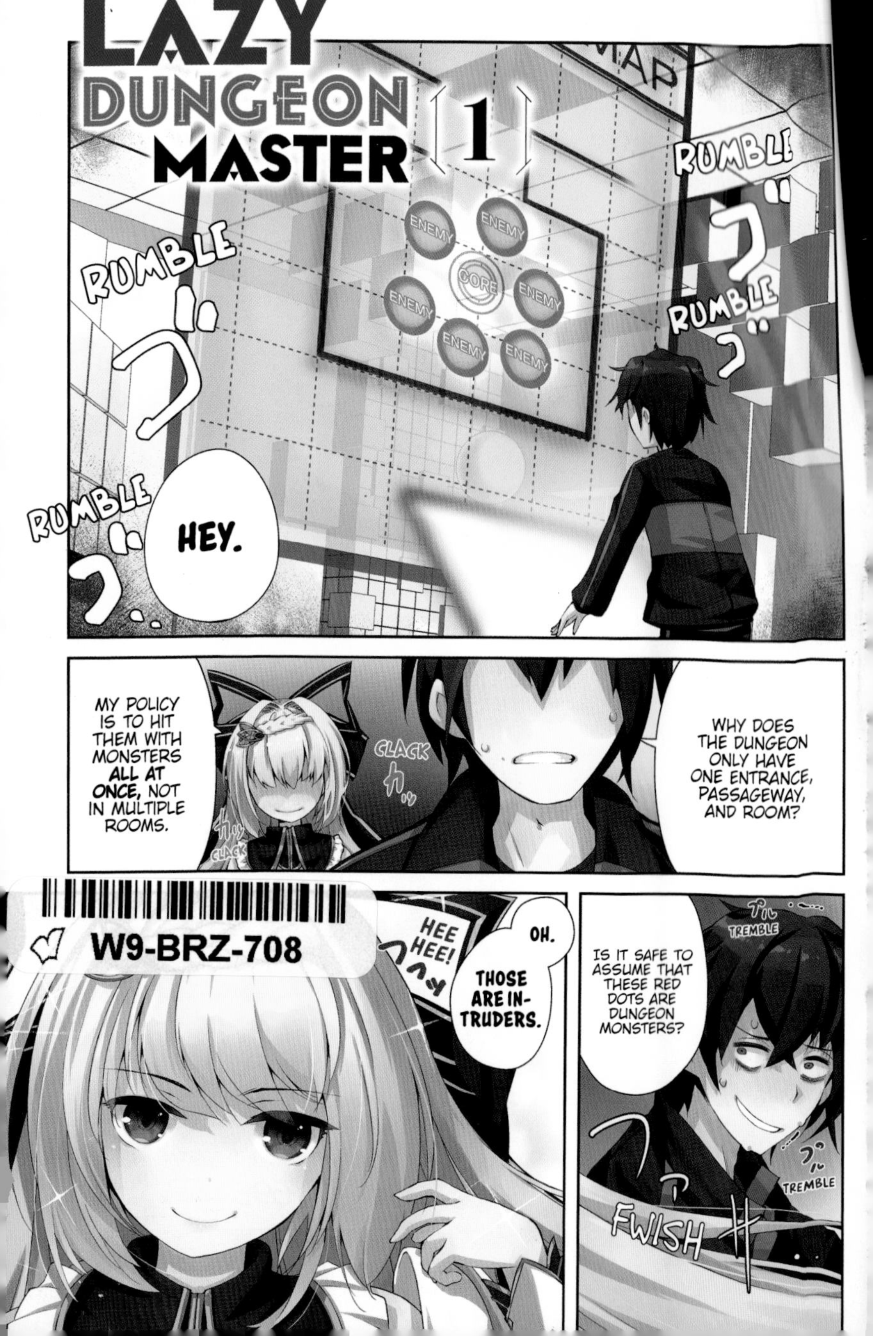
LAZY DUNGEON MASTER 1
MAP
ENEMY
ENEMY
CORE
ENEMY
ENEMY
ENEMY
ENEMY
RUMBLE
RUMBLE
RUMBLE
RUMBLE
HEY.
WHY DOES THE DUNGEON ONLY HAVE ONE ENTRANCE, PASSAGEWAY, AND ROOM?
CLACK
CLACK
MY POLICY IS TO HIT THEM WITH MONSTERS **ALL AT ONCE,** NOT IN MULTIPLE ROOMS.
TREMBLE
IS IT SAFE TO ASSUME THAT THESE RED DOTS ARE DUNGEON MONSTERS?
TREMBLE
FWISH
OH.
THOSE ARE IN-TRUDERS.
HEE HEE!

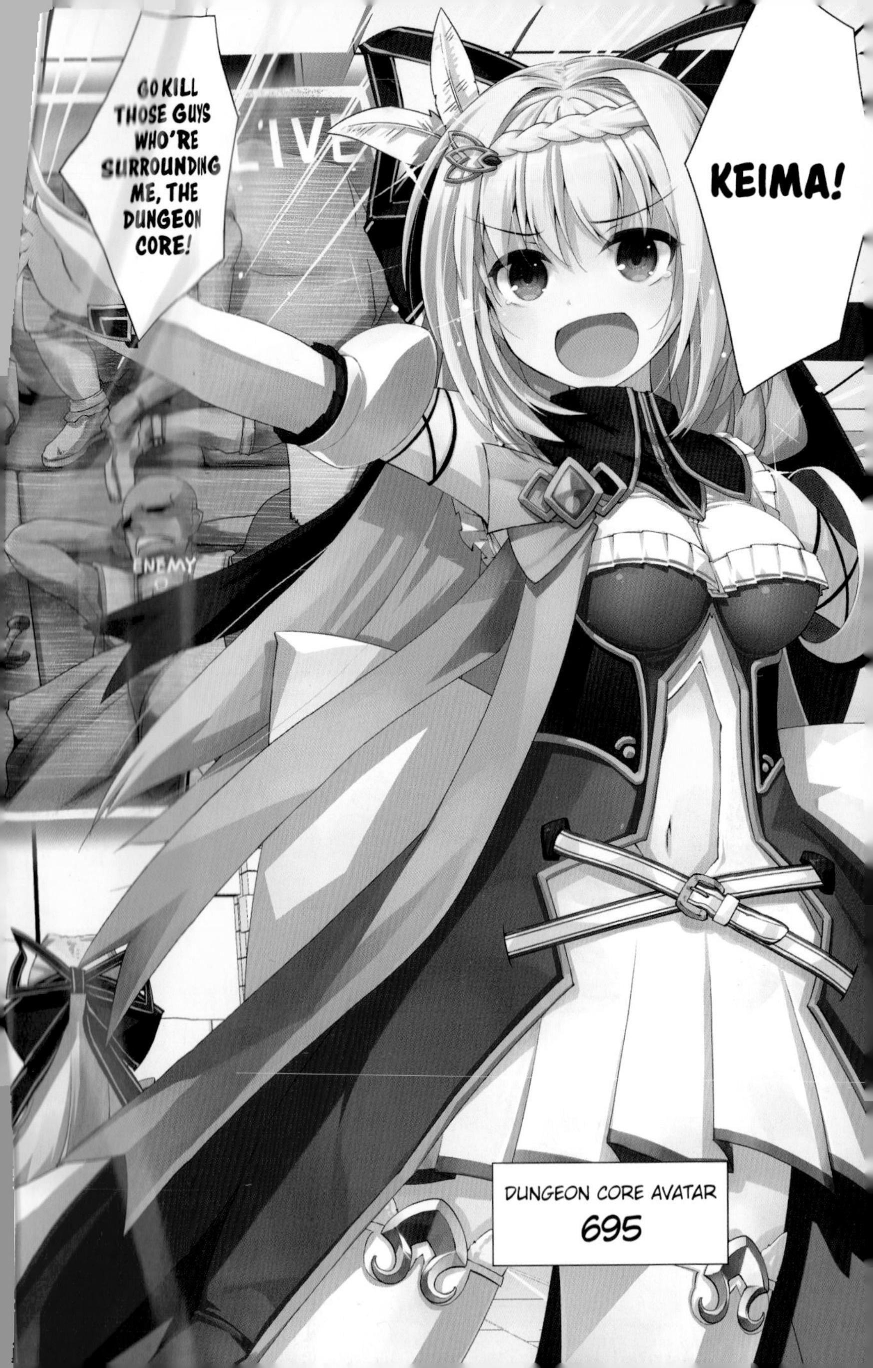
KEIMA!
GO KILL THOSE GUYS WHO'RE SURROUNDING ME, THE DUNGEON CORE!
ENEMY
DUNGEON CORE AVATAR
695

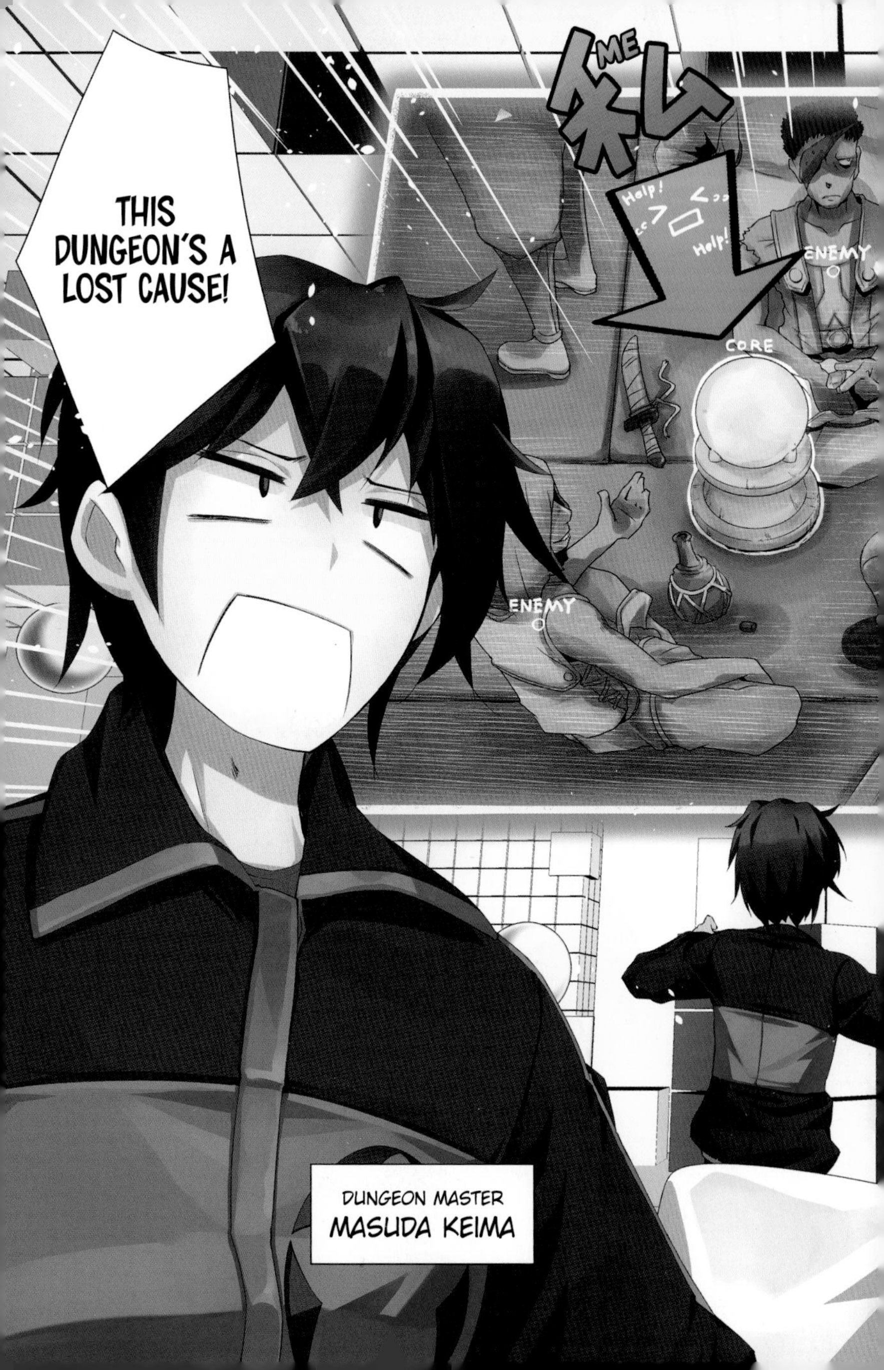
ME
Help!
Help!
ENEMY
CORE
THIS DUNGEON'S A LOST CAUSE!
ENEMY
DUNGEON MASTER
MASUDA KEIMA

LAZY DUNGEON MASTER

CONTENTS

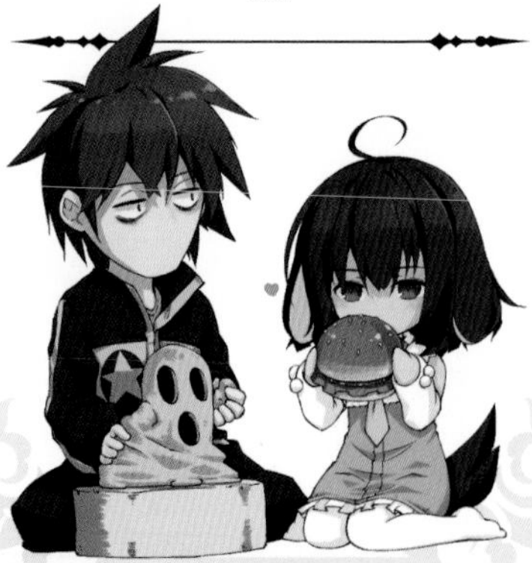

Chapter 1 The Lazy Dungeon Master

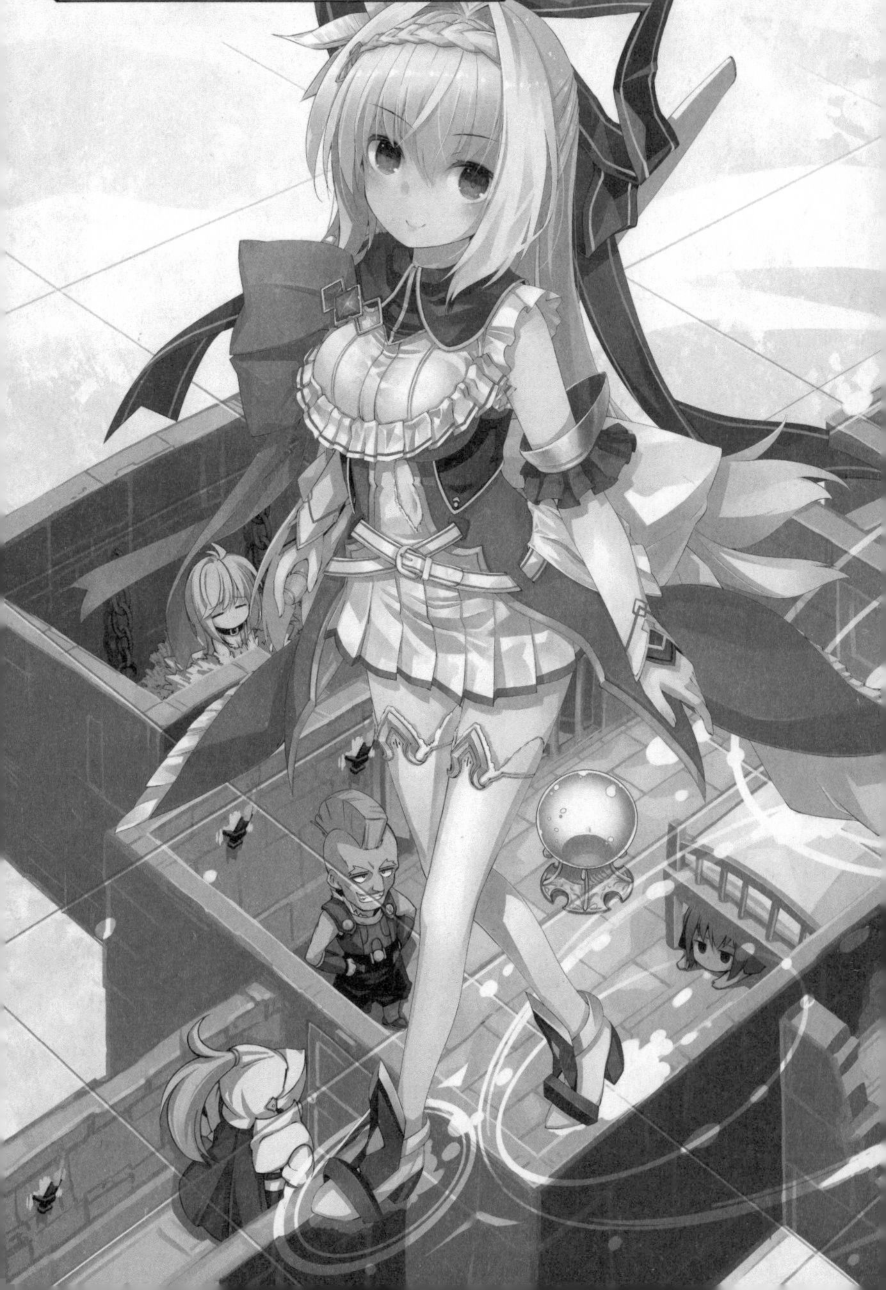

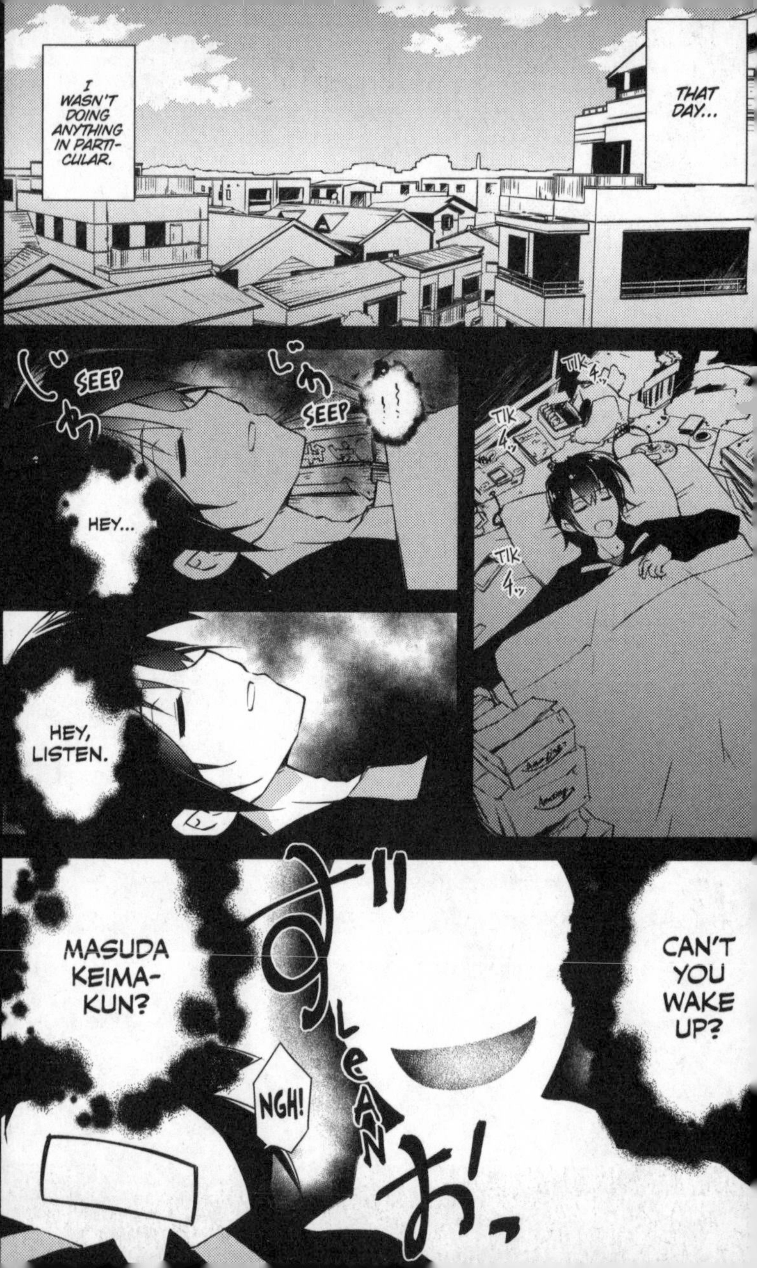

THAT DAY...
I WASN'T DOING ANYTHING IN PARTICULAR.
TIK
TIK
TIK
SEEP
SEEP
HEY...
HEY, LISTEN.
CAN'T YOU WAKE UP?
LEAN
MASUDA KEIMA-KUN?
NGH!

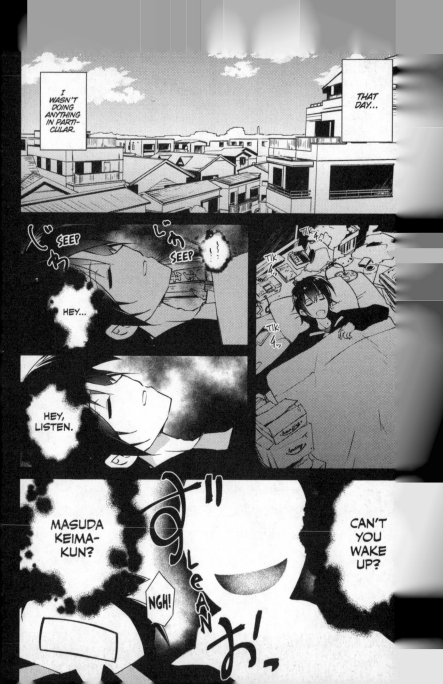

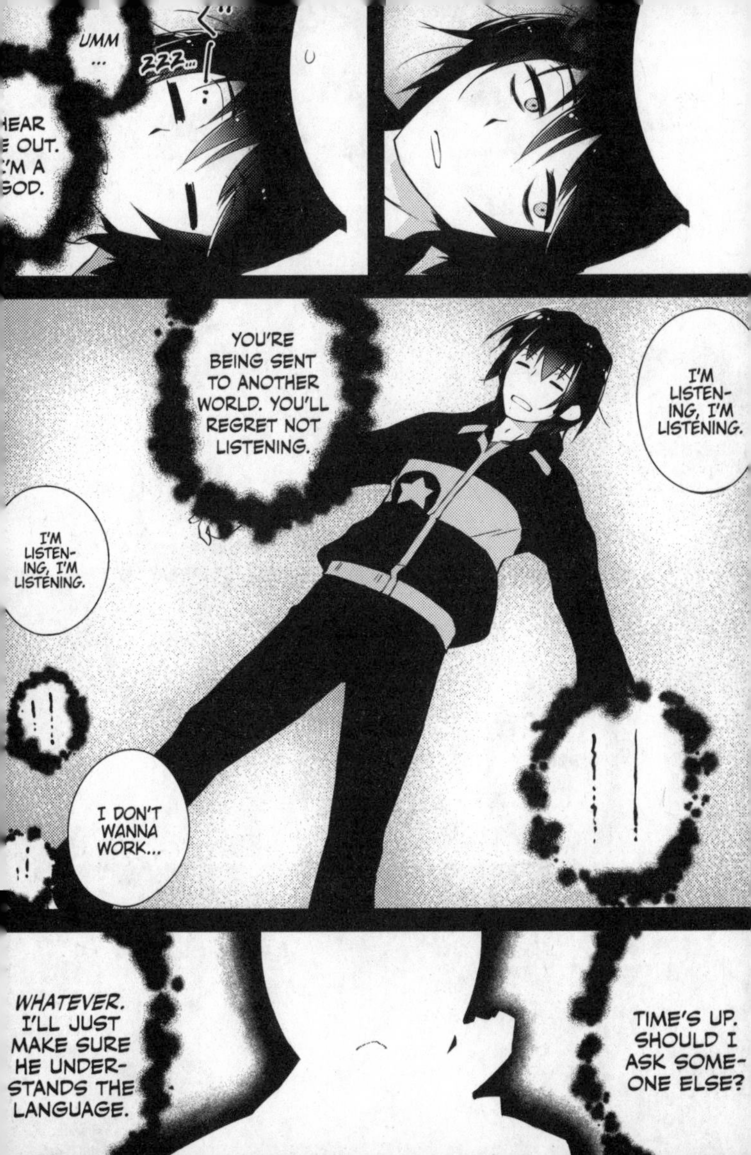
ZZZ...!
UMM...
HEAR
E OUT.
'M A
GOD.
I'M LISTENING, I'M LISTENING.
YOU'RE BEING SENT TO ANOTHER WORLD. YOU'LL REGRET NOT LISTENING.
I'M LISTENING, I'M LISTENING.
...!
!!
I DON'T WANNA WORK...
TIME'S UP. SHOULD I ASK SOMEONE ELSE?
WHATEVER. I'LL JUST MAKE SURE HE UNDERSTANDS THE LANGUAGE.

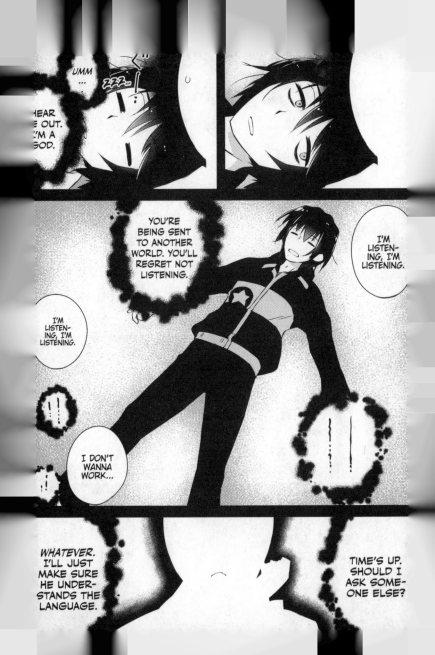

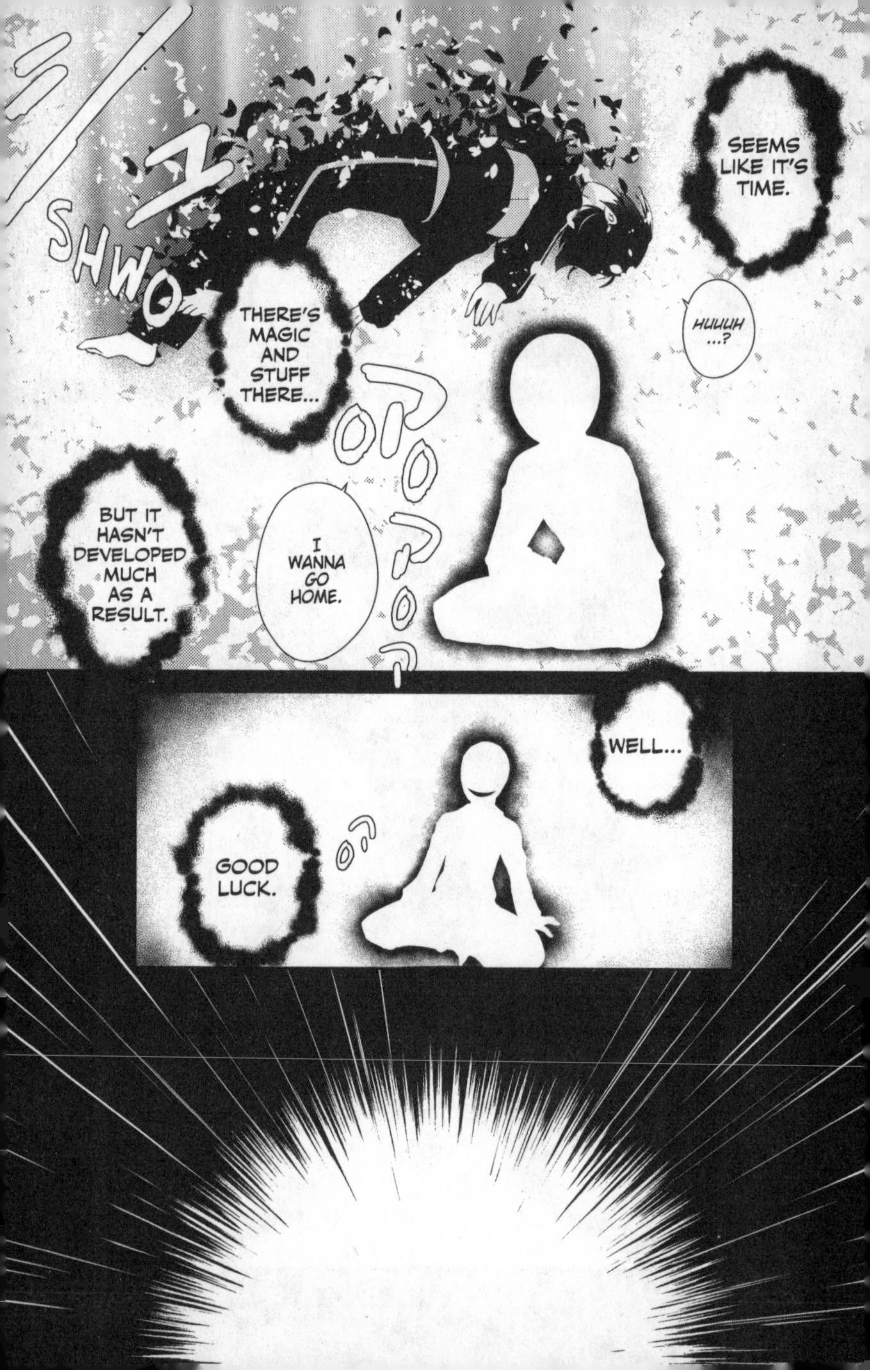
SEEMS LIKE IT'S TIME.
HUUUH ...?
SHWO
THERE'S MAGIC AND STUFF THERE...
I WANNA GO HOME.
BUT IT HASN'T DEVELOPED MUCH AS A RESULT.
WELL...
GOOD LUCK.

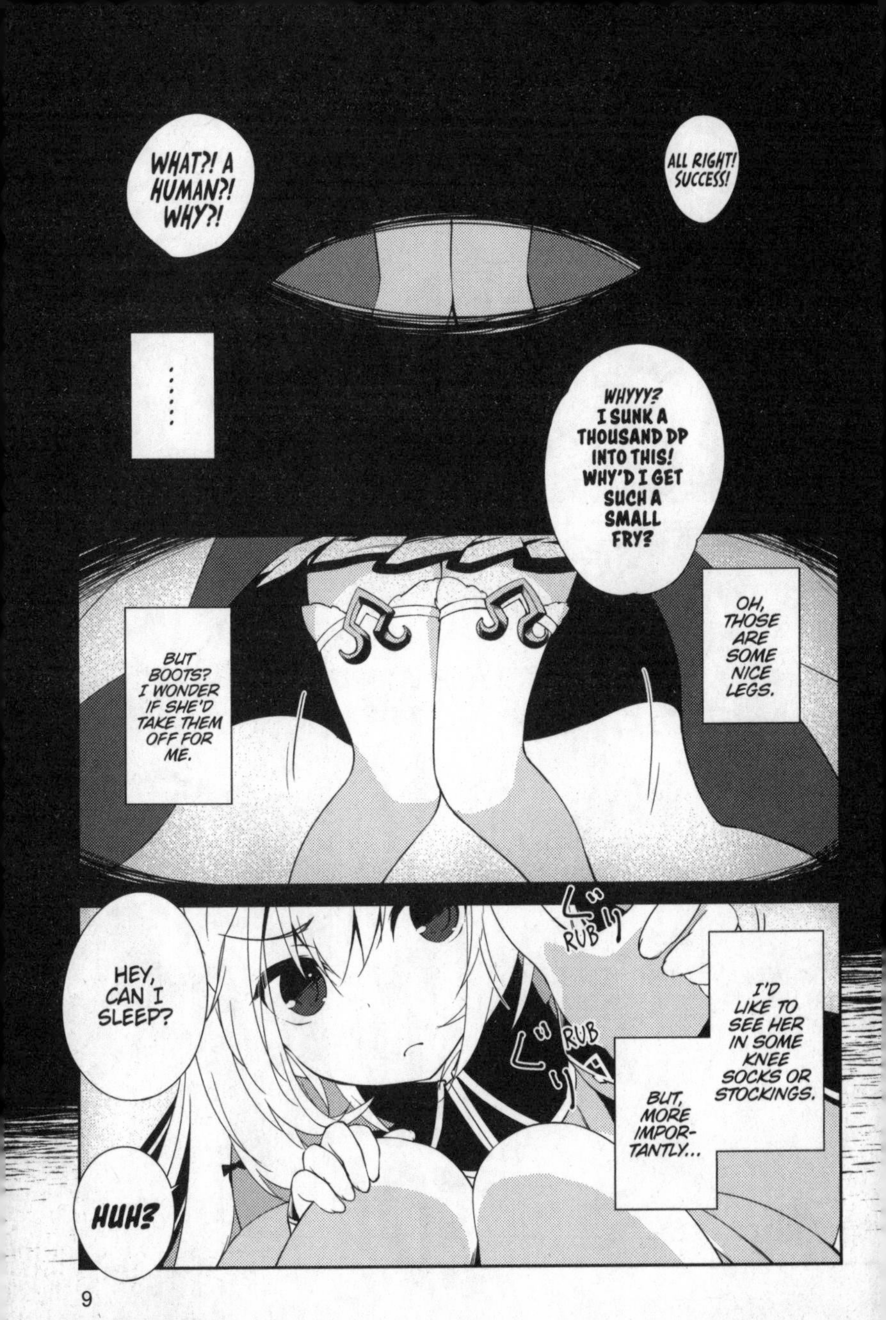
ALL RIGHT! SUCCESS!
WHAT?! A HUMAN?! WHY?!
......
WHYYY? I SUNK A THOUSAND DP INTO THIS! WHY'D I GET SUCH A SMALL FRY?
OH, THOSE ARE SOME NICE LEGS.
BUT BOOTS? I WONDER IF SHE'D TAKE THEM OFF FOR ME.
RUB
I'D LIKE TO SEE HER IN SOME KNEE SOCKS OR STOCKINGS.
RUB
BUT, MORE IMPOR-TANTLY...
HEY, CAN I SLEEP?
HUH?

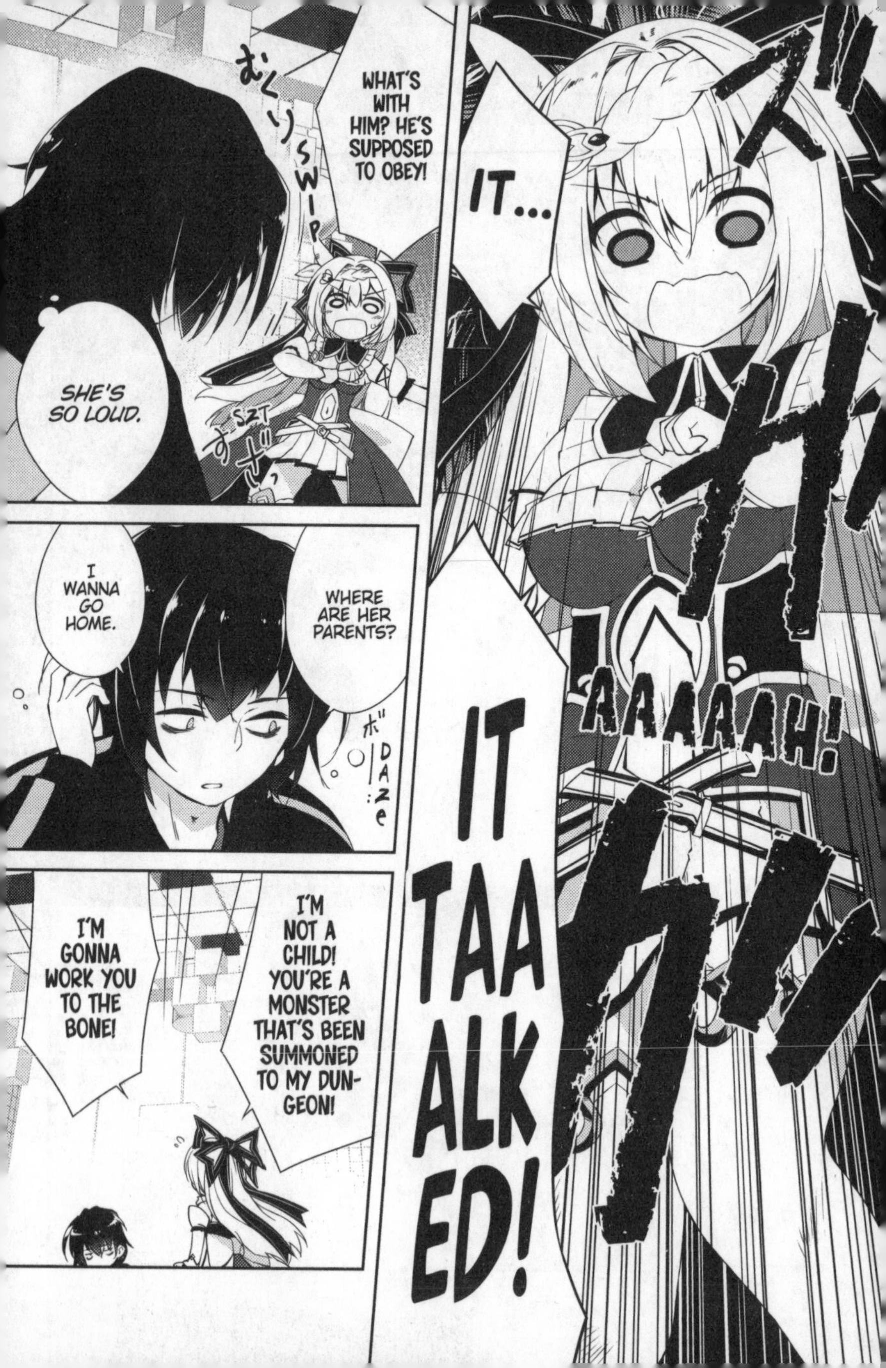
IT...
IT TAALKED!
AAAAAH!
WHAT'S WITH HIM? HE'S SUPPOSED TO OBEY!
SWIP
SHE'S SO LOUD.
SZT
WHERE ARE HER PARENTS?
I WANNA GO HOME.
DAZE
I'M NOT A CHILD! YOU'RE A MONSTER THAT'S BEEN SUMMONED TO MY DUN-GEON!
I'M GONNA WORK YOU TO THE BONE!

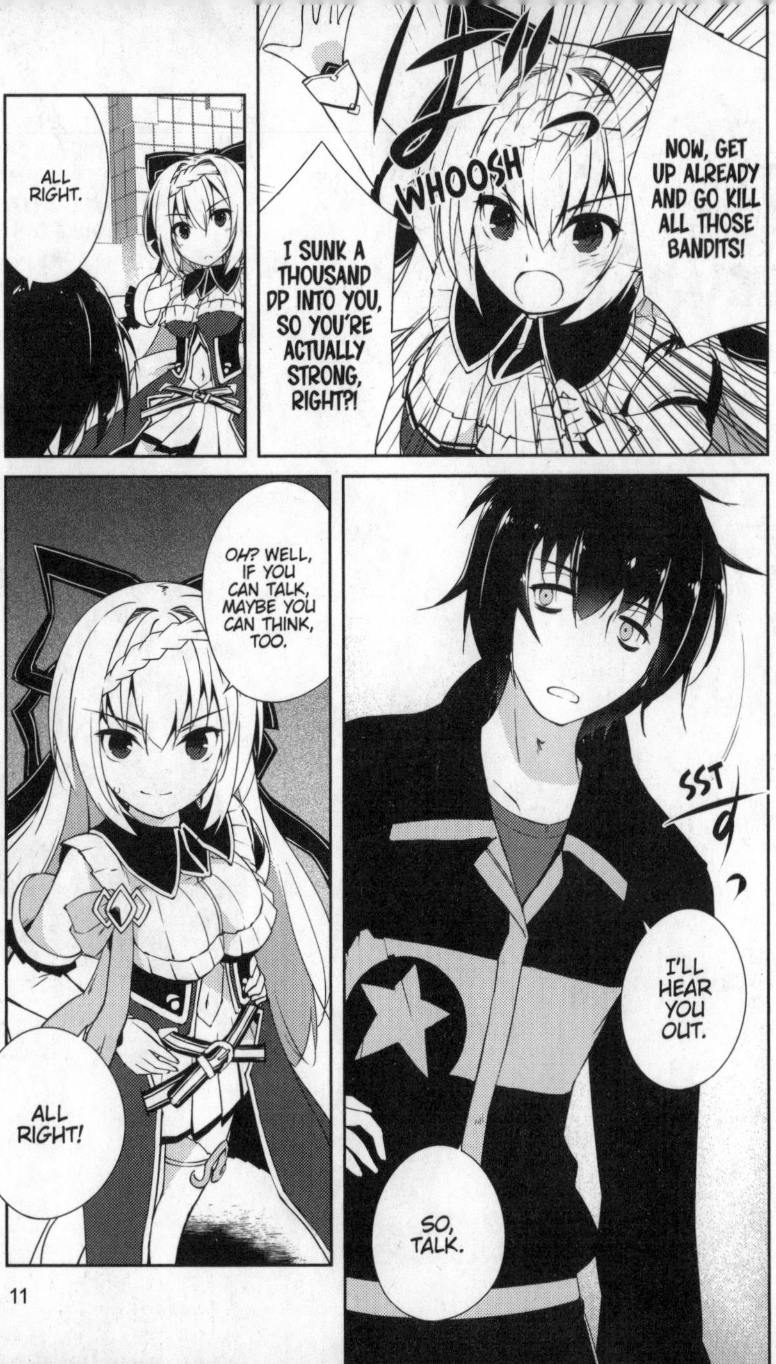
NOW, GET UP ALREADY AND GO KILL ALL THOSE BANDITS!
WHOOSH
I SUNK A THOUSAND DP INTO YOU, SO YOU'RE ACTUALLY STRONG, RIGHT?!
ALL RIGHT.
SST
I'LL HEAR YOU OUT.
SO, TALK.
OH? WELL, IF YOU CAN TALK, MAYBE YOU CAN THINK, TOO.
ALL RIGHT!

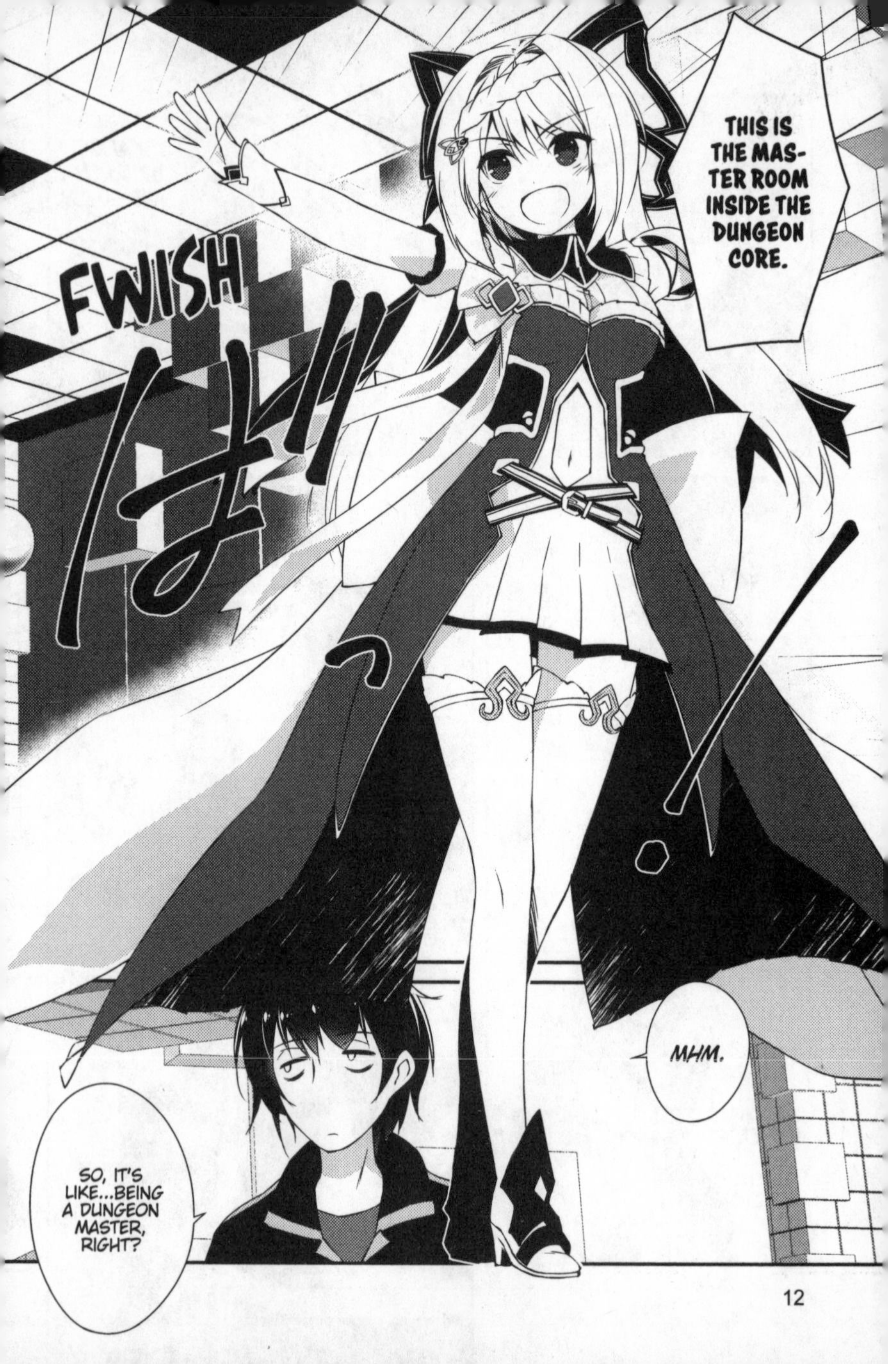
THIS IS THE MASTER ROOM INSIDE THE DUNGEON CORE.
FWISH
ばっ
MHM.
SO, IT'S LIKE...BEING A DUNGEON MASTER, RIGHT?

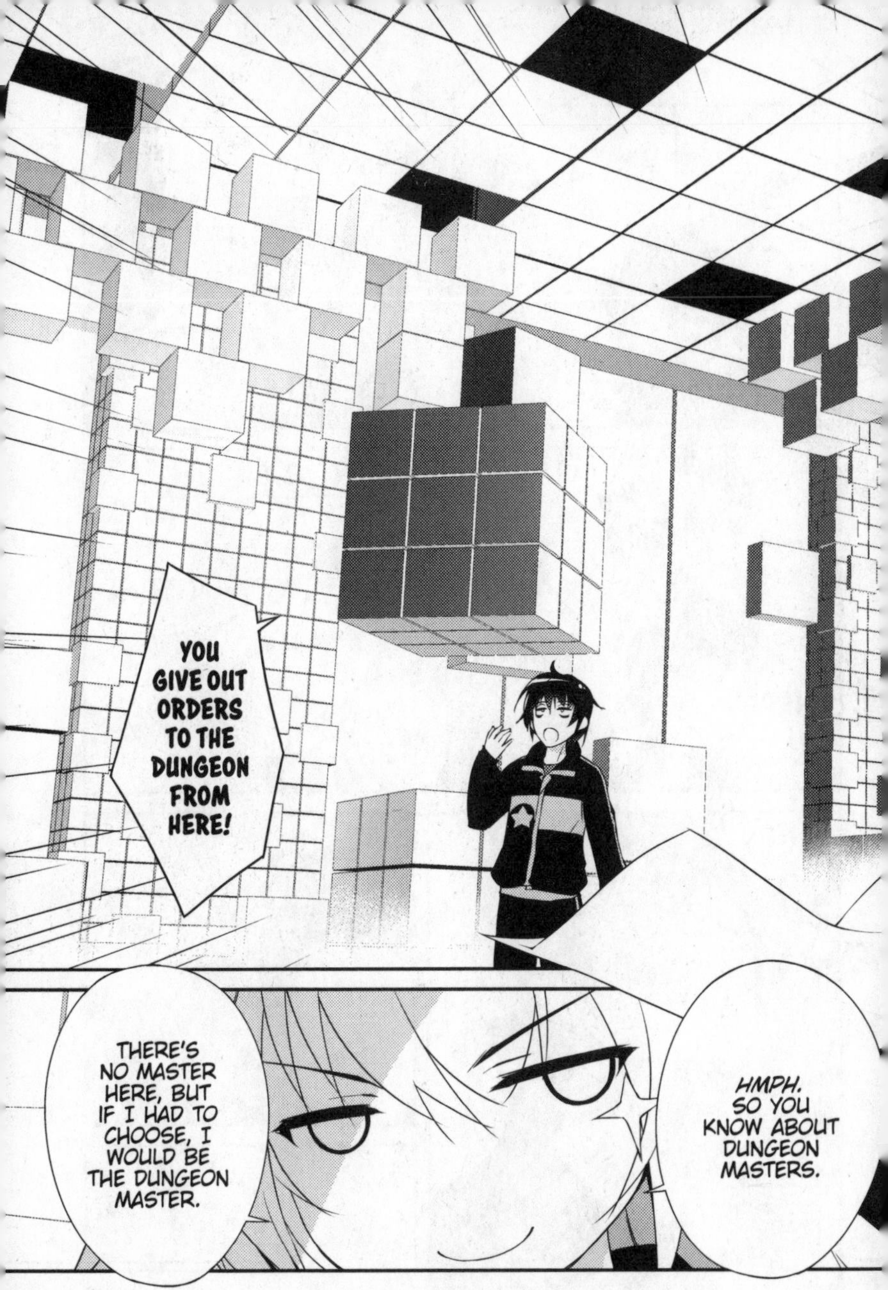
YOU GIVE OUT ORDERS TO THE DUNGEON FROM HERE!
HMPH. SO YOU KNOW ABOUT DUNGEON MASTERS.
THERE'S NO MASTER HERE, BUT IF I HAD TO CHOOSE, I WOULD BE THE DUNGEON MASTER.

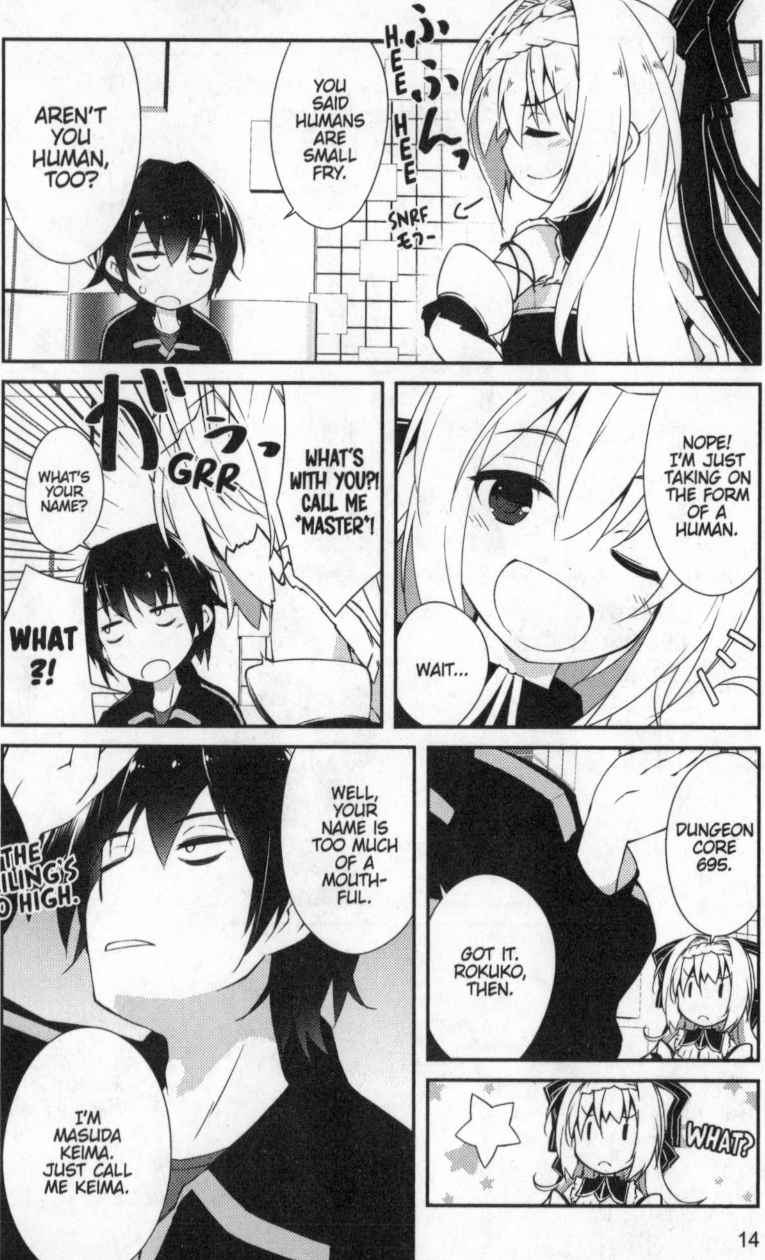
ふふんっ
HEE HEE HEE
SNRF
モフー
YOU SAID HUMANS ARE SMALL FRY.
AREN'T YOU HUMAN, TOO?
NOPE! I'M JUST TAKING ON THE FORM OF A HUMAN.
WAIT...
WHAT'S WITH YOU?! CALL ME "MASTER"!
がっ
GRR
WHAT'S YOUR NAME?
WHAT ?!
DUNGEON CORE 695.
GOT IT. ROKUKO, THEN.
WHAT?
WELL, YOUR NAME IS TOO MUCH OF A MOUTHFUL.
THE CEILING'S SO HIGH.
I'M MASUDA KEIMA. JUST CALL ME KEIMA.

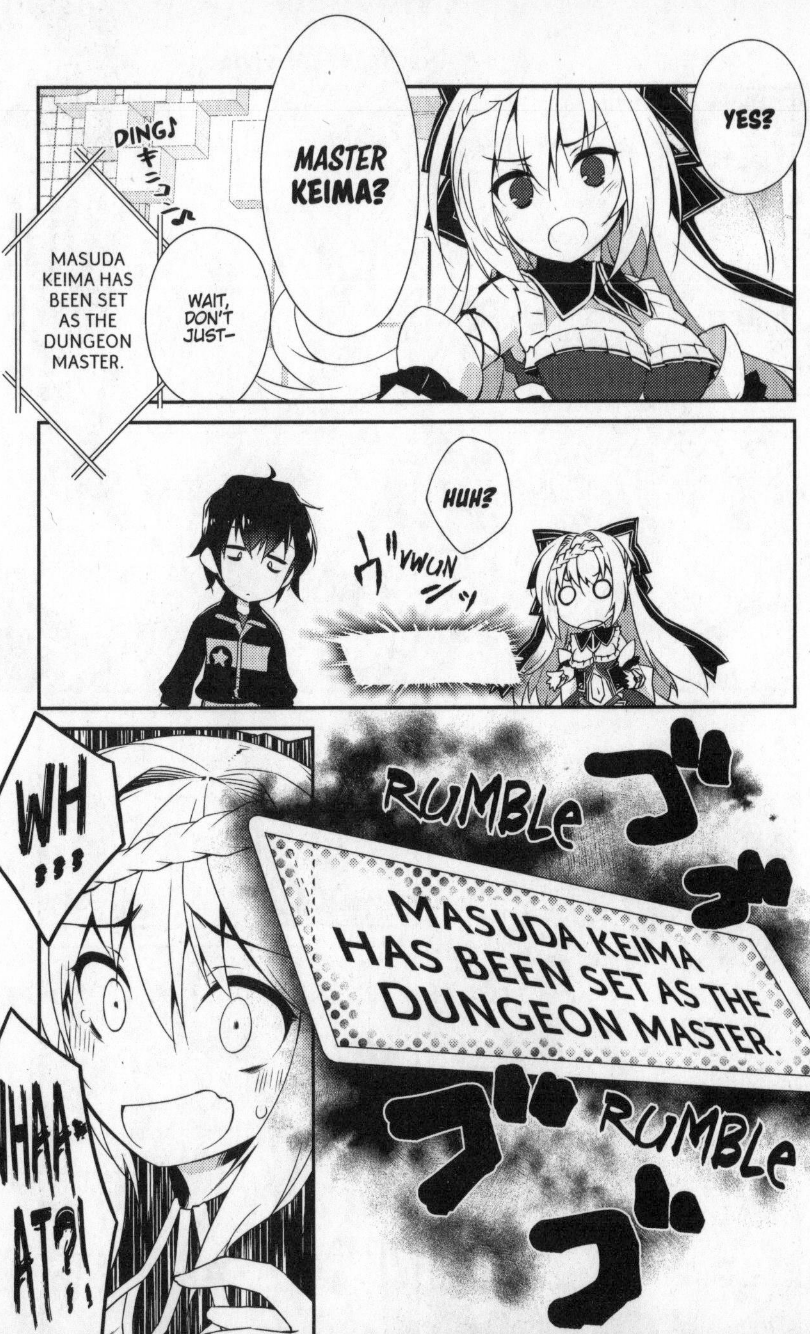
YES?
MASTER KEIMA?
WAIT, DON'T JUST-
DING♪
MASUDA KEIMA HAS BEEN SET AS THE DUNGEON MASTER.
HUH?
VWUN
RUMBLE
MASUDA KEIMA HAS BEEN SET AS THE DUNGEON MASTER.
RUMBLE
WH...
WHAA-AT?!

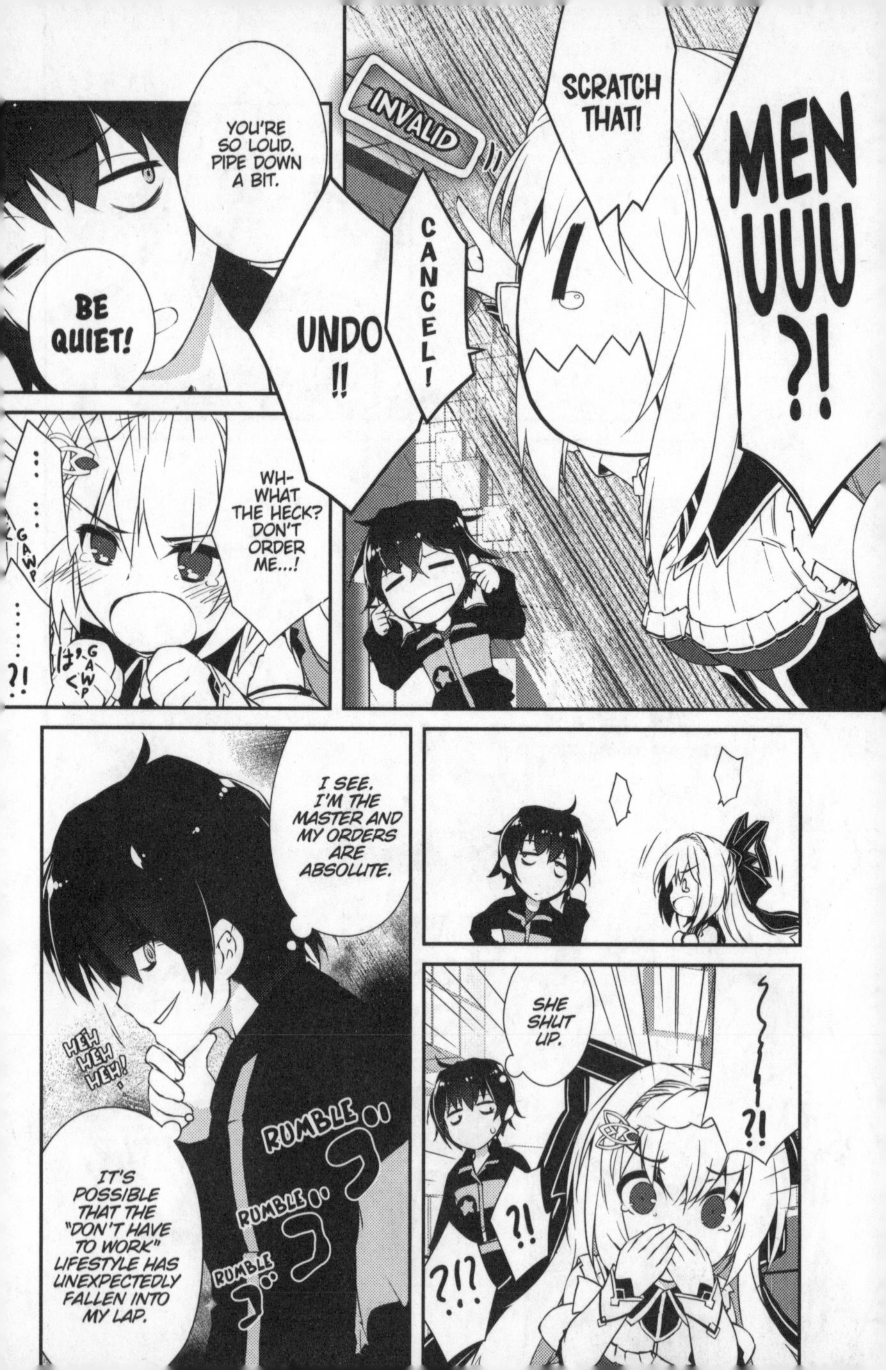
MENUUU?!
SCRATCH THAT!
INVALID
CANCEL!
UNDO!!
YOU'RE SO LOUD. PIPE DOWN A BIT.
BE QUIET!
...
...
GAWP
WH- WHAT THE HECK? DON'T ORDER ME...!
......?!
GAWP
SHE SHUT UP.
?!
?!
?!?
I SEE. I'M THE MASTER AND MY ORDERS ARE ABSOLUTE.
HEH HEH HEH!
RUMBLE
RUMBLE
RUMBLE
IT'S POSSIBLE THAT THE "DON'T HAVE TO WORK" LIFESTYLE HAS UNEXPECTEDLY FALLEN INTO MY LAP.

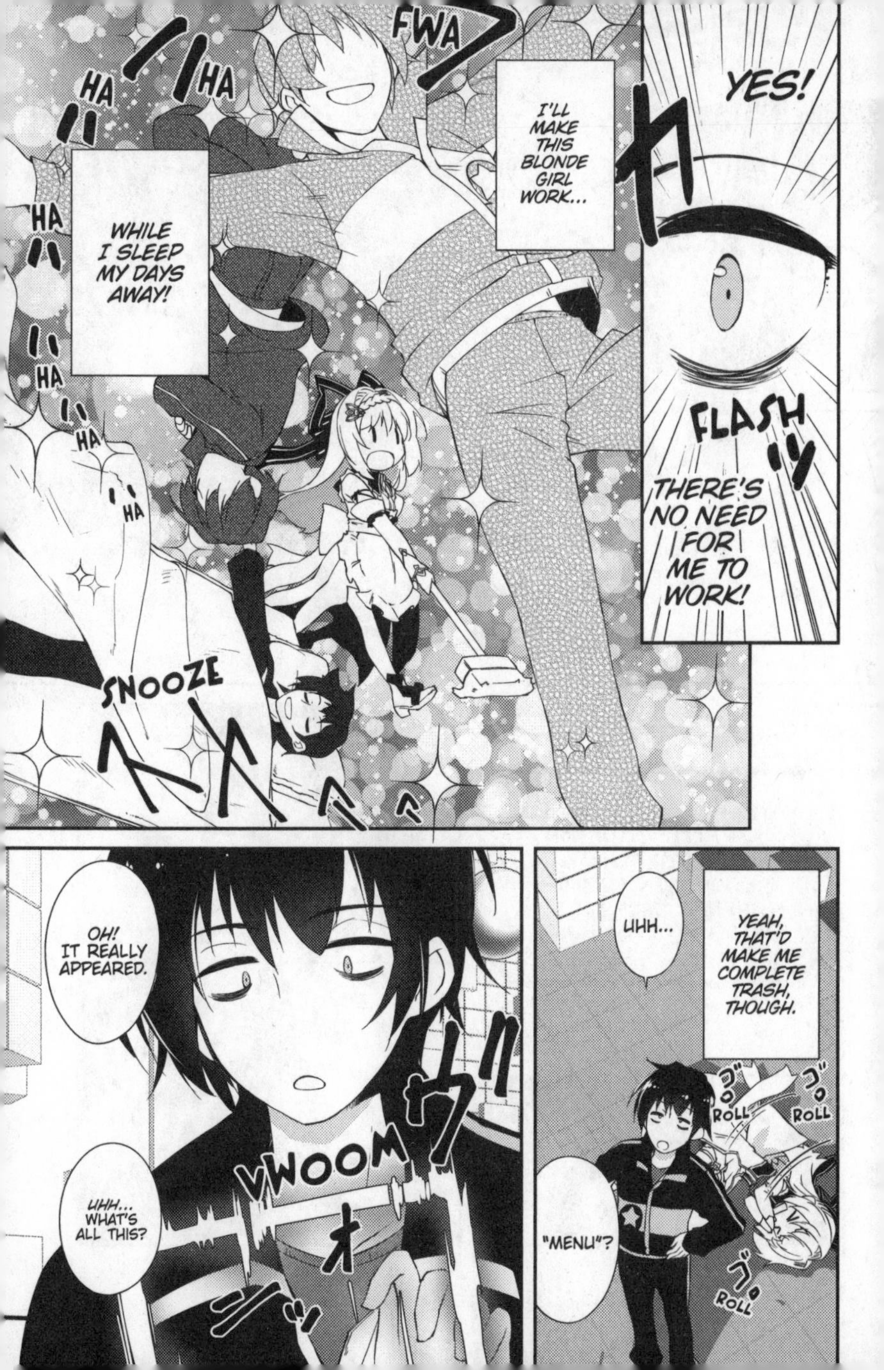
YES!
FLASH
THERE'S NO NEED FOR ME TO WORK!
FWA
I'LL MAKE THIS BLONDE GIRL WORK...
HA HA
WHILE I SLEEP MY DAYS AWAY!
HA
HA
HA
HA
SNOOZE
UHH...
YEAH, THAT'D MAKE ME COMPLETE TRASH, THOUGH.
ROLL
ROLL
"MENU"?
ROLL
OH! IT REALLY APPEARED.
VWOOM
UHH... WHAT'S ALL THIS?

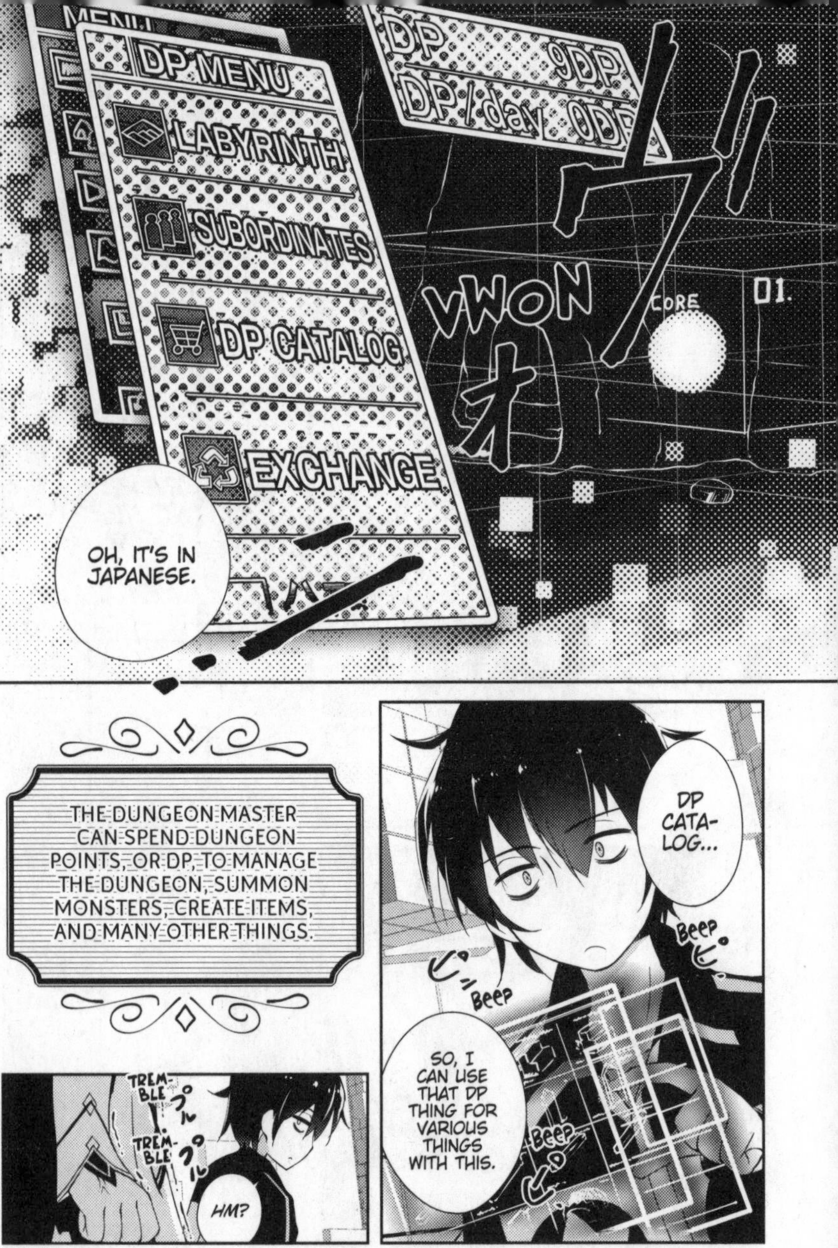
MENU
DP MENU
LABYRINTH
SUBORDINATES
DP CATALOG
EXCHANGE
DP 9DP
DP/day 0DP
VWON
CORE
01.
OH, IT'S IN JAPANESE.
DP CATA-LOG...
Beep
Beep
SO, I CAN USE THAT DP THING FOR VARIOUS THINGS WITH THIS.
Beep
THE DUNGEON MASTER CAN SPEND DUNGEON POINTS, OR DP, TO MANAGE THE DUNGEON, SUMMON MONSTERS, CREATE ITEMS, AND MANY OTHER THINGS.
TREM-BLE
TREM-BLE
HM?

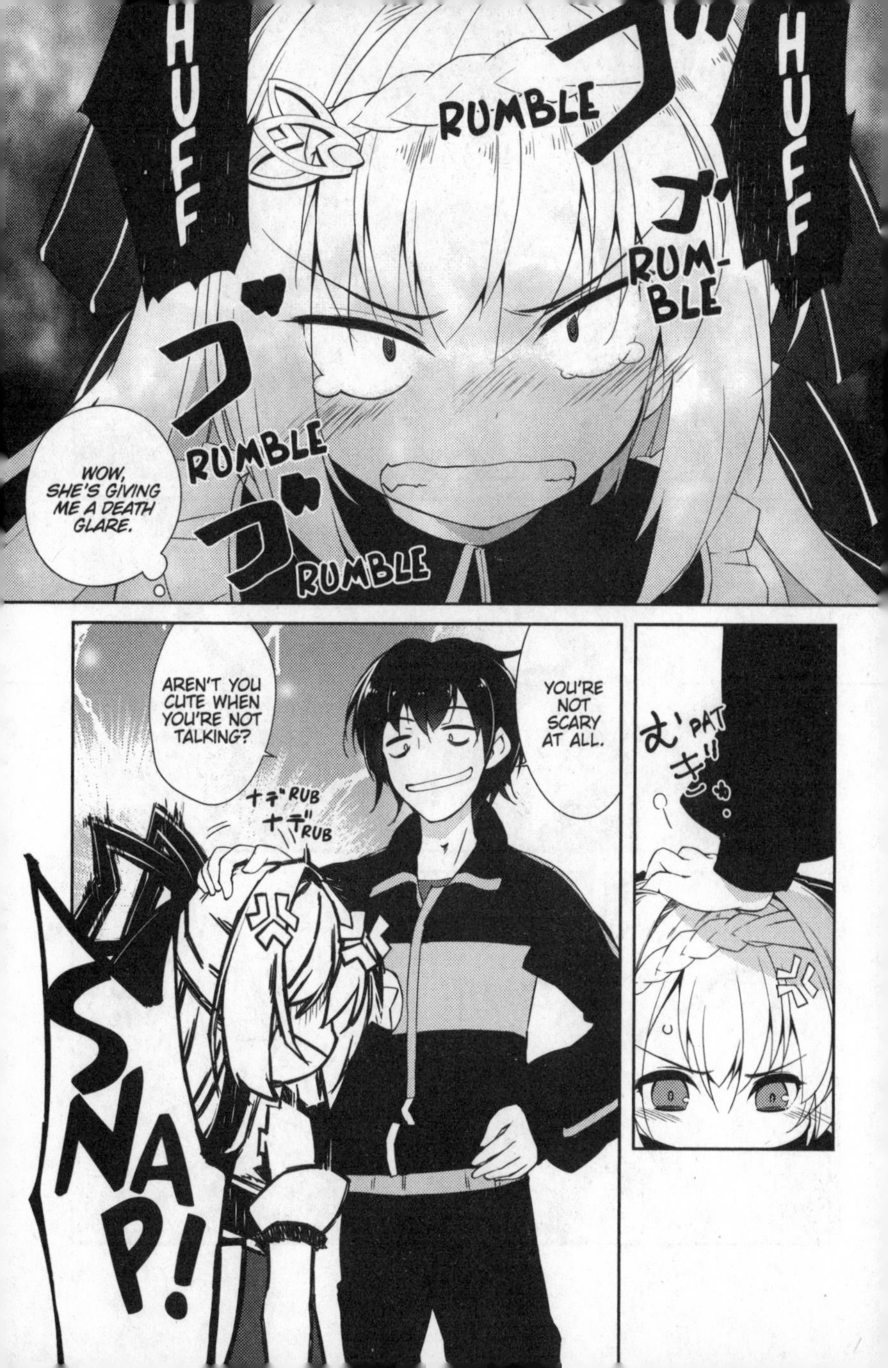
HUFF
RUMBLE
RUM-BLE
HUFF
RUMBLE
WOW, SHE'S GIVING ME A DEATH GLARE.
RUMBLE
PAT
YOU'RE NOT SCARY AT ALL.
AREN'T YOU CUTE WHEN YOU'RE NOT TALKING?
RUB
RUB
SNAP!

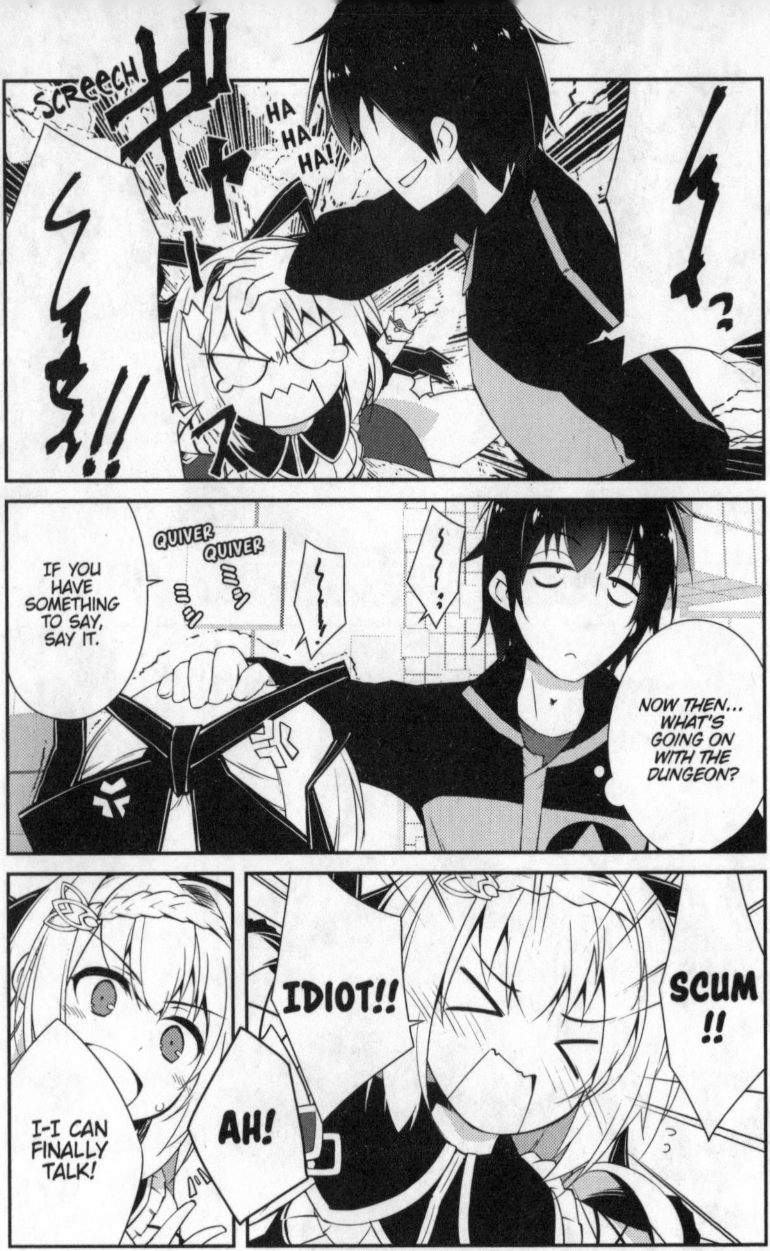
SCREECH
HA HA HA!
NOW THEN... WHAT'S GOING ON WITH THE DUNGEON?
QUIVER QUIVER
IF YOU HAVE SOMETHING TO SAY, SAY IT.
SCUM!!
IDIOT!!
AH!
I-I CAN FINALLY TALK!

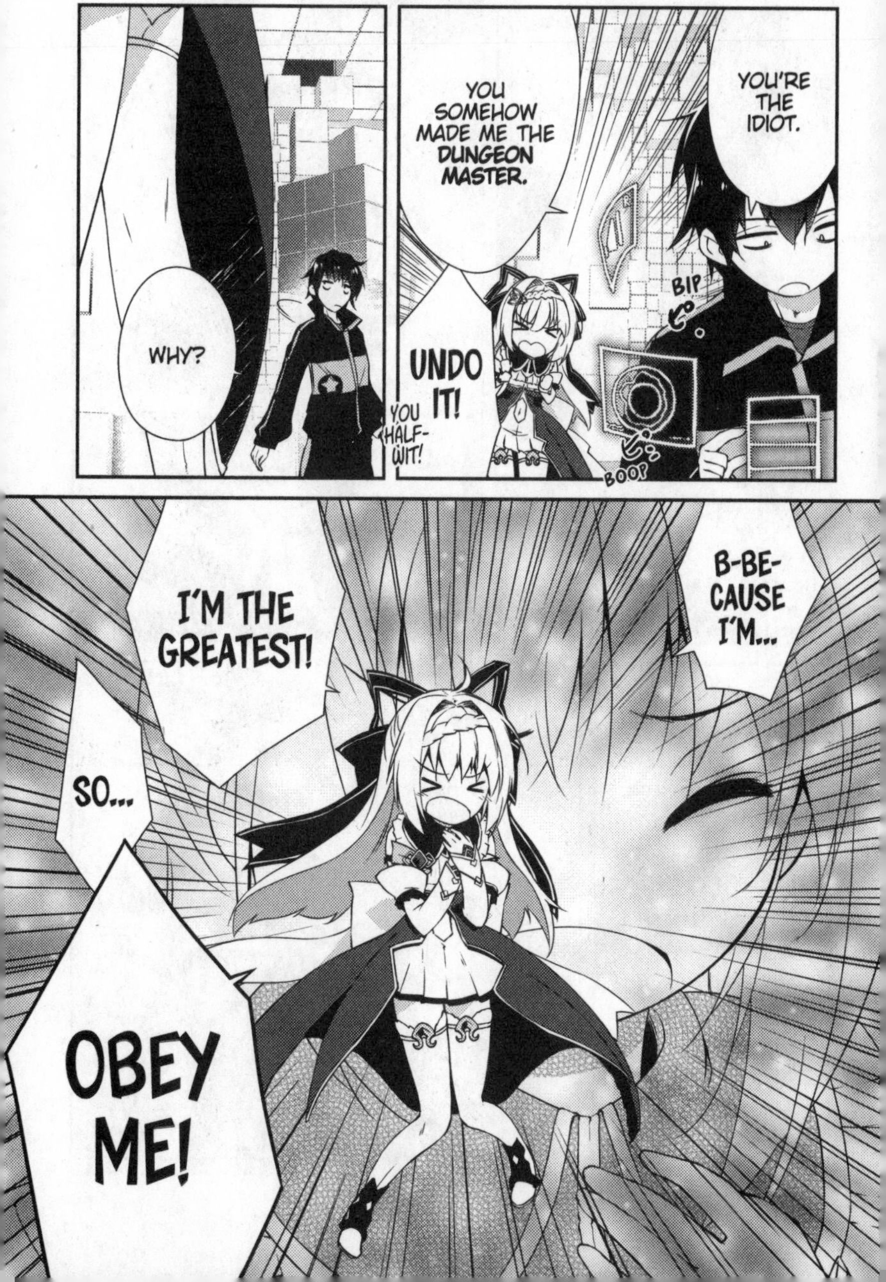

YOU'RE THE IDIOT.
YOU SOMEHOW MADE ME THE DUNGEON MASTER.
BIP
UNDO IT!
YOU HALF-WIT!
BOOP
WHY?
B-BE-CAUSE I'M...
I'M THE GREATEST!
SO...
OBEY ME!

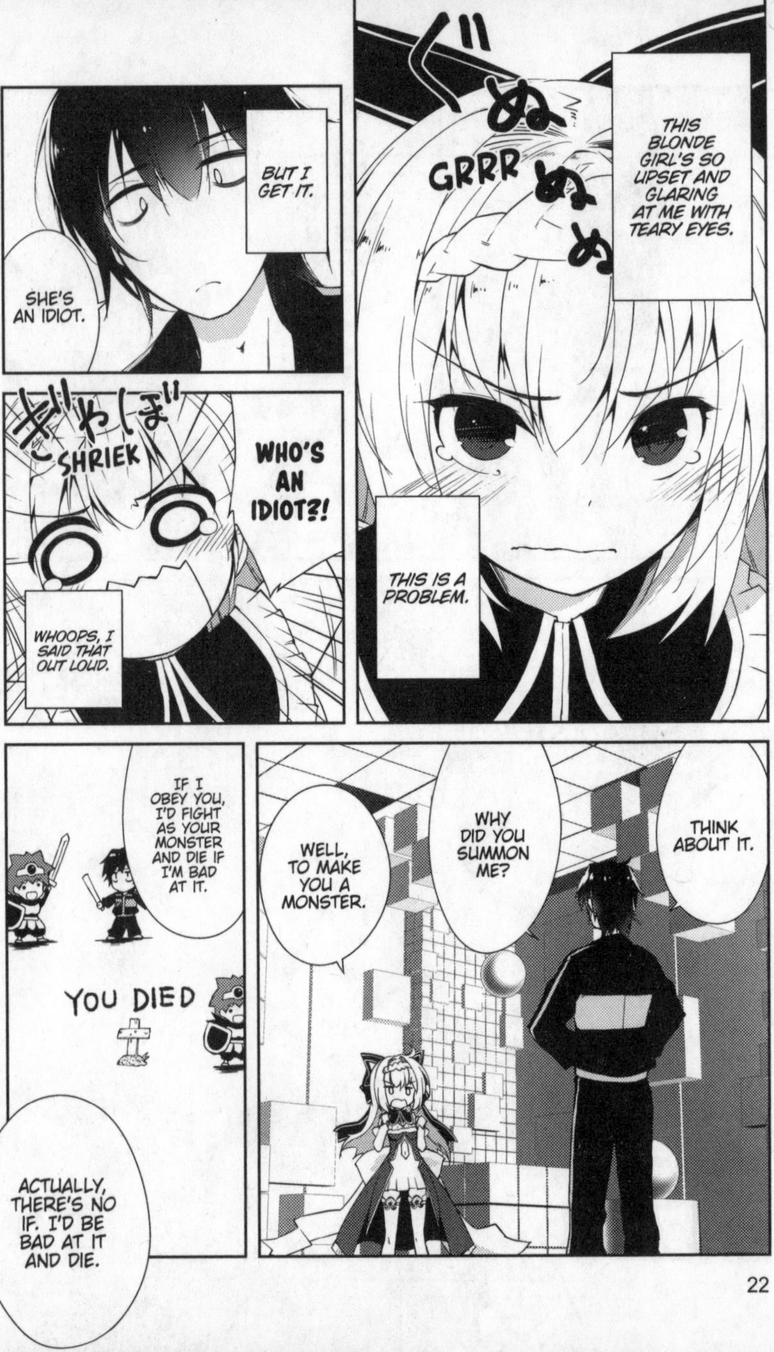
ぐぬぬぬ
GRRR
THIS BLONDE GIRL'S SO UPSET AND GLARING AT ME WITH TEARY EYES.
THIS IS A PROBLEM.
BUT I GET IT.
SHE'S AN IDIOT.
SHRIEK
WHO'S AN IDIOT?!
WHOOPS, I SAID THAT OUT LOUD.
THINK ABOUT IT.
WHY DID YOU SUMMON ME?
WELL, TO MAKE YOU A MONSTER.
IF I OBEY YOU, I'D FIGHT AS YOUR MONSTER AND DIE IF I'M BAD AT IT.
YOU DIED
ACTUALLY, THERE'S NO IF. I'D BE BAD AT IT AND DIE.

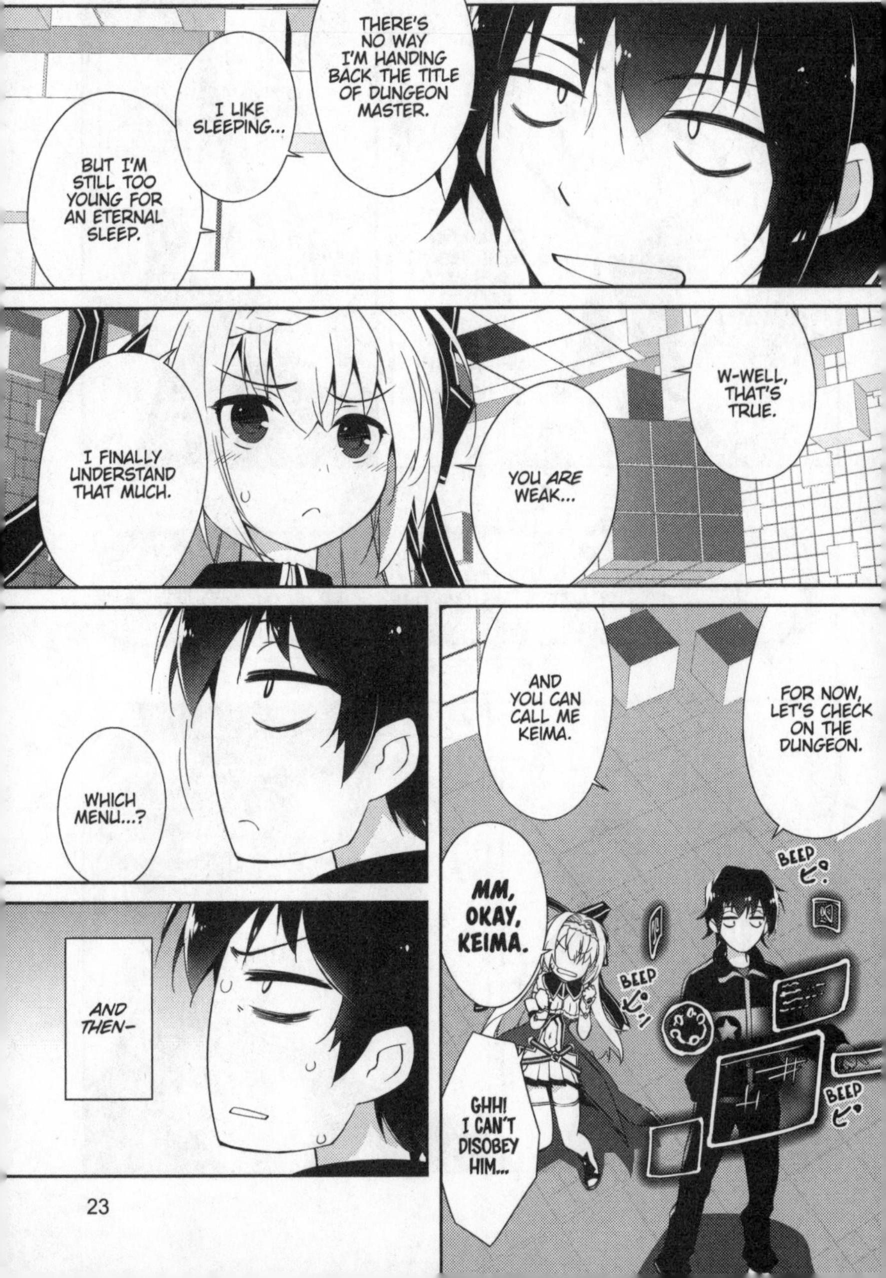

THERE'S NO WAY I'M HANDING BACK THE TITLE OF DUNGEON MASTER.
I LIKE SLEEPING...
BUT I'M STILL TOO YOUNG FOR AN ETERNAL SLEEP.
W-WELL, THAT'S TRUE.
YOU ARE WEAK...
I FINALLY UNDERSTAND THAT MUCH.
FOR NOW, LET'S CHECK ON THE DUNGEON.
AND YOU CAN CALL ME KEIMA.
BEEP
ピ。
MM, OKAY, KEIMA.
BEEP
ピ。
BEEP
ピ。
GHH! I CAN'T DISOBEY HIM...
WHICH MENU...?
AND THEN-

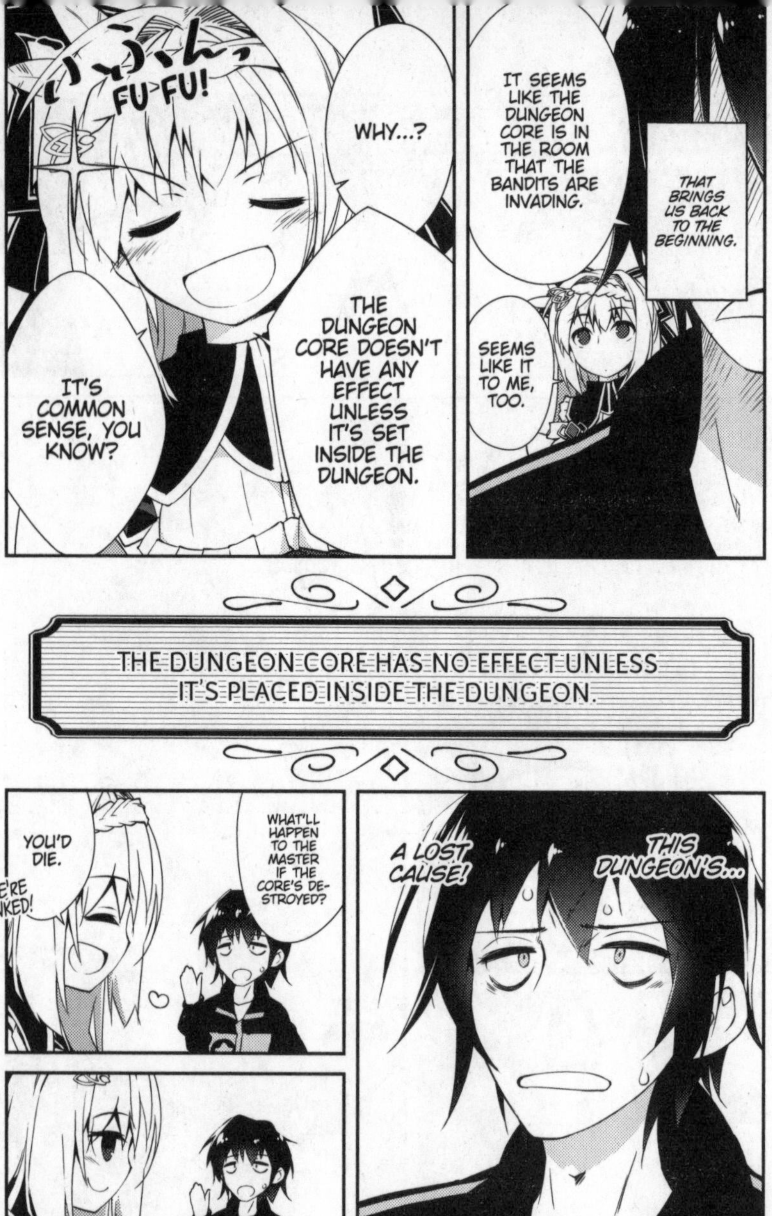
IT SEEMS LIKE THE DUNGEON CORE IS IN THE ROOM THAT THE BANDITS ARE INVADING.
THAT BRINGS US BACK TO THE BEGINNING.
SEEMS LIKE IT TO ME, TOO.
WHY...?
FU-FU!
THE DUNGEON CORE DOESN'T HAVE ANY EFFECT UNLESS IT'S SET INSIDE THE DUNGEON.
IT'S COMMON SENSE, YOU KNOW?
THE DUNGEON CORE HAS NO EFFECT UNLESS IT'S PLACED INSIDE THE DUNGEON.
THIS DUNGEON'S...
A LOST CAUSE!
WHAT'LL HAPPEN TO THE MASTER IF THE CORE'S DESTROYED?
YOU'D DIE.
WE'RE LINKED!

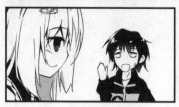

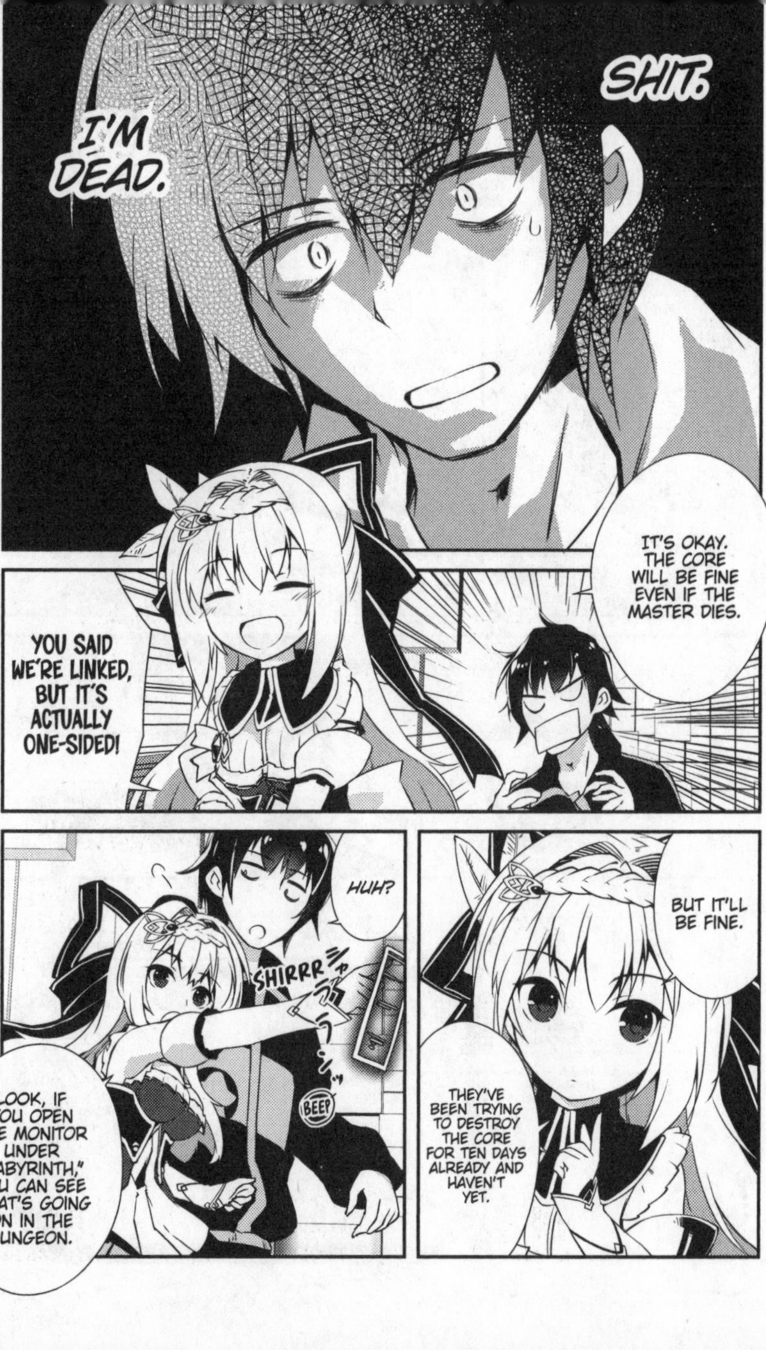
SHIT.
I'M DEAD.
IT'S OKAY. THE CORE WILL BE FINE EVEN IF THE MASTER DIES.
YOU SAID WE'RE LINKED, BUT IT'S ACTUALLY ONE-SIDED!
BUT IT'LL BE FINE.
THEY'VE BEEN TRYING TO DESTROY THE CORE FOR TEN DAYS ALREADY AND HAVEN'T YET.
HUH?
SHIRRR
BEEP
LOOK, IF YOU OPEN THE MONITOR UNDER "LABYRINTH," YOU CAN SEE WHAT'S GOING ON IN THE DUNGEON.

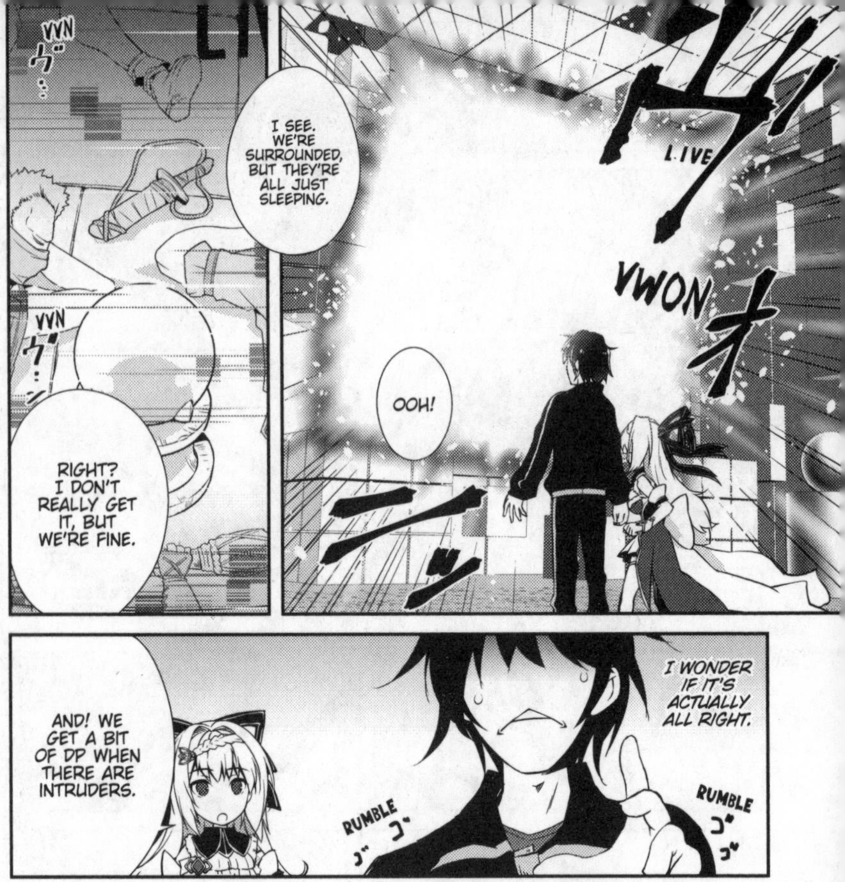
LIVE
VWON
OOH!
I SEE. WE'RE SURROUNDED, BUT THEY'RE ALL JUST SLEEPING.
VVN
VVN
RIGHT? I DON'T REALLY GET IT, BUT WE'RE FINE.
I WONDER IF IT'S ACTUALLY ALL RIGHT.
AND! WE GET A BIT OF DP WHEN THERE ARE INTRUDERS.
RUMBLE
RUMBLE

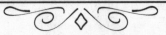

CONDITIONS TO INCREASE DP

- AUTO-REGENERATION FROM LEY LINE (10 P / DAY)
- KEEP INTRUDERS INSIDE THE DUNGEON (INCREASE DEPENDS ON THEIR STRENGTH)
- KILL INTRUDERS (INCREASE DEPENDS ON THEIR STRENGTH)
- SACRIFICE A CORPSE (DEPENDS ON THEIR STRENGTH WHEN THEY WERE ALIVE)
- OFFER TREASURE

IT SEEMS THAT WE'VE ACCUMULATED EIGHTY FROM THE BANDITS SLEEPING HERE FOR TEN DAYS.

AND AFTER SAVING UP ONE THOUSAND DP LIKE SO, SHE ROLLED THE MONSTER GACHA.

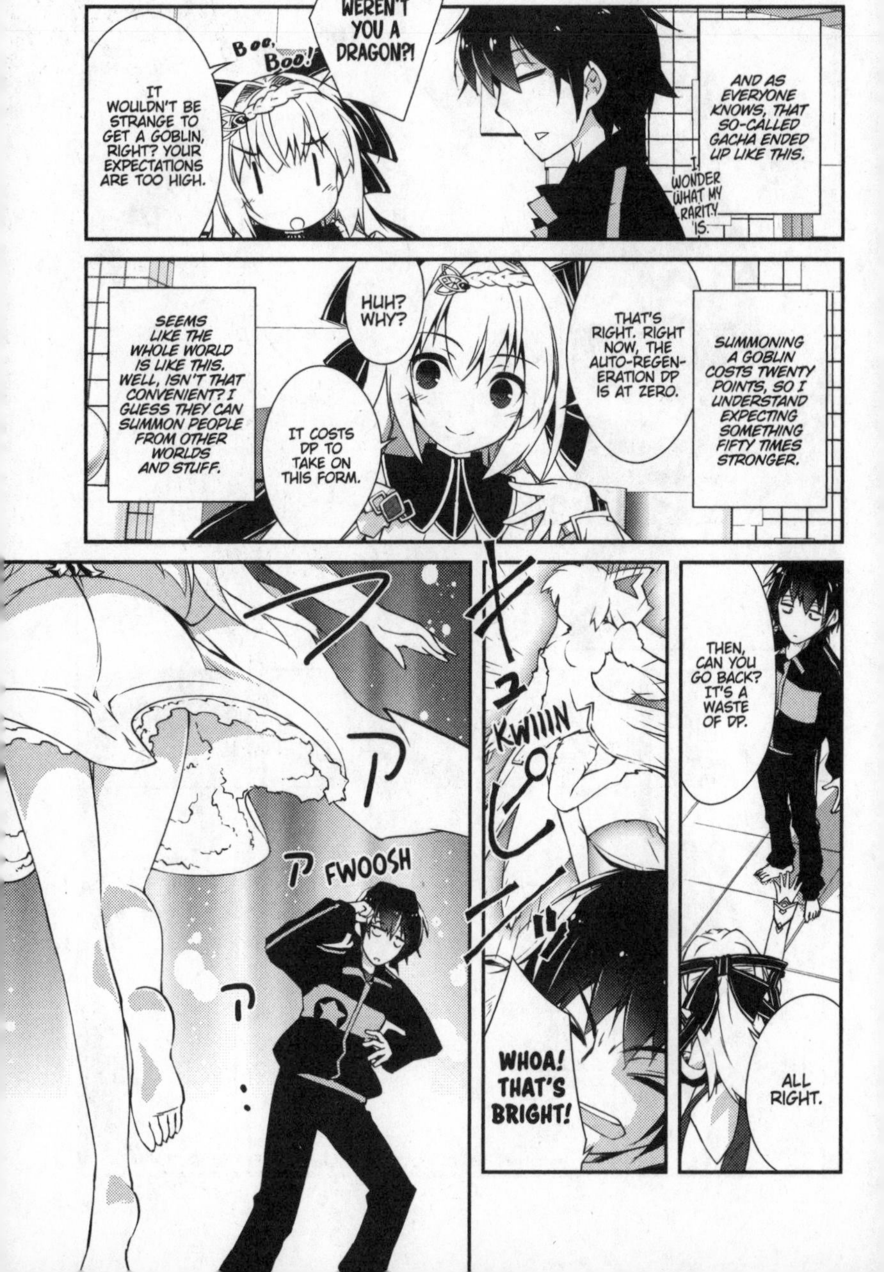
AND AS EVERYONE KNOWS, THAT SO-CALLED GACHA ENDED UP LIKE THIS.
I WONDER WHAT MY RARITY IS.
WHY WEREN'T YOU A DRAGON?!
Boo, Boo!
IT WOULDN'T BE STRANGE TO GET A GOBLIN, RIGHT? YOUR EXPECTATIONS ARE TOO HIGH.
SUMMONING A GOBLIN COSTS TWENTY POINTS, SO I UNDERSTAND EXPECTING SOMETHING FIFTY TIMES STRONGER.
THAT'S RIGHT. RIGHT NOW, THE AUTO-REGEN-ERATION DP IS AT ZERO.
HUH? WHY?
IT COSTS DP TO TAKE ON THIS FORM.
SEEMS LIKE THE WHOLE WORLD IS LIKE THIS. WELL, ISN'T THAT CONVENIENT? I GUESS THEY CAN SUMMON PEOPLE FROM OTHER WORLDS AND STUFF.
THEN, CAN YOU GO BACK? IT'S A WASTE OF DP.
ALL RIGHT.
KWIIIN
WHOA! THAT'S BRIGHT!
FWOOSH

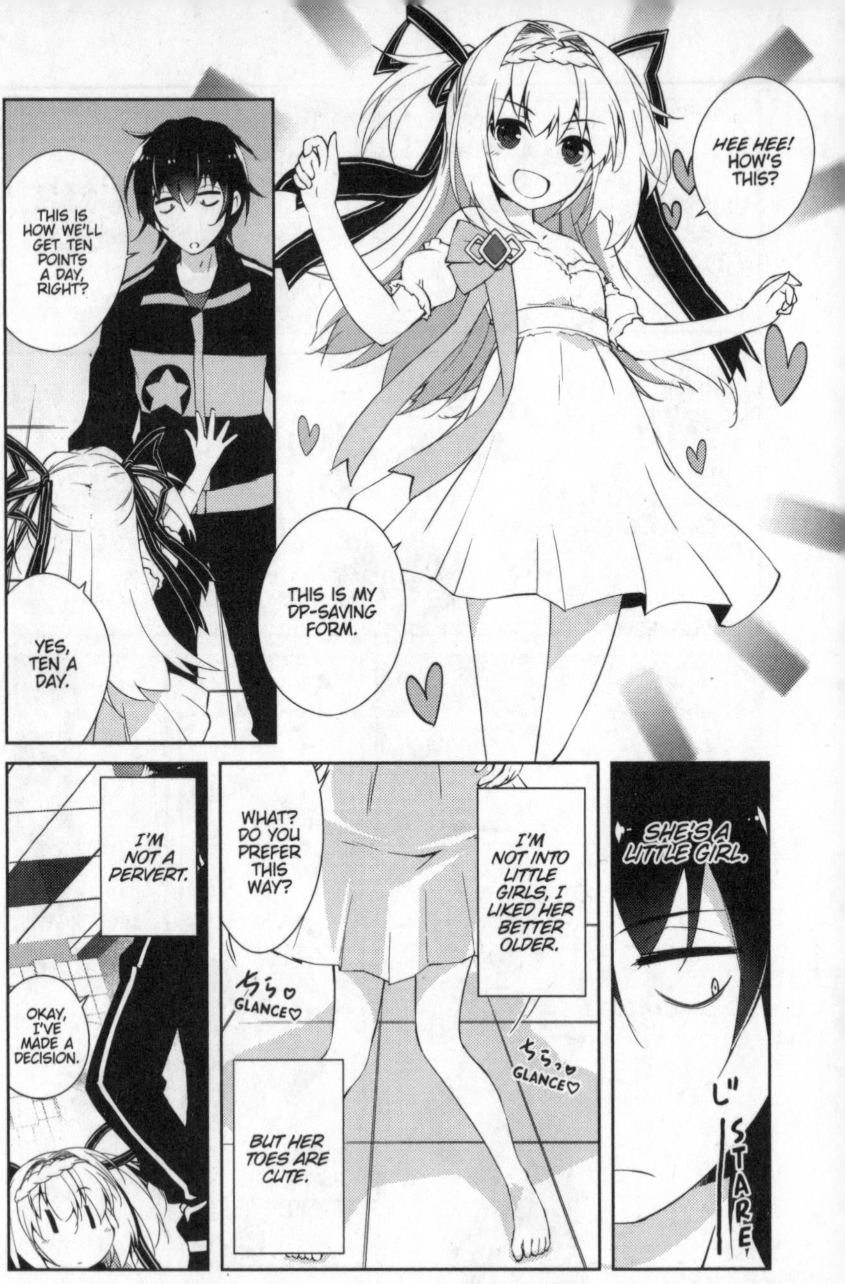
HEE HEE! HOW'S THIS?
THIS IS MY DP-SAVING FORM.
THIS IS HOW WE'LL GET TEN POINTS A DAY, RIGHT?
YES, TEN A DAY.
SHE'S A LITTLE GIRL.
じ
STARE
I'M NOT INTO LITTLE GIRLS, I LIKED HER BETTER OLDER.
WHAT? DO YOU PREFER THIS WAY?
ちらっ
GLANCE♡
ちらっ
GLANCE♡
BUT HER TOES ARE CUTE.
I'M NOT A PERVERT.
OKAY, I'VE MADE A DECISION.

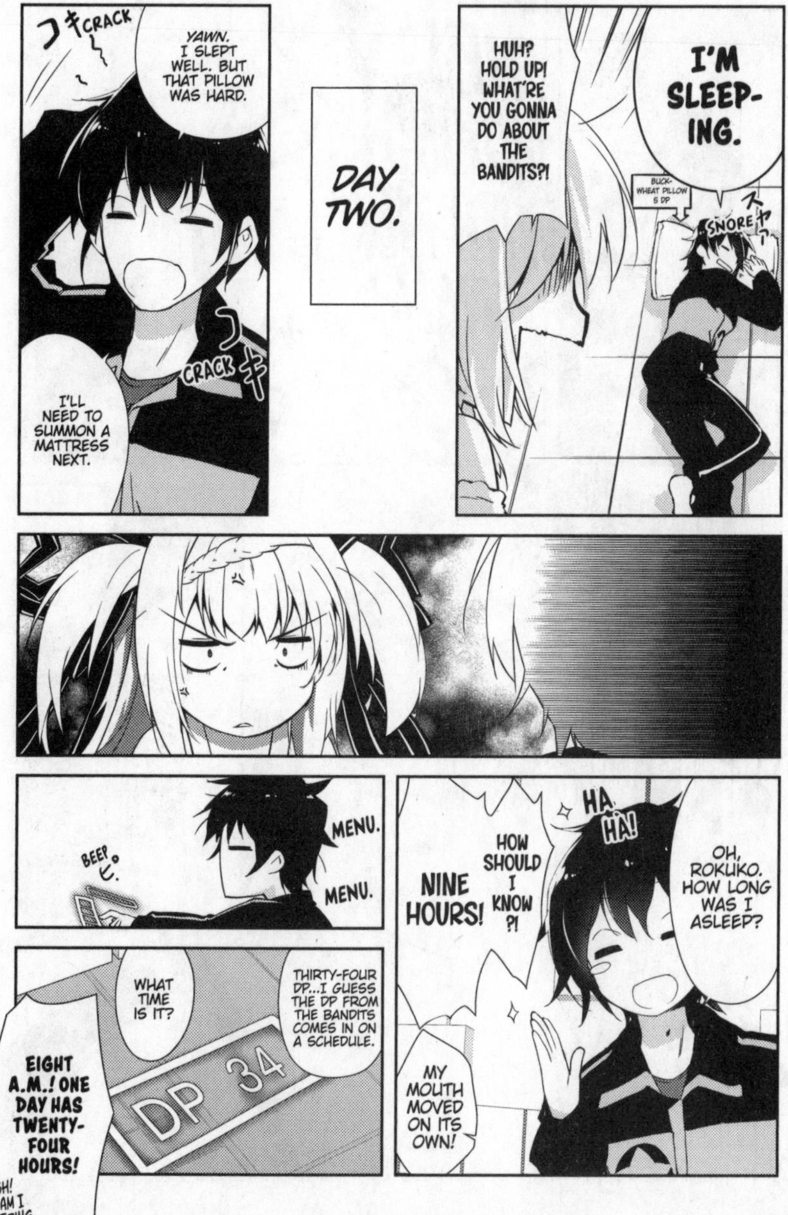
I'M SLEEP-ING.
HUH? HOLD UP! WHAT'RE YOU GONNA DO ABOUT THE BANDITS?!
BUCK-WHEAT PILLOW 5 DP
SNORE
DAY TWO.
YAWN. I SLEPT WELL. BUT THAT PILLOW WAS HARD.
CRACK
CRACK
I'LL NEED TO SUMMON A MATTRESS NEXT.
OH, ROKUKO. HOW LONG WAS I ASLEEP?
HA HA!
HOW SHOULD I KNOW ?!
NINE HOURS!
MY MOUTH MOVED ON ITS OWN!
MENU.
MENU.
BEEP
THIRTY-FOUR DP...I GUESS THE DP FROM THE BANDITS COMES IN ON A SCHEDULE.
WHAT TIME IS IT?
DP 34
EIGHT A.M.! ONE DAY HAS TWENTY-FOUR HOURS!
ARGH! WHY AM I ANSWERING HIM?!

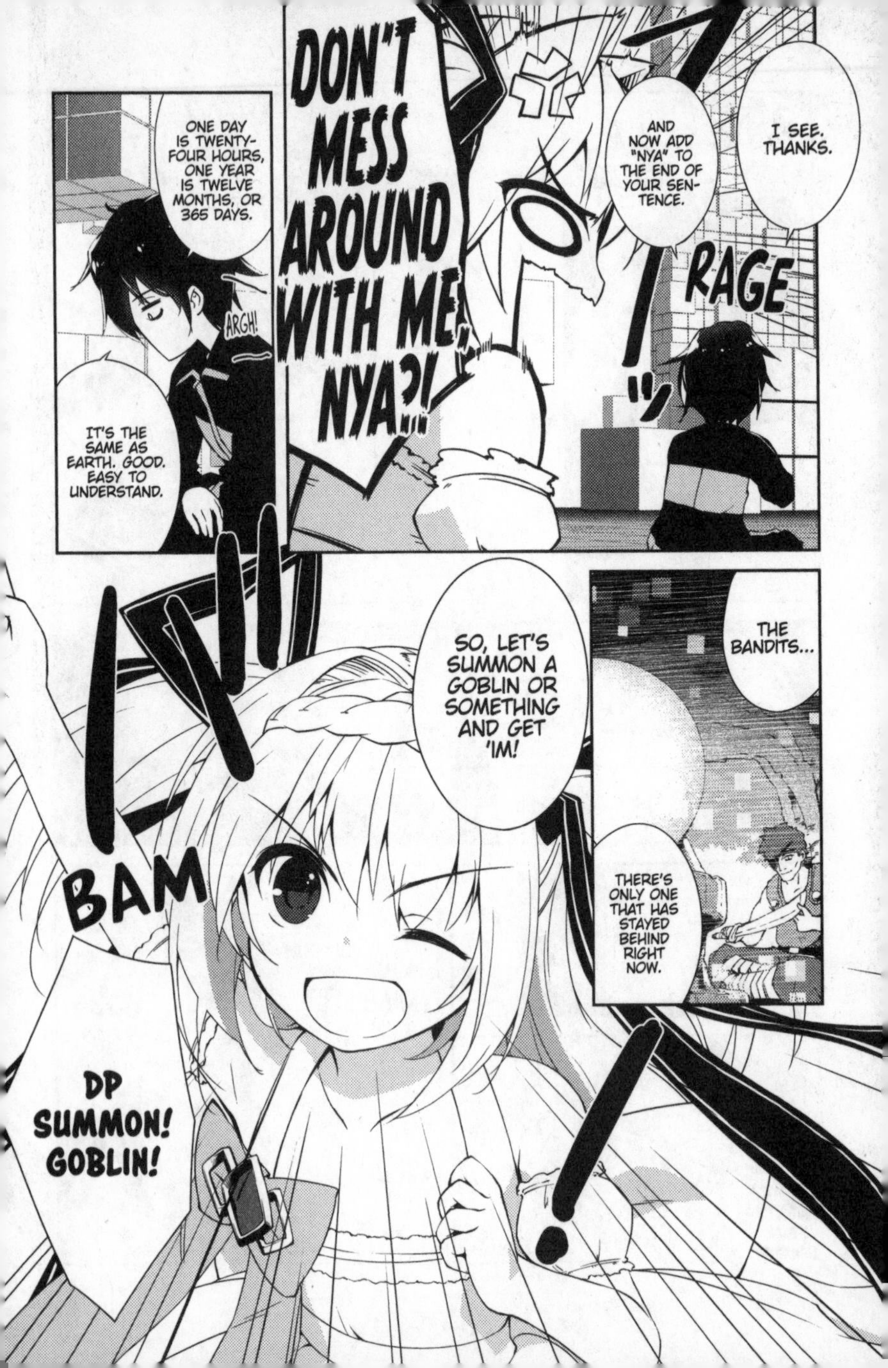
I SEE. THANKS.
AND NOW ADD "NYA" TO THE END OF YOUR SEN-TENCE.
RAGE
DON'T MESS AROUND WITH ME, NYA?!
ONE DAY IS TWENTY-FOUR HOURS, ONE YEAR IS TWELVE MONTHS, OR 365 DAYS.
ARGH!
IT'S THE SAME AS EARTH. GOOD. EASY TO UNDERSTAND.
THE BANDITS...
THERE'S ONLY ONE THAT HAS STAYED BEHIND RIGHT NOW.
SO, LET'S SUMMON A GOBLIN OR SOMETHING AND GET 'IM!
BAM
DP SUMMON! GOBLIN!

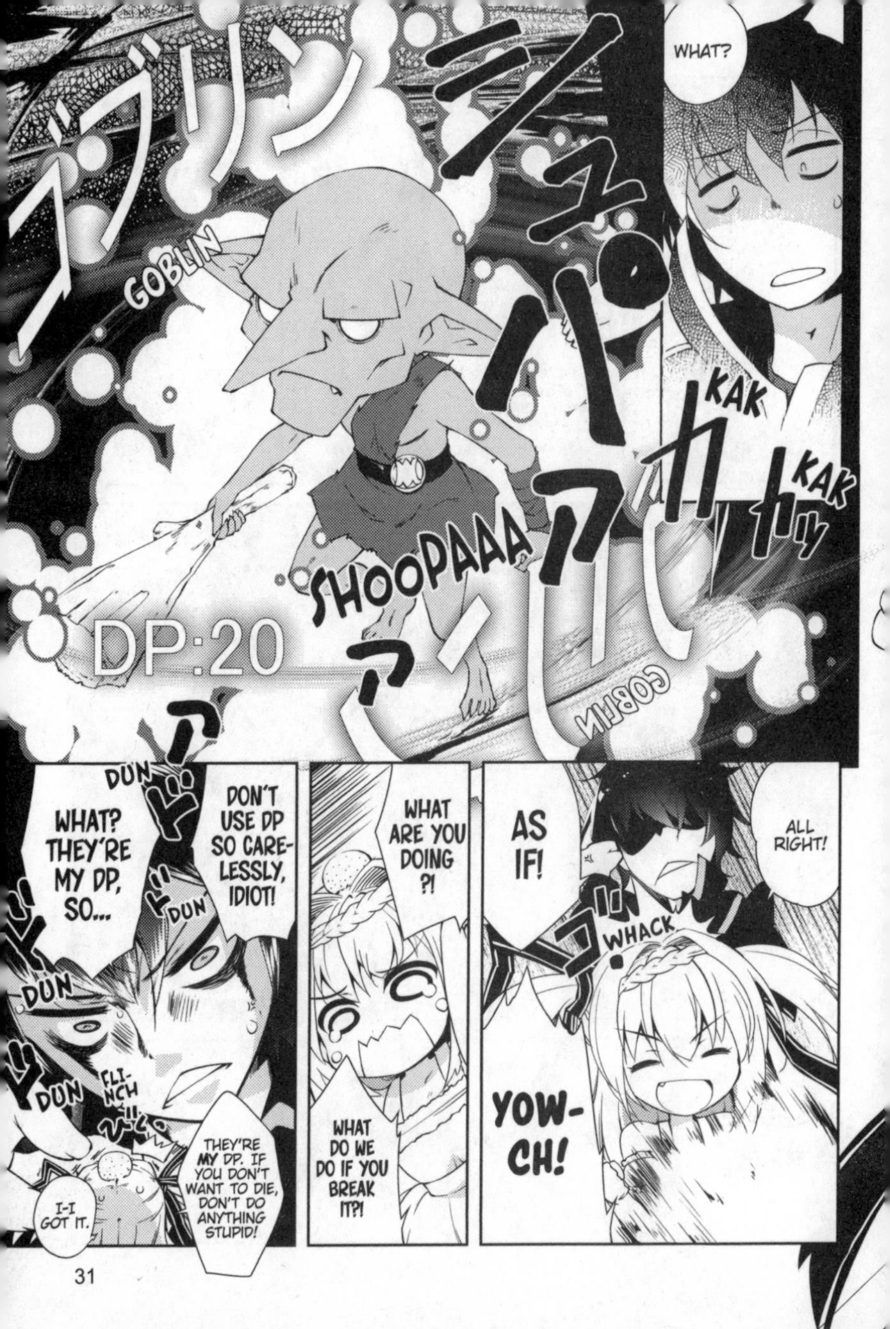
WHAT?
KAK
KAK
SHOOPAAA
GOBLIN
GOBLIN
DP:20
ALL RIGHT!
AS IF!
WHACK
YOW-CH!
WHAT ARE YOU DOING?!
WHAT DO WE DO IF YOU BREAK IT?!
DON'T USE DP SO CARE-LESSLY, IDIOT!
DUN
WHAT? THEY'RE MY DP, SO...
DUN
DUN
DUN
FLI-NCH
THEY'RE MY DP. IF YOU DON'T WANT TO DIE, DON'T DO ANYTHING STUPID!
I-I GOT IT.

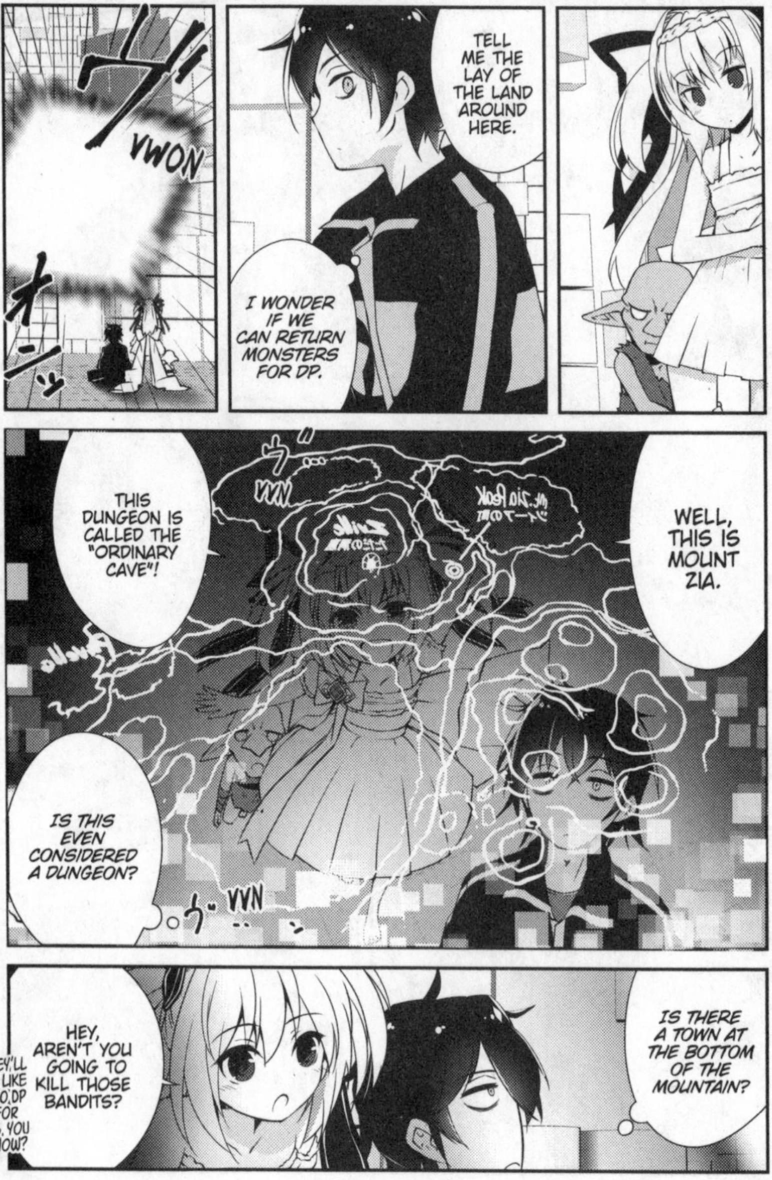
TELL ME THE LAY OF THE LAND AROUND HERE.
I WONDER IF WE CAN RETURN MONSTERS FOR DP.
VWON
WELL, THIS IS MOUNT ZIA.
VVN
THIS DUNGEON IS CALLED THE "ORDINARY CAVE"!
IS THIS EVEN CONSIDERED A DUNGEON?
VVN
IS THERE A TOWN AT THE BOTTOM OF THE MOUNTAIN?
HEY, AREN'T YOU GOING TO KILL THOSE BANDITS?
THEY'LL BE LIKE 200 DP FOR US, YOU KNOW?

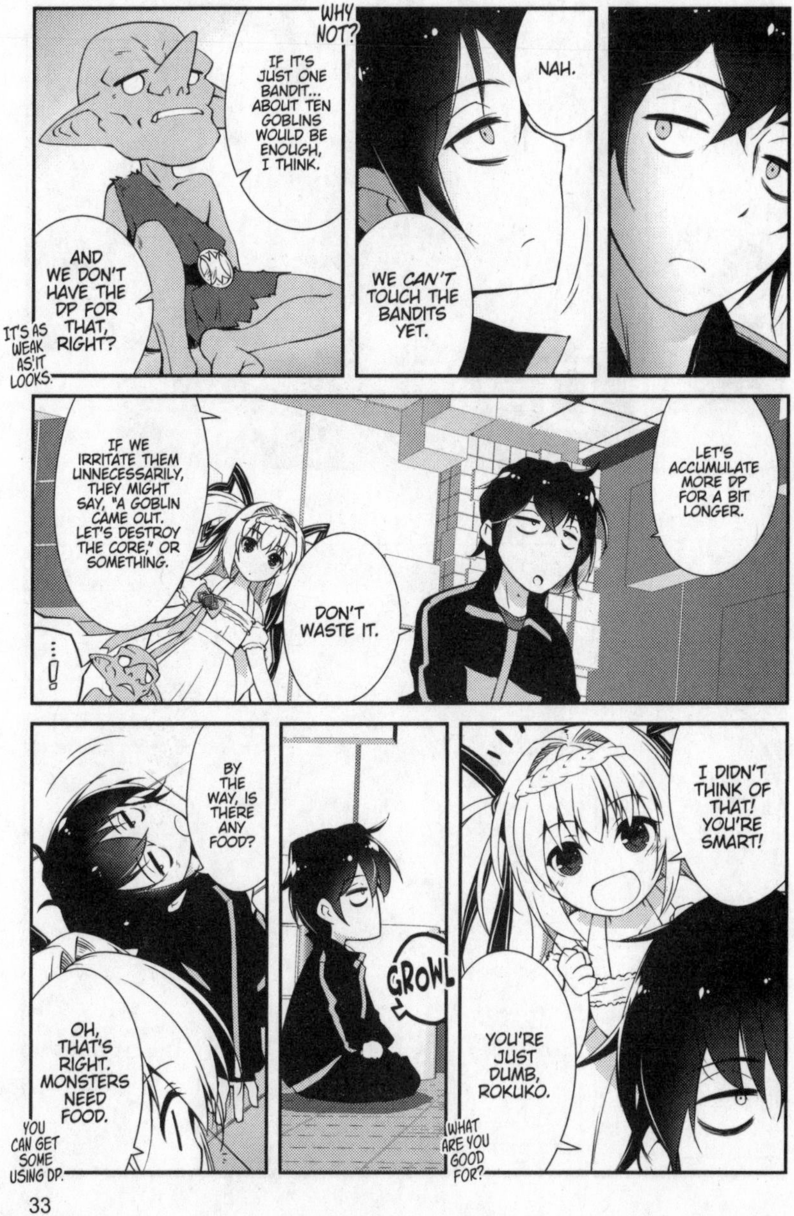
NAH.
WE *CAN'T* TOUCH THE BANDITS YET.
WHY NOT?
IF IT'S JUST ONE BANDIT... ABOUT TEN GOBLINS WOULD BE ENOUGH, I THINK.
AND WE DON'T HAVE THE DP FOR THAT, RIGHT?
IT'S AS WEAK AS IT LOOKS.
LET'S ACCUMULATE MORE DP FOR A BIT LONGER.
DON'T WASTE IT.
IF WE IRRITATE THEM UNNECESSARILY, THEY MIGHT SAY, "A GOBLIN CAME OUT. LET'S DESTROY THE CORE," OR SOMETHING.
...!
I DIDN'T THINK OF THAT! YOU'RE SMART!
YOU'RE JUST DUMB, ROKUKO.
WHAT ARE YOU GOOD FOR?
BY THE WAY, IS THERE ANY FOOD?
GROWL
OH, THAT'S RIGHT. MONSTERS NEED FOOD.
YOU CAN GET SOME USING DP.

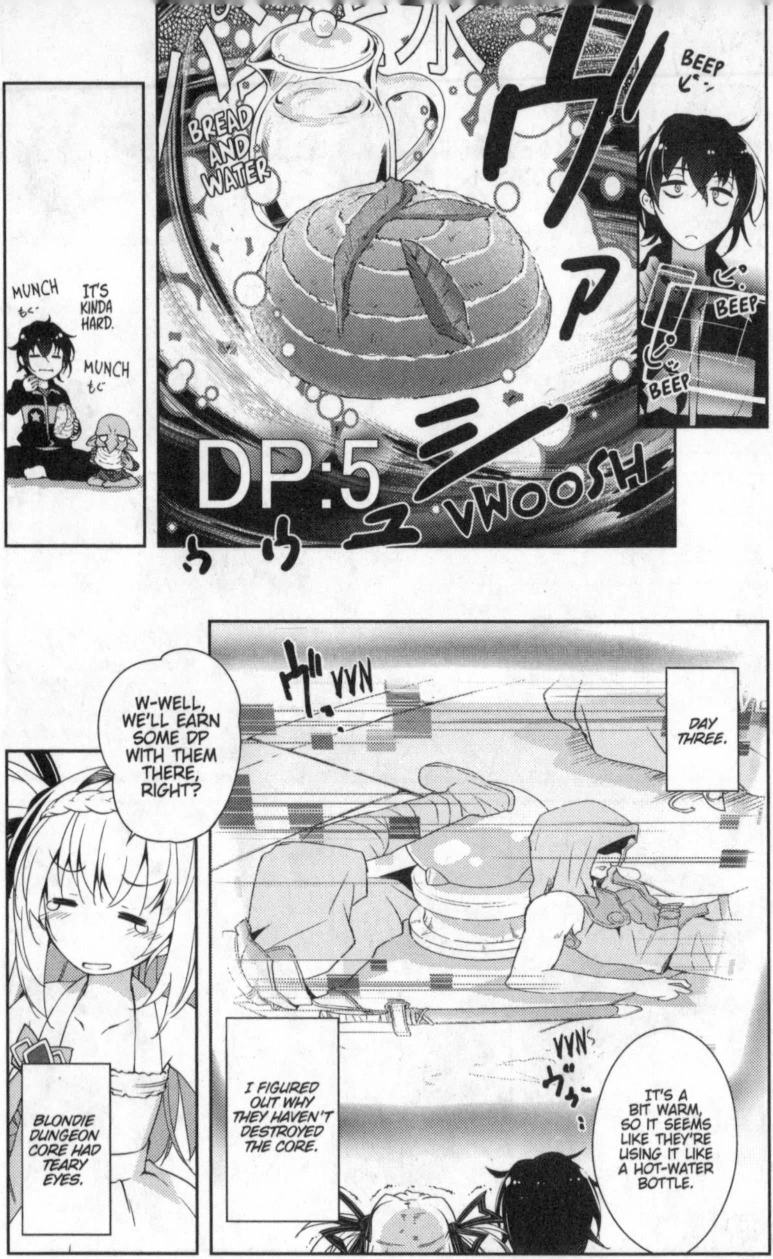
BEEP
BEEP
BEEP
BREAD AND WATER
DP:5
VWOOSH
MUNCH
IT'S KINDA HARD.
MUNCH
DAY THREE.
VVN
IT'S A BIT WARM, SO IT SEEMS LIKE THEY'RE USING IT LIKE A HOT-WATER BOTTLE.
VVN
I FIGURED OUT WHY THEY HAVEN'T DESTROYED THE CORE.
W-WELL, WE'LL EARN SOME DP WITH THEM THERE, RIGHT?
BLONDIE DUNGEON CORE HAD TEARY EYES.

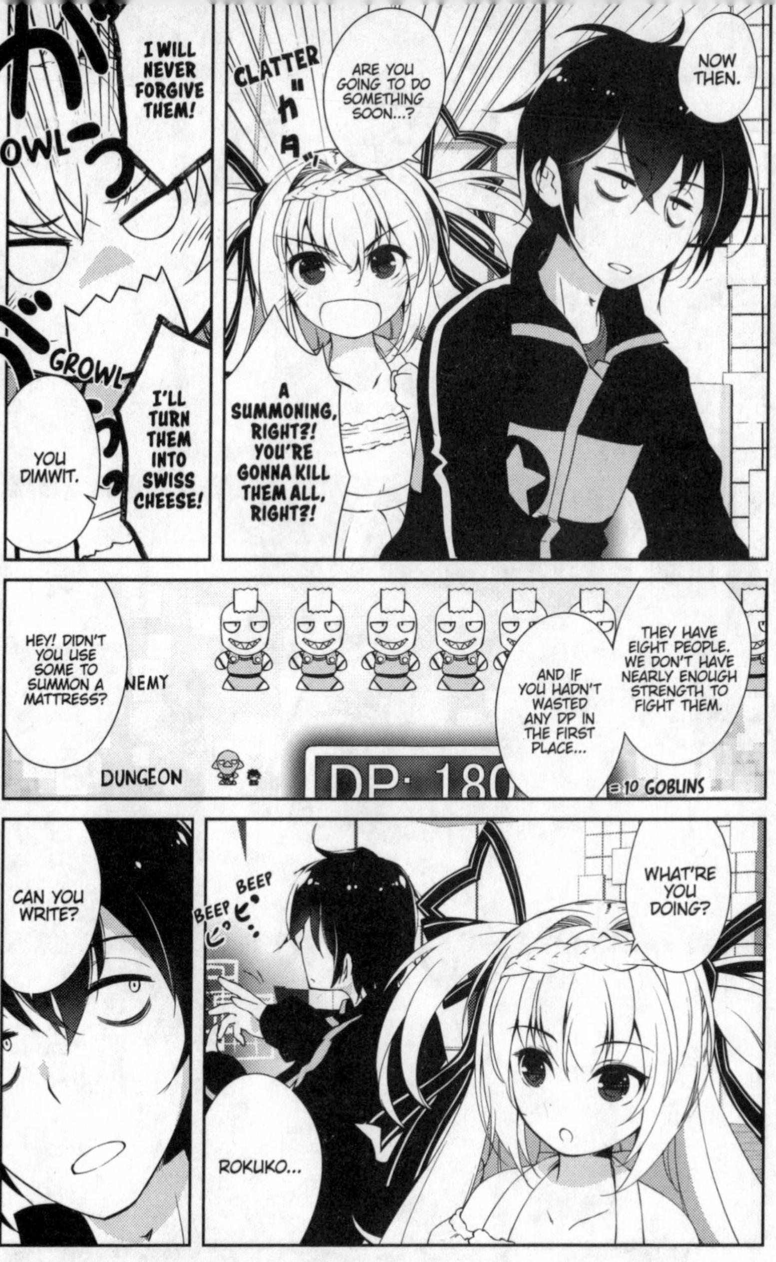
NOW THEN.
ARE YOU GOING TO DO SOMETHING SOON...?
CLATTER
A SUMMONING, RIGHT?! YOU'RE GONNA KILL THEM ALL, RIGHT?!
I WILL NEVER FORGIVE THEM!
GROWL
I'LL TURN THEM INTO SWISS CHEESE!
GROWL
YOU DIMWIT.
THEY HAVE EIGHT PEOPLE. WE DON'T HAVE NEARLY ENOUGH STRENGTH TO FIGHT THEM.
AND IF YOU HADN'T WASTED ANY DP IN THE FIRST PLACE...
= 10 GOBLINS
DUNGEON
HEY! DIDN'T YOU USE SOME TO SUMMON A MATTRESS?
WHAT'RE YOU DOING?
BEEP BEEP
ROKUKO...
CAN YOU WRITE?

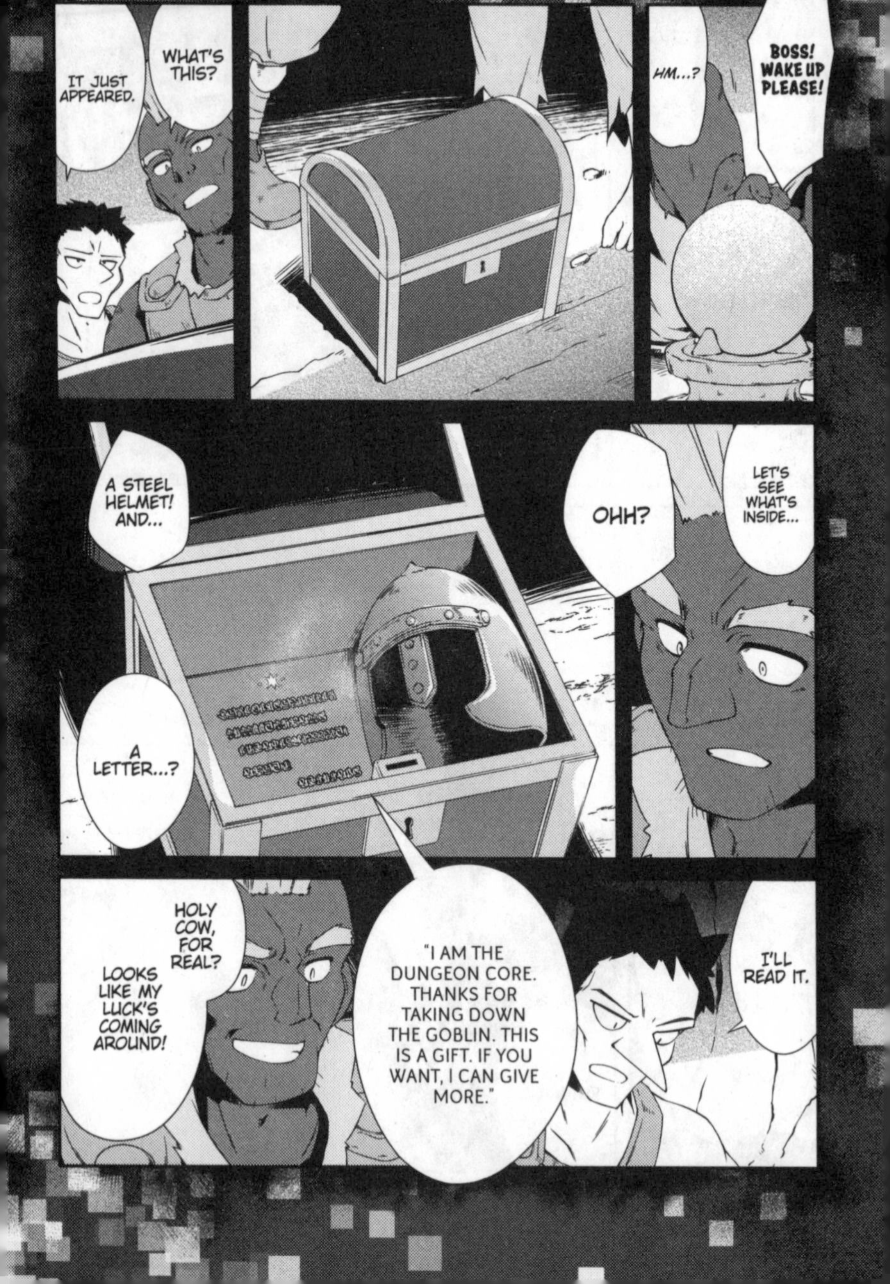
BOSS! WAKE UP PLEASE!
HM...?
WHAT'S THIS?
IT JUST APPEARED.
LET'S SEE WHAT'S INSIDE...
OHH?
A STEEL HELMET! AND...
A LETTER...?
I'LL READ IT.
"I AM THE DUNGEON CORE. THANKS FOR TAKING DOWN THE GOBLIN. THIS IS A GIFT. IF YOU WANT, I CAN GIVE MORE."
HOLY COW, FOR REAL?
LOOKS LIKE MY LUCK'S COMING AROUND!

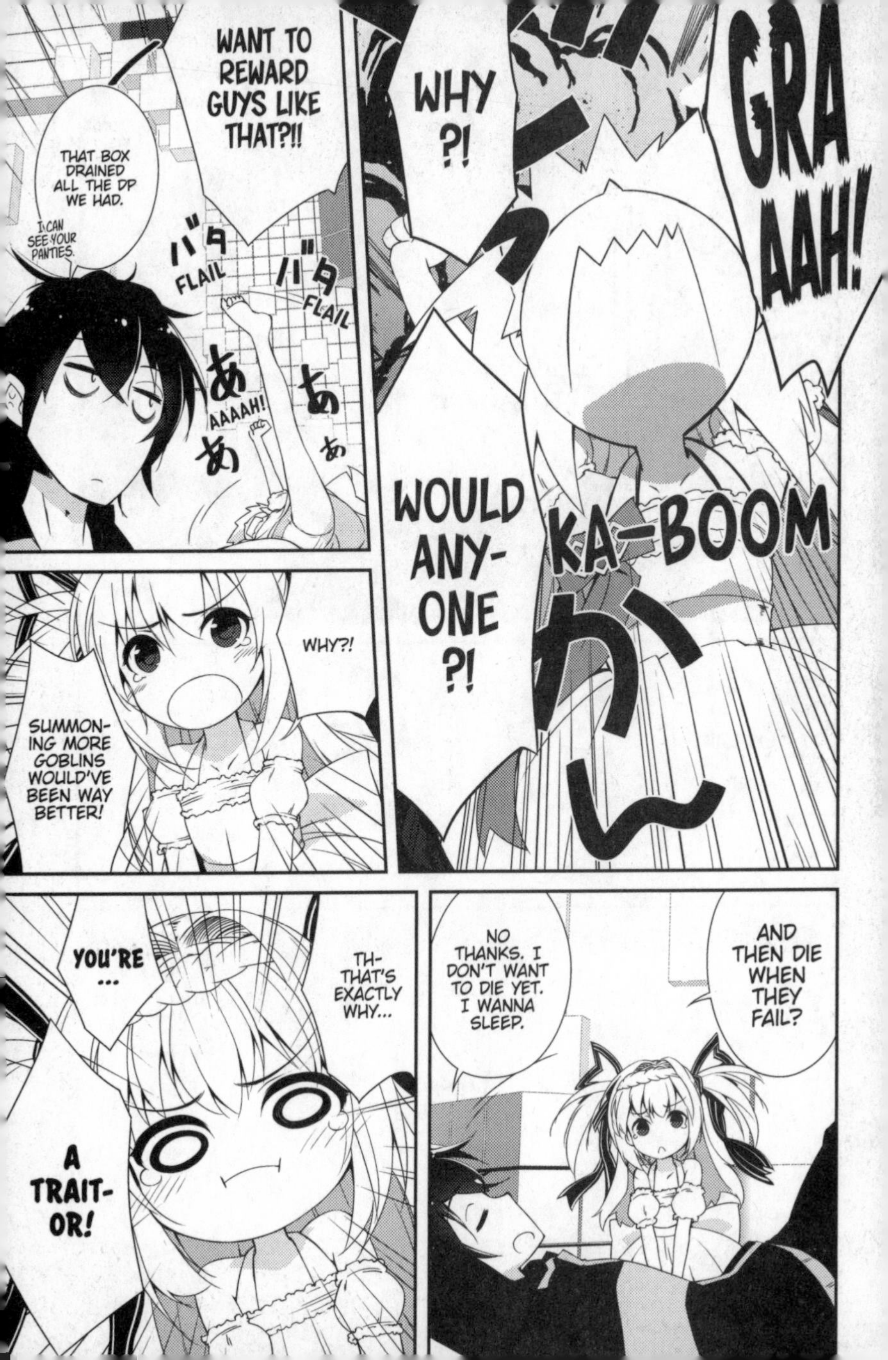
GRA AAH!
WHY ?!
WOULD ANY-ONE ?!
KA-BOOM
わ～
WANT TO REWARD GUYS LIKE THAT?!!
THAT BOX DRAINED ALL THE DP WE HAD.
I CAN SEE YOUR PANTIES.
バタ
FLAIL
バタ
FLAIL
あ
あ
AAAAH!
あ
あ
WHY?!
SUMMON-ING MORE GOBLINS WOULD'VE BEEN WAY BETTER!
AND THEN DIE WHEN THEY FAIL?
NO THANKS. I DON'T WANT TO DIE YET. I WANNA SLEEP.
TH-THAT'S EXACTLY WHY...
YOU'RE ...
A TRAIT-OR!

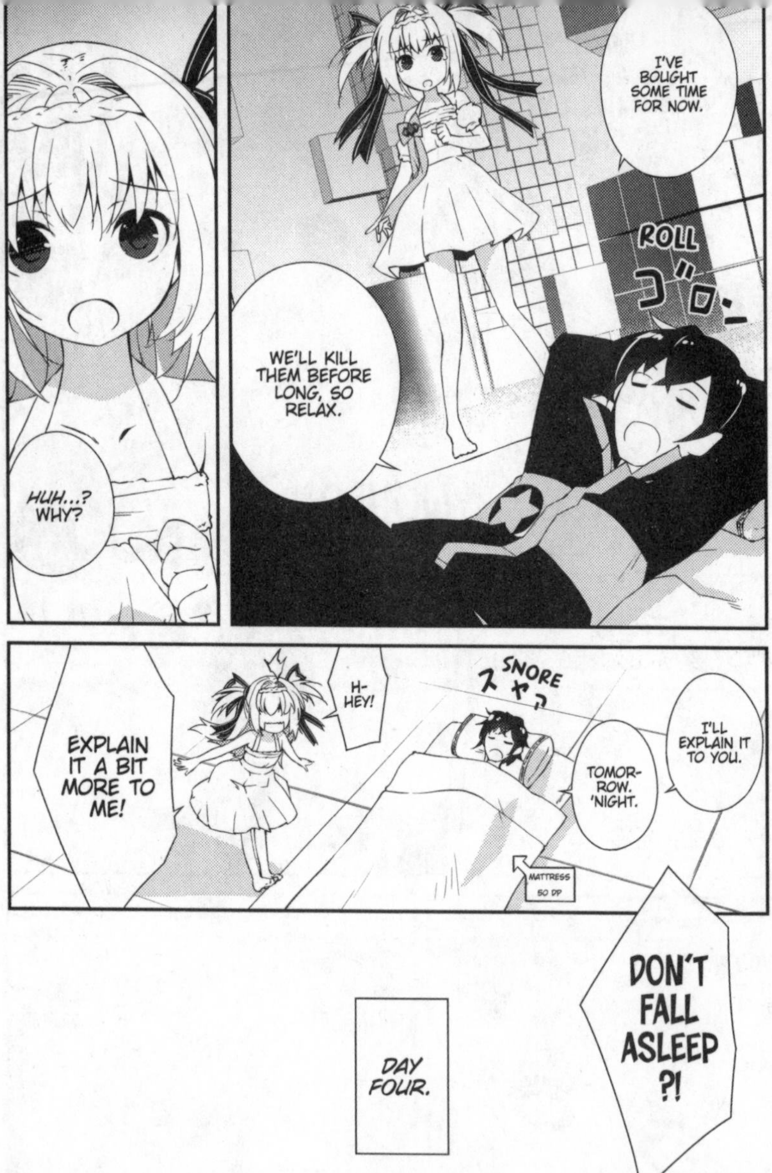
I'VE BOUGHT SOME TIME FOR NOW.
ROLL
ゴロン
WE'LL KILL THEM BEFORE LONG, SO RELAX.
HUH...? WHY?
I'LL EXPLAIN IT TO YOU.
TOMOR-ROW. 'NIGHT.
SNORE
スヤァ
MATTRESS 50 DP
H-HEY!
EXPLAIN IT A BIT MORE TO ME!
DON'T FALL ASLEEP?!
DAY FOUR.

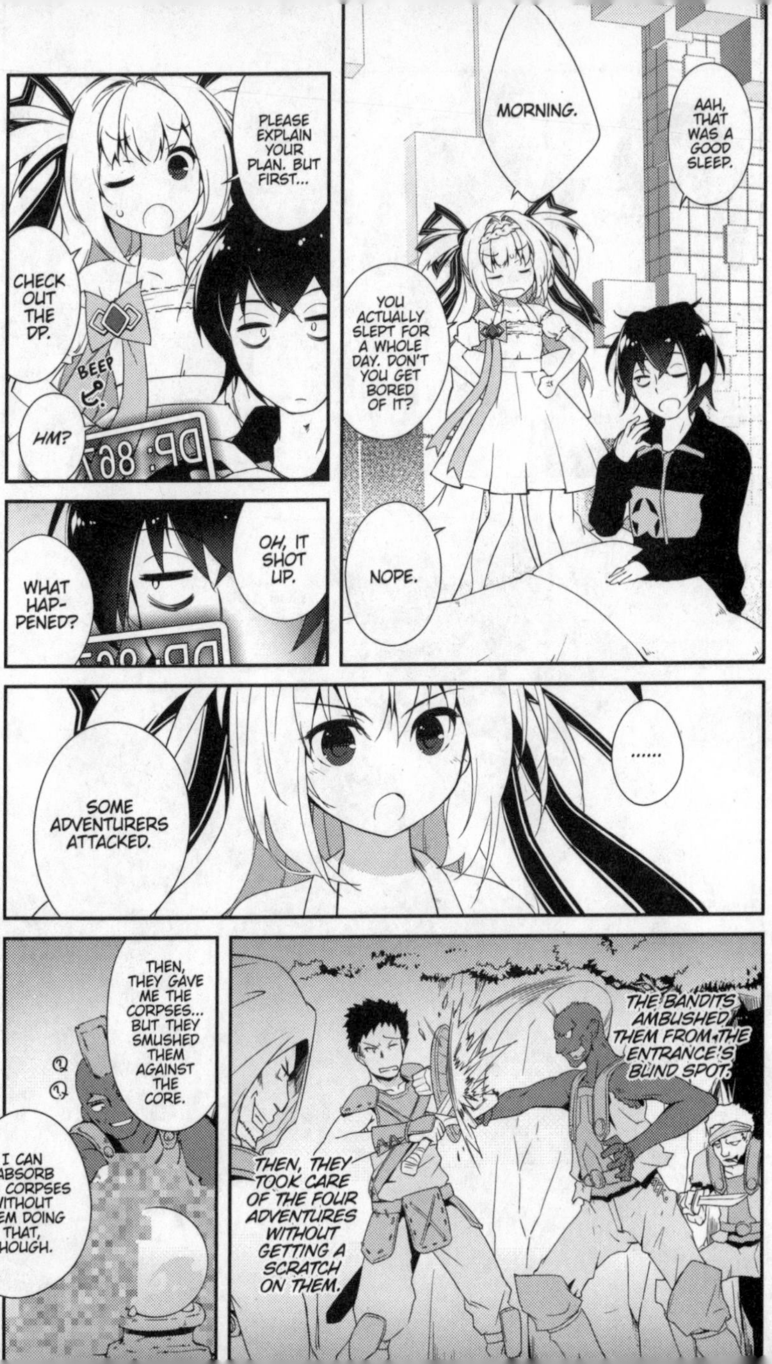

AAH, THAT WAS A GOOD SLEEP.
MORNING.
YOU ACTUALLY SLEPT FOR A WHOLE DAY. DON'T YOU GET BORED OF IT?
NOPE.
PLEASE EXPLAIN YOUR PLAN. BUT FIRST...
CHECK OUT THE DP.
BEEP
HM?
OH, IT SHOT UP.
WHAT HAP-PENED?
......
SOME ADVENTURERS ATTACKED.
THE BANDITS AMBUSHED THEM FROM THE ENTRANCE'S BLIND SPOT.
THEN, THEY TOOK CARE OF THE FOUR ADVENTURES WITHOUT GETTING A SCRATCH ON THEM.
THEN, THEY GAVE ME THE CORPSES... BUT THEY SMUSHED THEM AGAINST THE CORE.
I CAN ABSORB THE CORPSES WITHOUT THEM DOING THAT, THOUGH.

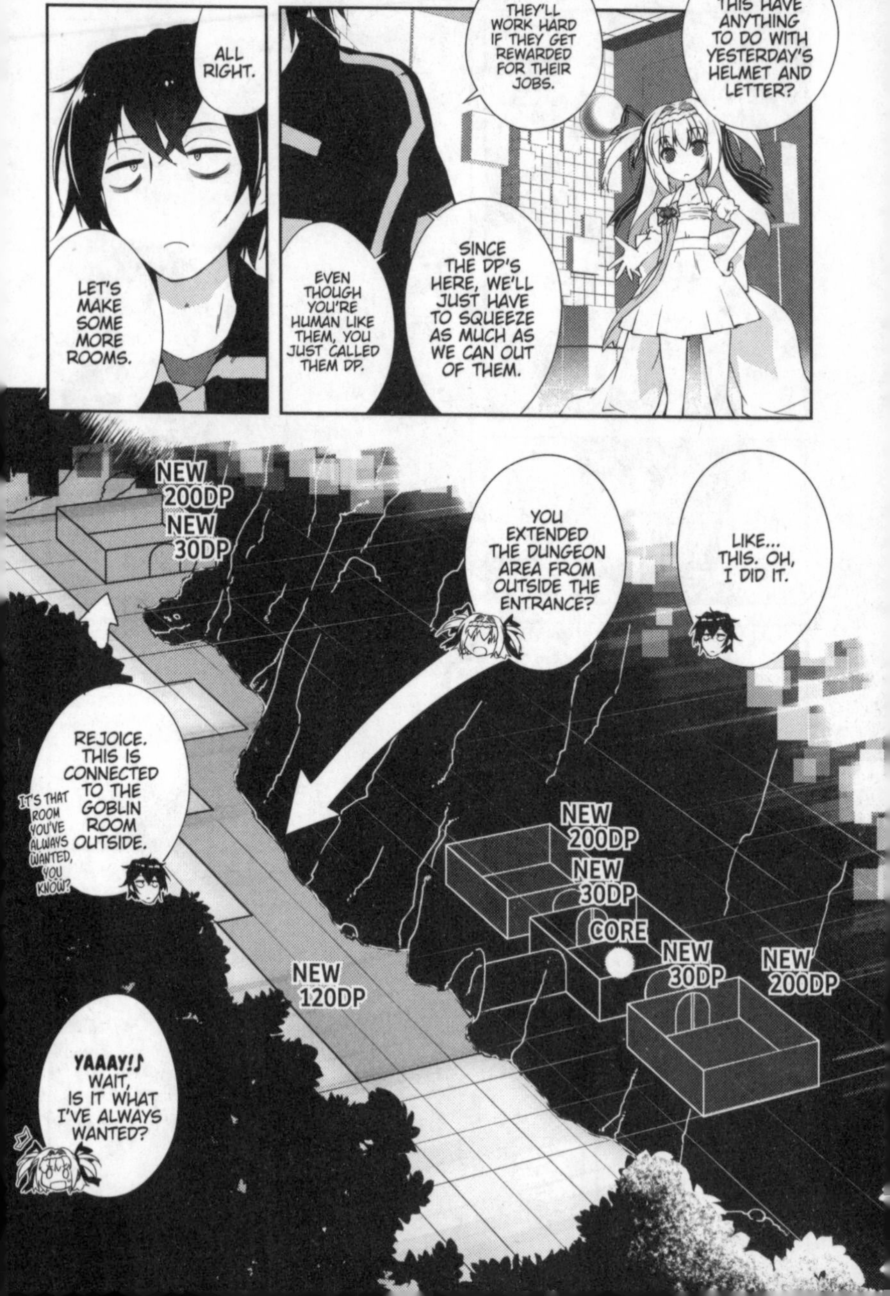
DOES THIS HAVE ANYTHING TO DO WITH YESTERDAY'S HELMET AND LETTER?
THEY'LL WORK HARD IF THEY GET REWARDED FOR THEIR JOBS.
SINCE THE DP'S HERE, WE'LL JUST HAVE TO SQUEEZE AS MUCH AS WE CAN OUT OF THEM.
EVEN THOUGH YOU'RE HUMAN LIKE THEM, YOU JUST CALLED THEM DP.
ALL RIGHT.
LET'S MAKE SOME MORE ROOMS.
LIKE... THIS. OH, I DID IT.
YOU EXTENDED THE DUNGEON AREA FROM OUTSIDE THE ENTRANCE?
NEW 200DP
NEW 30DP
REJOICE. THIS IS CONNECTED TO THE GOBLIN ROOM OUTSIDE.
IT'S THAT ROOM YOU'VE ALWAYS WANTED, YOU KNOW?
NEW 200DP
NEW 30DP
CORE
NEW 30DP
NEW 200DP
NEW 120DP
YAAAY!♪ WAIT, IS IT WHAT I'VE ALWAYS WANTED?

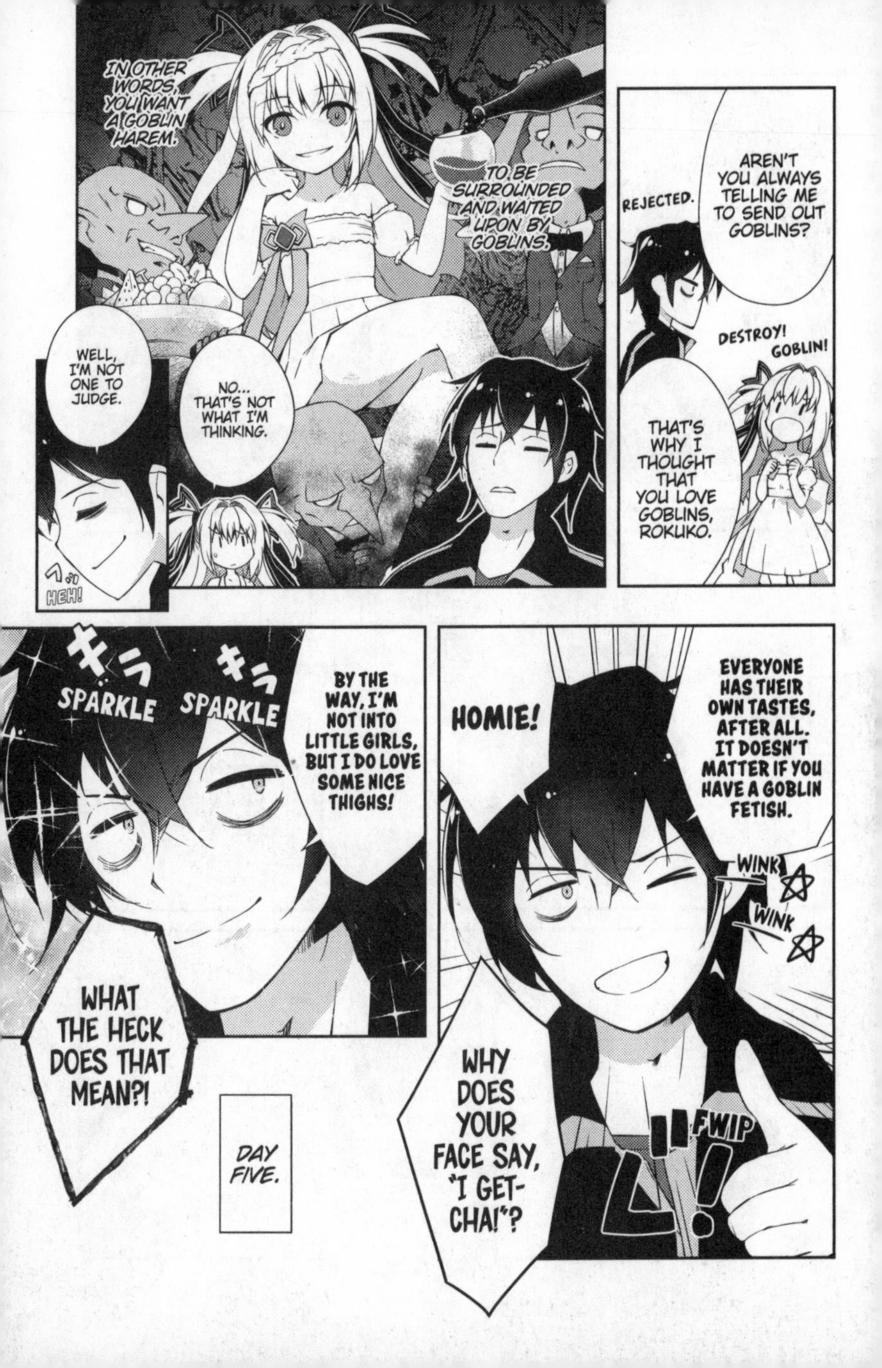

AREN'T YOU ALWAYS TELLING ME TO SEND OUT GOBLINS?
REJECTED.
DESTROY! GOBLIN!
THAT'S WHY I THOUGHT THAT YOU LOVE GOBLINS, ROKUKO.
IN OTHER WORDS, YOU WANT A GOBLIN HAREM.
TO BE SURROUNDED AND WAITED UPON BY GOBLINS.
NO... THAT'S NOT WHAT I'M THINKING.
WELL, I'M NOT ONE TO JUDGE.
HEH!
EVERYONE HAS THEIR OWN TASTES, AFTER ALL. IT DOESN'T MATTER IF YOU HAVE A GOBLIN FETISH.
HOMIE!
WINK
WINK
WHY DOES YOUR FACE SAY, "I GET-CHA!"?
FWIP
BY THE WAY, I'M NOT INTO LITTLE GIRLS, BUT I DO LOVE SOME NICE THIGHS!
キラ SPARKLE
キラ SPARKLE
WHAT THE HECK DOES THAT MEAN?!
DAY FIVE.

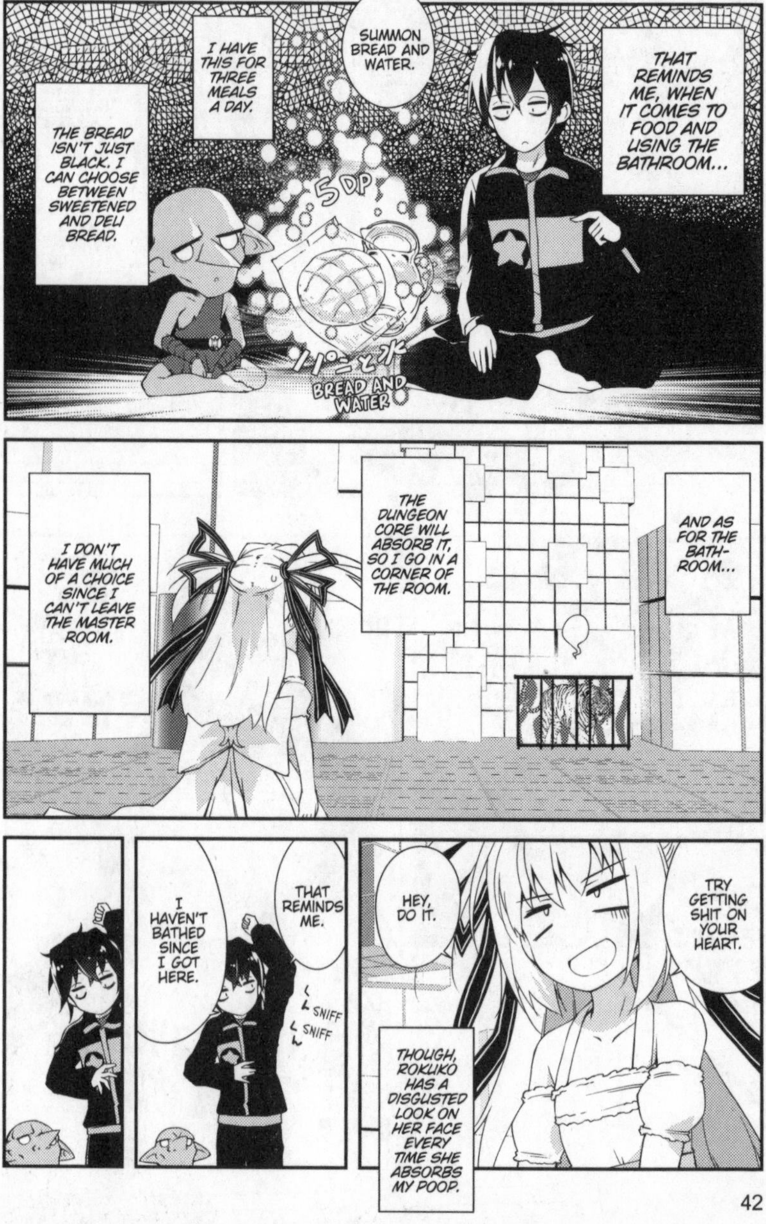
THAT REMINDS ME, WHEN IT COMES TO FOOD AND USING THE BATHROOM...
SUMMON BREAD AND WATER.
I HAVE THIS FOR THREE MEALS A DAY.
THE BREAD ISN'T JUST BLACK. I CAN CHOOSE BETWEEN SWEETENED AND DELI BREAD.
5 DP
BREAD AND WATER
AND AS FOR THE BATH-ROOM...
THE DUNGEON CORE WILL ABSORB IT, SO I GO IN A CORNER OF THE ROOM.
I DON'T HAVE MUCH OF A CHOICE SINCE I CAN'T LEAVE THE MASTER ROOM.
TRY GETTING SHIT ON YOUR HEART.
HEY, DO IT.
THOUGH, ROKUKO HAS A DISGUSTED LOOK ON HER FACE EVERY TIME SHE ABSORBS MY POOP.
THAT REMINDS ME.
I HAVEN'T BATHED SINCE I GOT HERE.
SNIFF
SNIFF

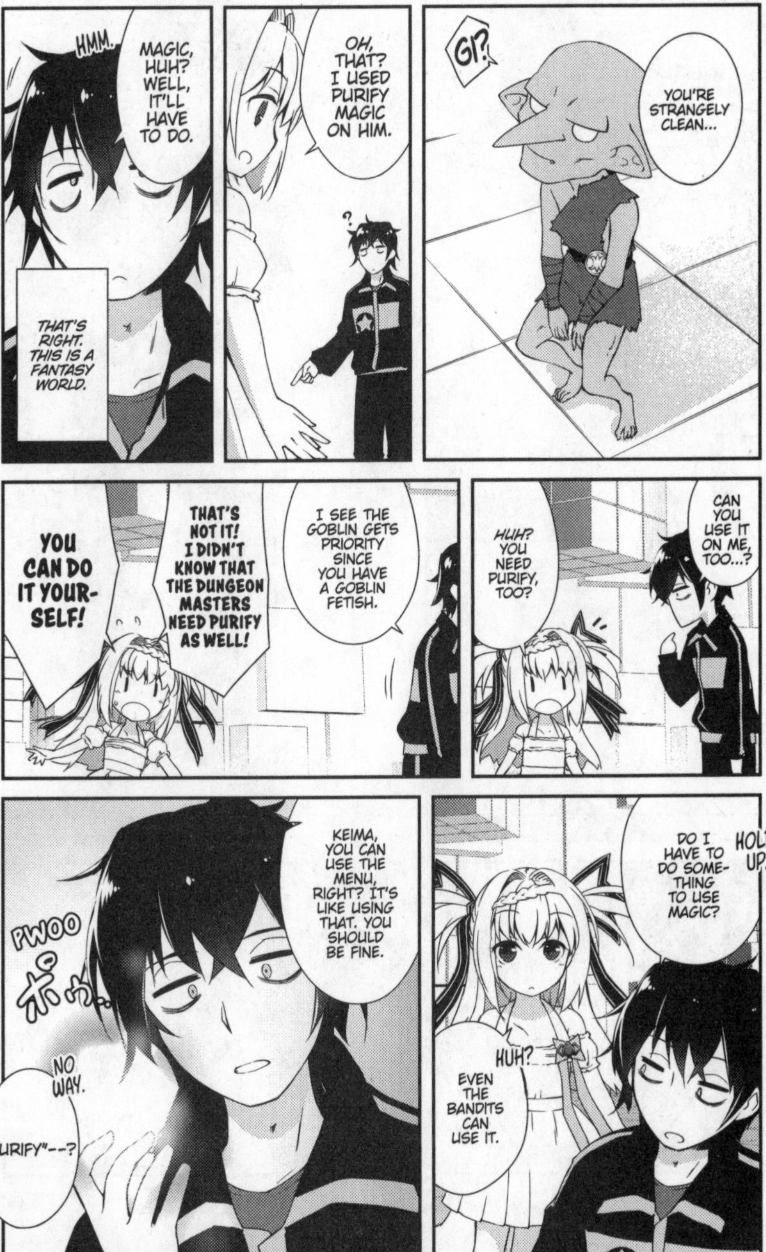
GI?
YOU'RE STRANGELY CLEAN...
OH, THAT? I USED PURIFY MAGIC ON HIM.
HMM.
MAGIC, HUH? WELL, IT'LL HAVE TO DO.
THAT'S RIGHT. THIS IS A FANTASY WORLD.
CAN YOU USE IT ON ME, TOO...?
HUH? YOU NEED PURIFY, TOO?
I SEE THE GOBLIN GETS PRIORITY SINCE YOU HAVE A GOBLIN FETISH.
THAT'S NOT IT! I DIDN'T KNOW THAT THE DUNGEON MASTERS NEED PURIFY AS WELL!
YOU CAN DO IT YOUR-SELF!
DO I HAVE TO DO SOME-THING TO USE MAGIC?
HOLD UP.
HUH?
EVEN THE BANDITS CAN USE IT.
KEIMA, YOU CAN USE THE MENU, RIGHT? IT'S LIKE USING THAT. YOU SHOULD BE FINE.
PWOO
NO WAY.
"PURIFY"--?

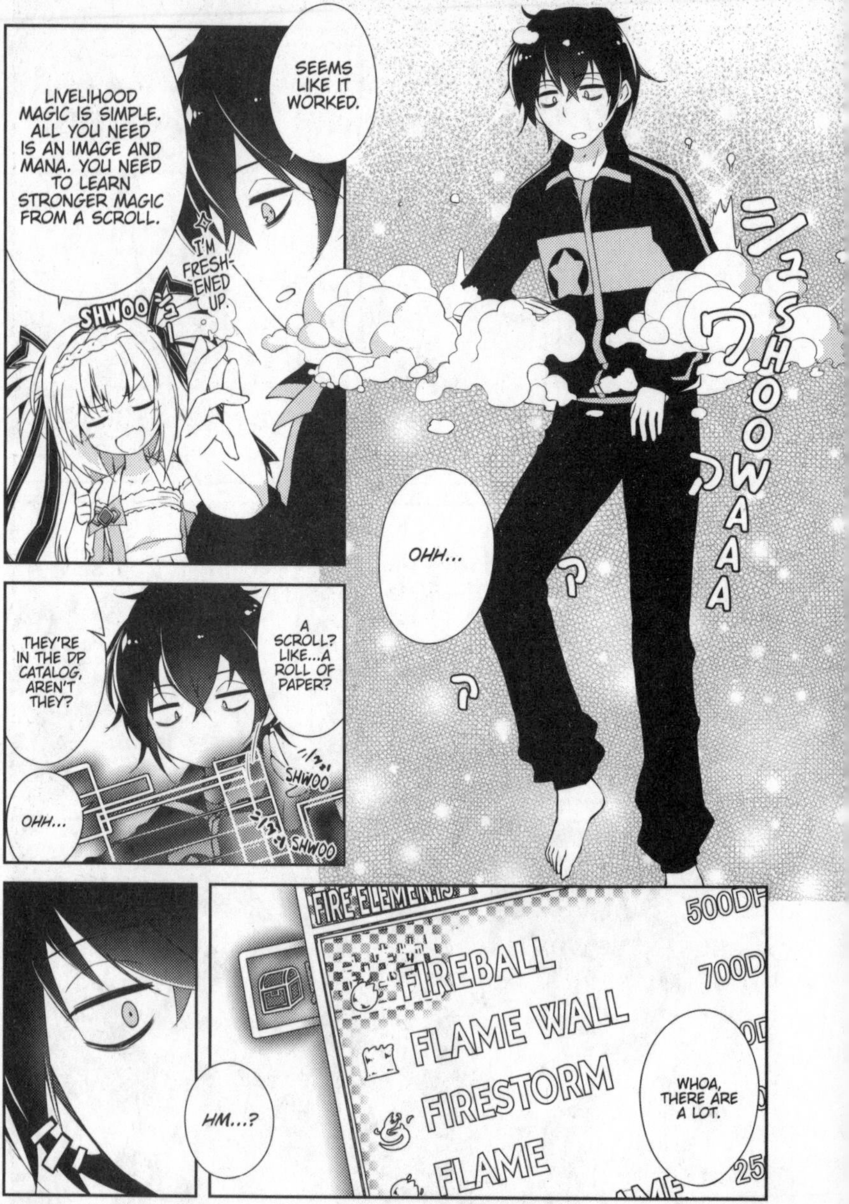
SHOOOWAAAA
OHH...
SEEMS LIKE IT WORKED.
LIVELIHOOD MAGIC IS SIMPLE. ALL YOU NEED IS AN IMAGE AND MANA. YOU NEED TO LEARN STRONGER MAGIC FROM A SCROLL.
I'M FRESHENED UP.
SHWOO
A SCROLL? LIKE...A ROLL OF PAPER?
THEY'RE IN THE DP CATALOG, AREN'T THEY?
SHWOO
SHWOO
OHH...
FIRE ELEMENTS
500D
FIREBALL
700D
FLAME WALL
FIRESTORM
FLAME
25
WHOA, THERE ARE A LOT.
HM...?

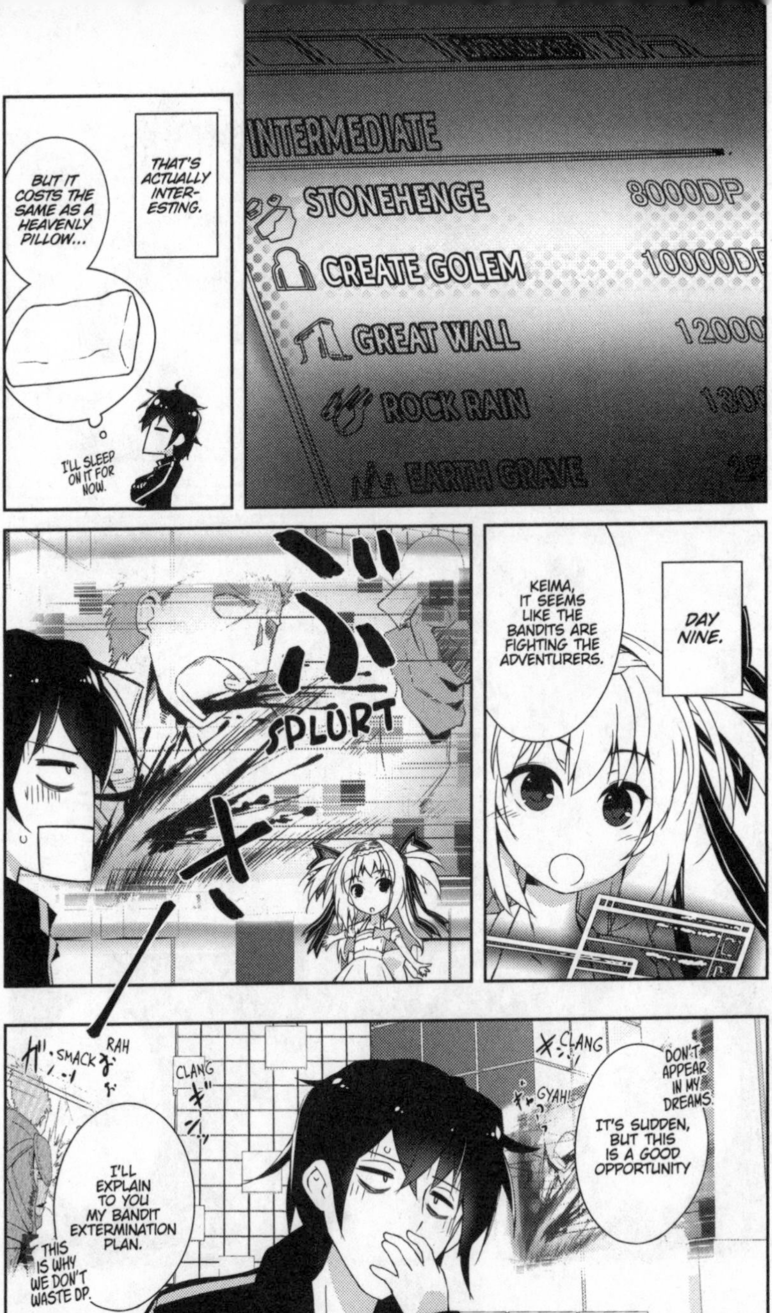
INTERMEDIATE
STONEHENGE 8000DP
CREATE GOLEM 10000DP
GREAT WALL 12000
ROCK RAIN
EARTH GRAVE
THAT'S ACTUALLY INTERESTING.
BUT IT COSTS THE SAME AS A HEAVENLY PILLOW...
I'LL SLEEP ON IT FOR NOW.
DAY NINE.
KEIMA, IT SEEMS LIKE THE BANDITS ARE FIGHTING THE ADVENTURERS.
SPLURT
DON'T APPEAR IN MY DREAMS.
IT'S SUDDEN, BUT THIS IS A GOOD OPPORTUNITY
CLANG
GYAH!
I'LL EXPLAIN TO YOU MY BANDIT EXTERMINATION PLAN.
CLANG
RAH
SMACK
THIS IS WHY WE DON'T WASTE DP.

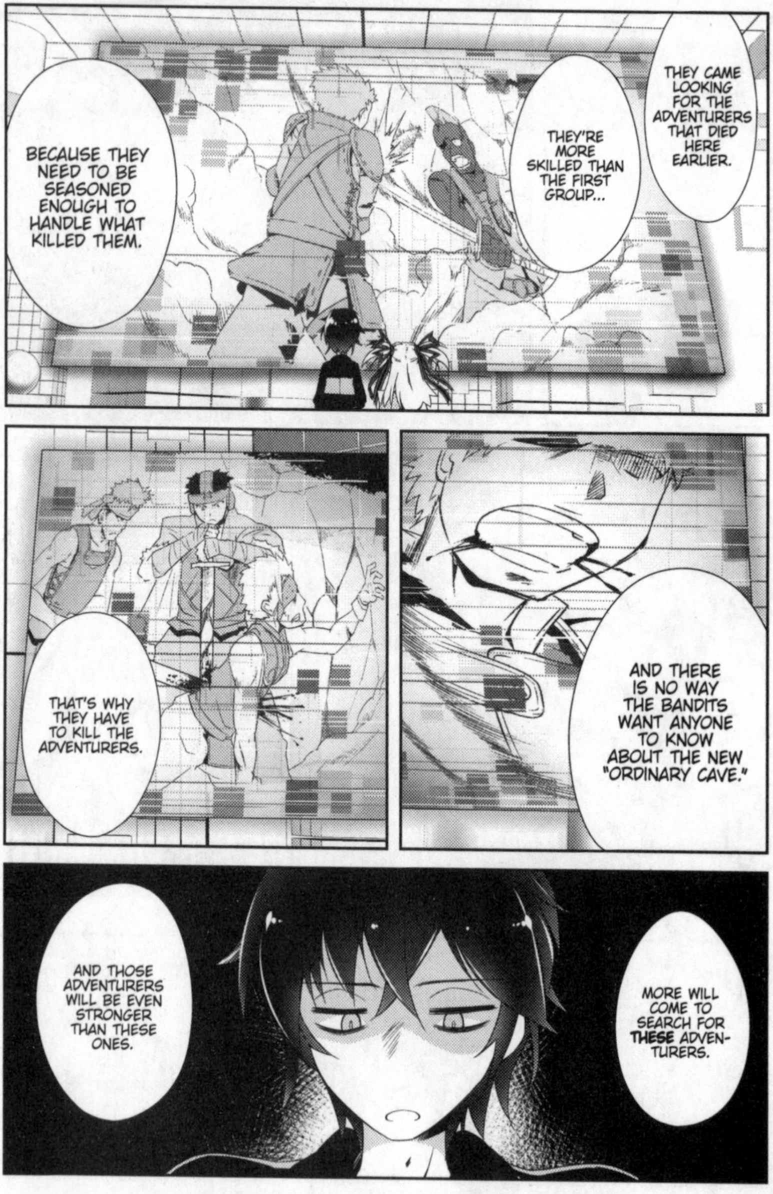
THEY CAME LOOKING FOR THE ADVENTURERS THAT DIED HERE EARLIER.
THEY'RE MORE SKILLED THAN THE FIRST GROUP...
BECAUSE THEY NEED TO BE SEASONED ENOUGH TO HANDLE WHAT KILLED THEM.
AND THERE IS NO WAY THE BANDITS WANT ANYONE TO KNOW ABOUT THE NEW "ORDINARY CAVE."
THAT'S WHY THEY HAVE TO KILL THE ADVENTURERS.
MORE WILL COME TO SEARCH FOR **THESE** ADVEN-TURERS.
AND THOSE ADVENTURERS WILL BE EVEN STRONGER THAN THESE ONES.

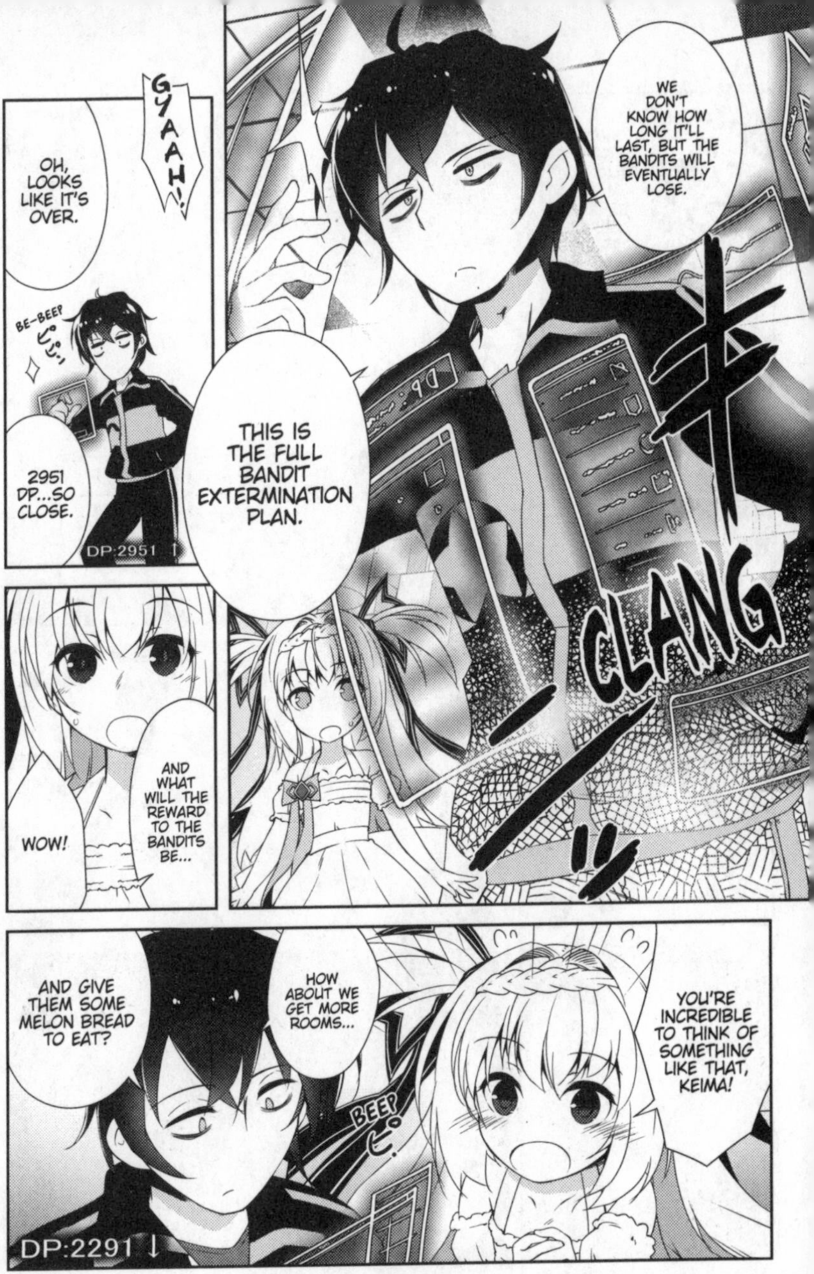
WE DON'T KNOW HOW LONG IT'LL LAST, BUT THE BANDITS WILL EVENTUALLY LOSE.
THIS IS THE FULL BANDIT EXTERMINATION PLAN.
CLANG
GYAAH!!
OH, LOOKS LIKE IT'S OVER.
BE-BEEP
ピピッ
2951 DP...SO CLOSE.
DP:2951 ↑
AND WHAT WILL THE REWARD TO THE BANDITS BE...
WOW!
YOU'RE INCREDIBLE TO THINK OF SOMETHING LIKE THAT, KEIMA!
HOW ABOUT WE GET MORE ROOMS...
AND GIVE THEM SOME MELON BREAD TO EAT?
BEEP
ピ
DP:2291 ↓

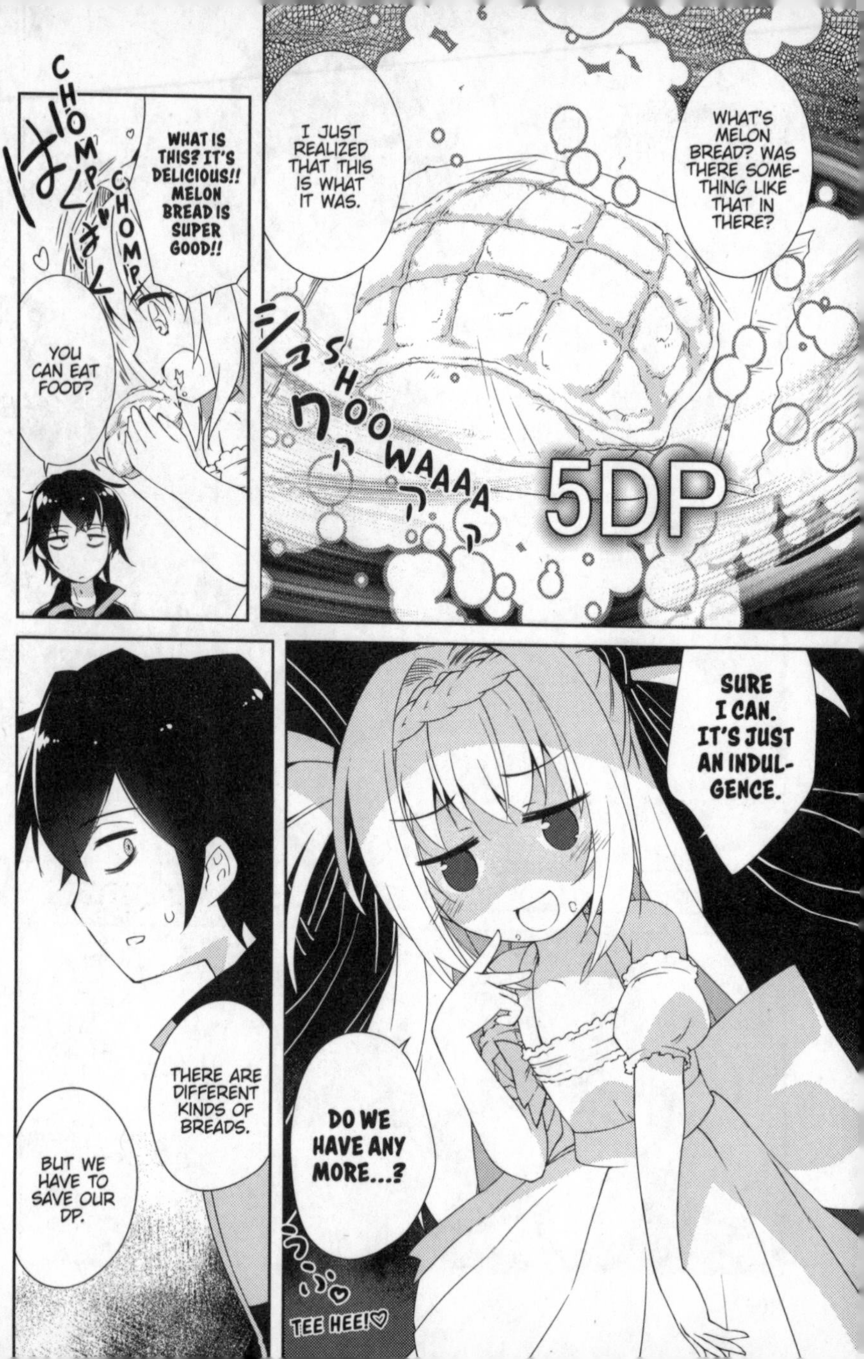
WHAT'S MELON BREAD? WAS THERE SOME-THING LIKE THAT IN THERE?
I JUST REALIZED THAT THIS IS WHAT IT WAS.
SHOOWAAAA
5DP
CHOMP
CHOMP
WHAT IS THIS? IT'S DELICIOUS!! MELON BREAD IS SUPER GOOD!!
YOU CAN EAT FOOD?
SURE I CAN. IT'S JUST AN INDUL-GENCE.
DO WE HAVE ANY MORE...?
TEE HEE!♡
THERE ARE DIFFERENT KINDS OF BREADS.
BUT WE HAVE TO SAVE OUR DP.

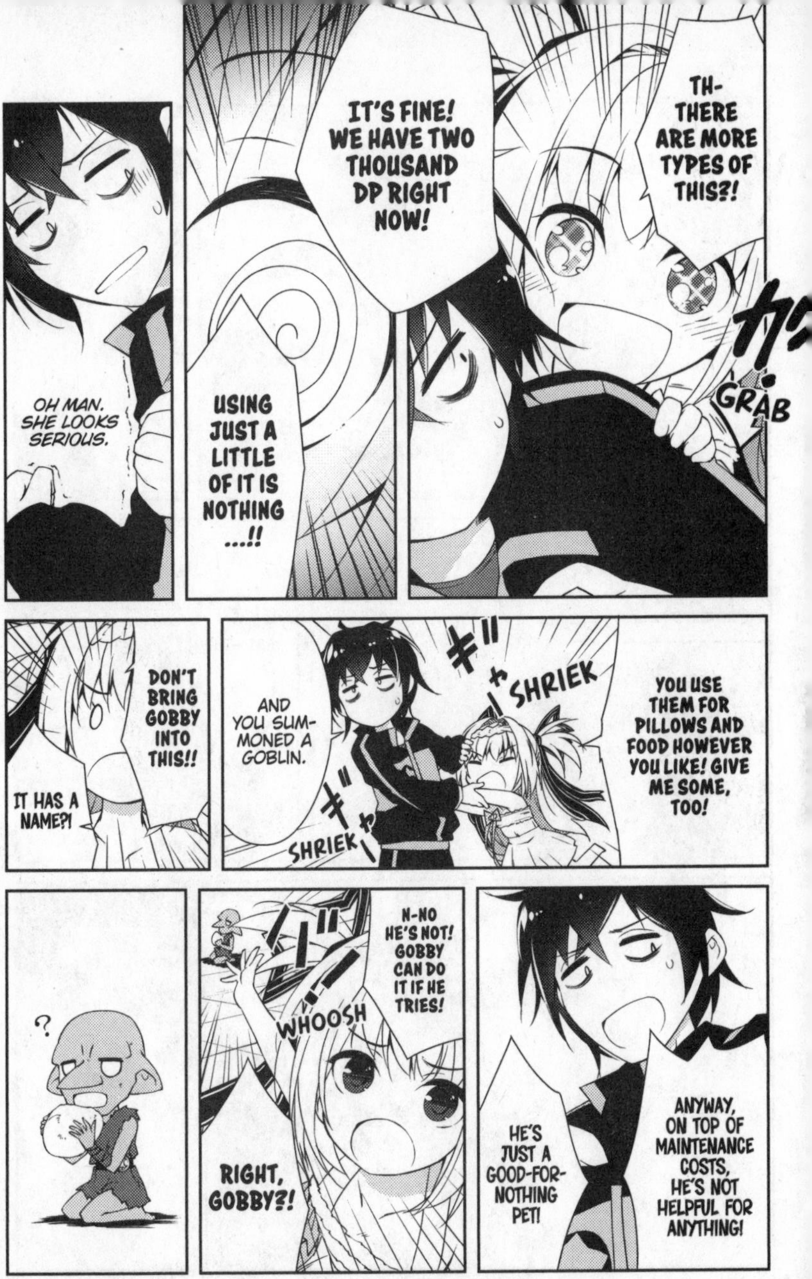
TH- THERE ARE MORE TYPES OF THIS?!
GRAB
IT'S FINE! WE HAVE TWO THOUSAND DP RIGHT NOW!
USING JUST A LITTLE OF IT IS NOTHING ...!!
OH MAN. SHE LOOKS SERIOUS.
YOU USE THEM FOR PILLOWS AND FOOD HOWEVER YOU LIKE! GIVE ME SOME, TOO!
SHRIEK
AND YOU SUMMONED A GOBLIN.
SHRIEK
DON'T BRING GOBBY INTO THIS!!
IT HAS A NAME?!
ANYWAY, ON TOP OF MAINTENANCE COSTS, HE'S NOT HELPFUL FOR ANYTHING!
HE'S JUST A GOOD-FOR-NOTHING PET!
N-NO HE'S NOT! GOBBY CAN DO IT IF HE TRIES!
WHOOSH
RIGHT, GOBBY?!
?

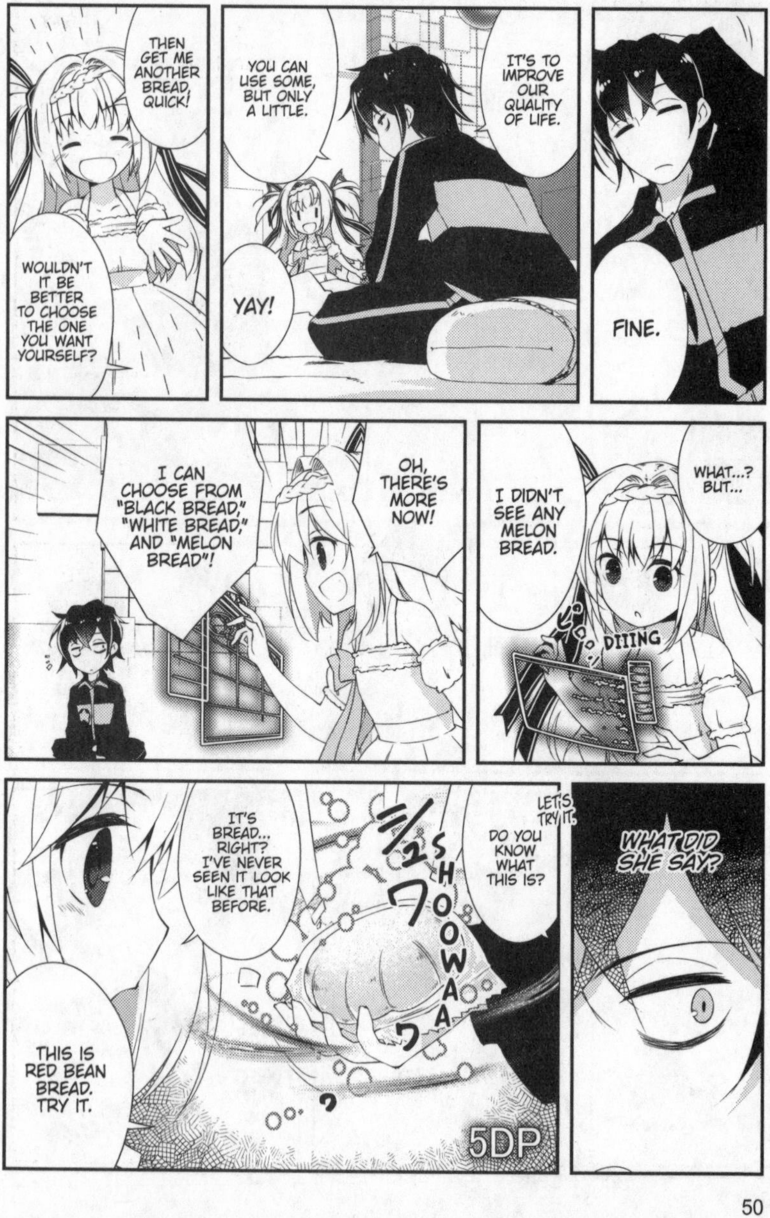
FINE.
IT'S TO IMPROVE OUR QUALITY OF LIFE.
YOU CAN USE SOME, BUT ONLY A LITTLE.
YAY!
THEN GET ME ANOTHER BREAD, QUICK!
WOULDN'T IT BE BETTER TO CHOOSE THE ONE YOU WANT YOURSELF?
WHAT...? BUT...
I DIDN'T SEE ANY MELON BREAD.
DIIING
OH, THERE'S MORE NOW!
I CAN CHOOSE FROM "BLACK BREAD," "WHITE BREAD," AND "MELON BREAD"!
WHAT DID SHE SAY?
LET'S TRY IT.
DO YOU KNOW WHAT THIS IS?
SHOOWAA
IT'S BREAD... RIGHT? I'VE NEVER SEEN IT LOOK LIKE THAT BEFORE.
THIS IS RED BEAN BREAD. TRY IT.
5DP

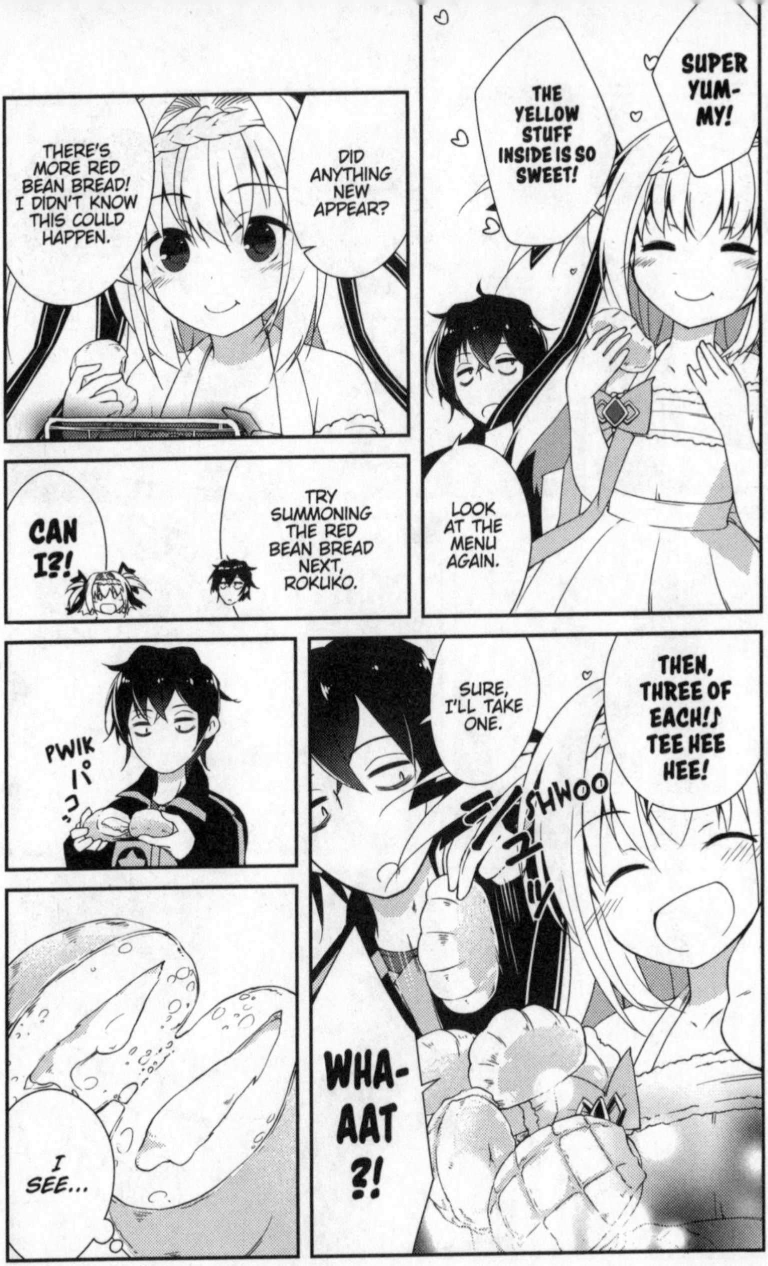
SUPER YUM-MY!
THE YELLOW STUFF INSIDE IS SO SWEET!
LOOK AT THE MENU AGAIN.
DID ANYTHING NEW APPEAR?
THERE'S MORE RED BEAN BREAD! I DIDN'T KNOW THIS COULD HAPPEN.
TRY SUMMONING THE RED BEAN BREAD NEXT, ROKUKO.
CAN I?!
THEN, THREE OF EACH!♪ TEE HEE HEE!
SURE, I'LL TAKE ONE.
SHWOO
WHA-AAT?!
PWIK
パッ
I SEE...

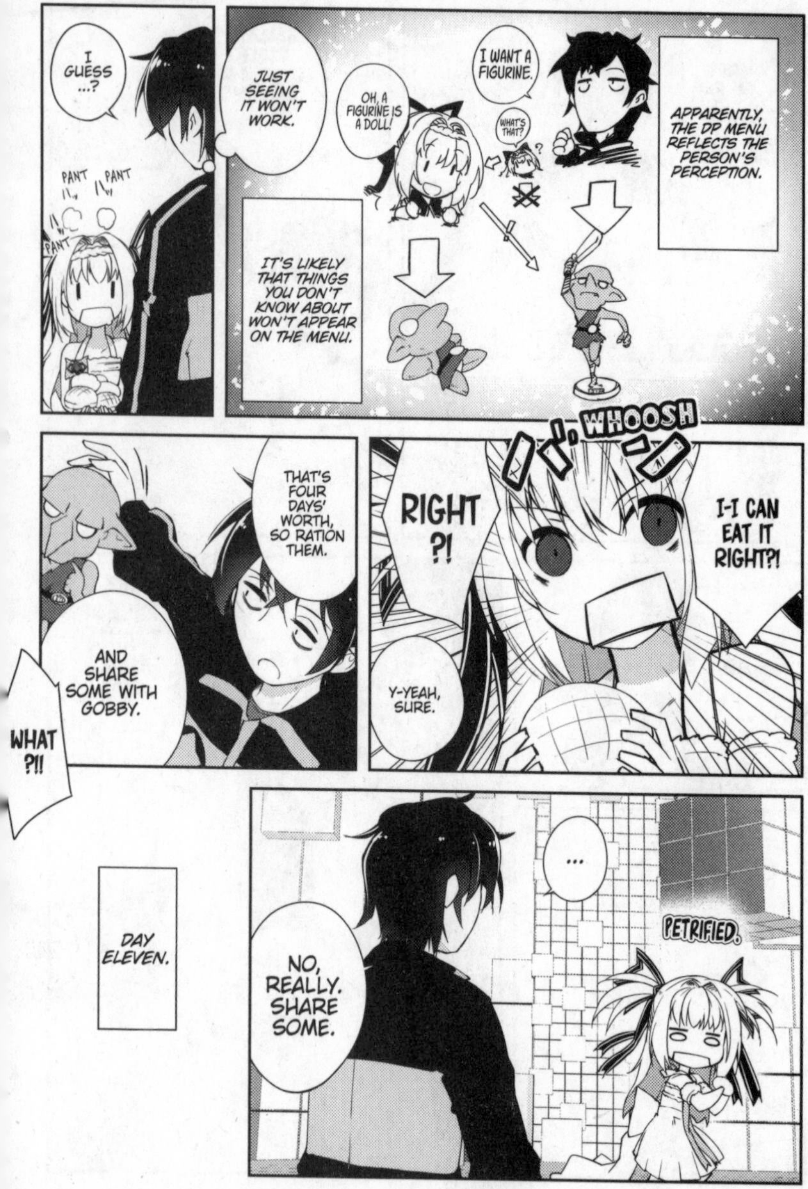
APPARENTLY, THE DP MENU REFLECTS THE PERSON'S PERCEPTION.
I WANT A FIGURINE.
WHAT'S THAT?
OH, A FIGURINE IS A DOLL!
IT'S LIKELY THAT THINGS YOU DON'T KNOW ABOUT WON'T APPEAR ON THE MENU.
JUST SEEING IT WON'T WORK.
I GUESS ...?
PANT PANT
PANT
WHOOSH
I-I CAN EAT IT RIGHT?!
RIGHT ?!
Y-YEAH, SURE.
THAT'S FOUR DAYS' WORTH, SO RATION THEM.
AND SHARE SOME WITH GOBBY.
WHAT ?!!
...
PETRIFIED.
NO, REALLY. SHARE SOME.
DAY ELEVEN.

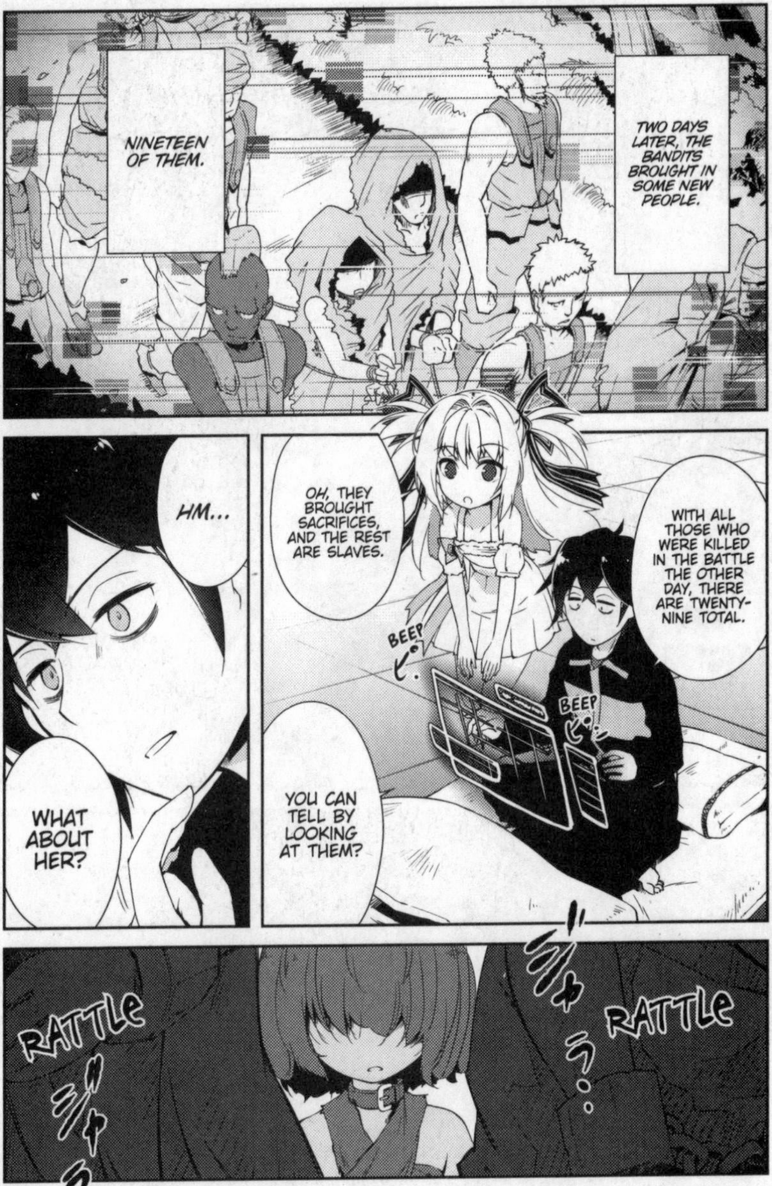
TWO DAYS LATER, THE BANDITS BROUGHT IN SOME NEW PEOPLE.
NINETEEN OF THEM.
WITH ALL THOSE WHO WERE KILLED IN THE BATTLE THE OTHER DAY, THERE ARE TWENTY-NINE TOTAL.
OH, THEY BROUGHT SACRIFICES, AND THE REST ARE SLAVES.
BEEP
BEEP
YOU CAN TELL BY LOOKING AT THEM?
HM...
WHAT ABOUT HER?
RATTLE
RATTLE

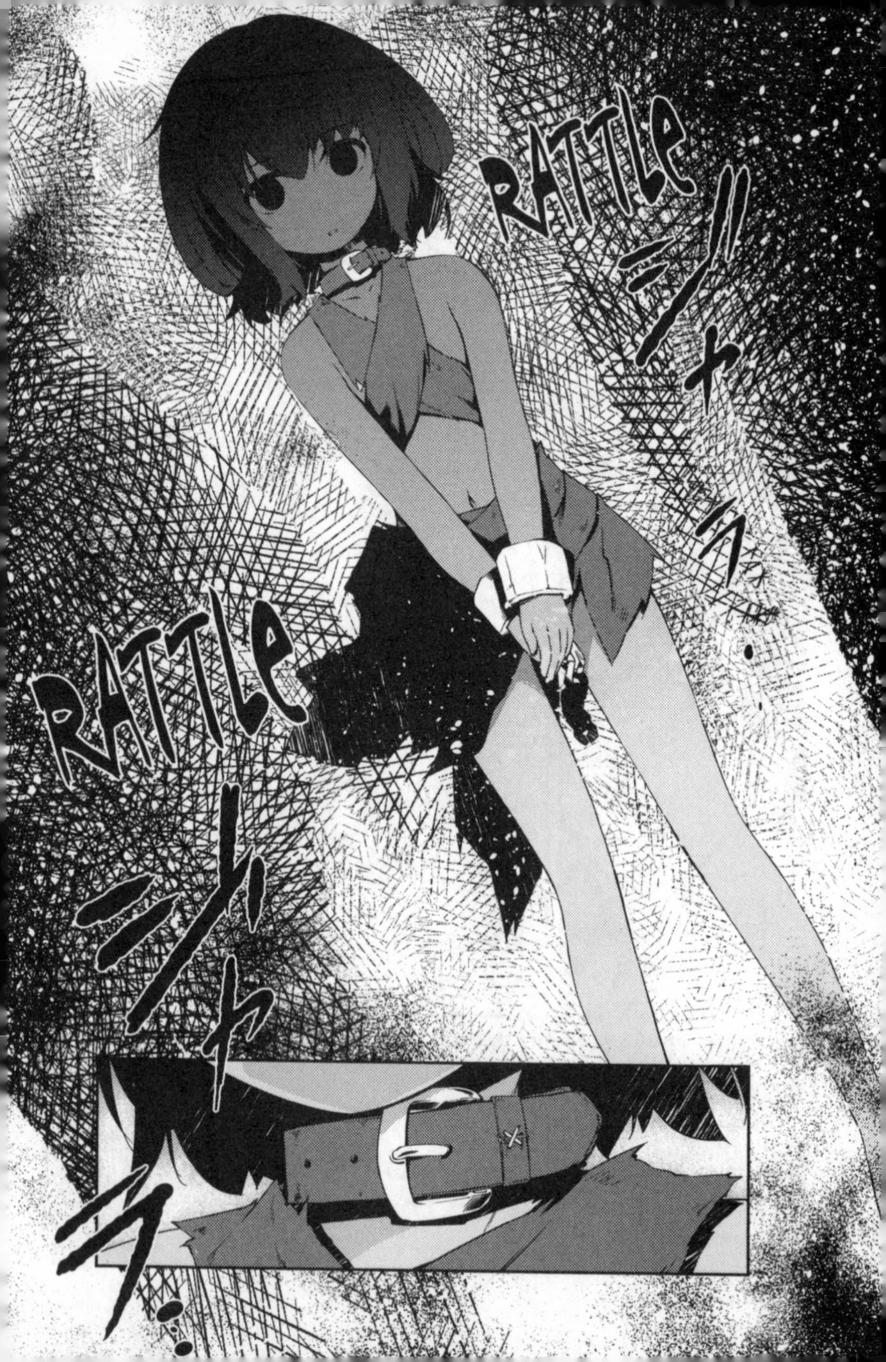
RATTLE
RATTLE

LAZY
DUNGEON
MASTER

LAZY
DUNGEON
MASTER

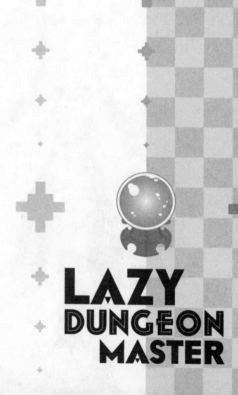

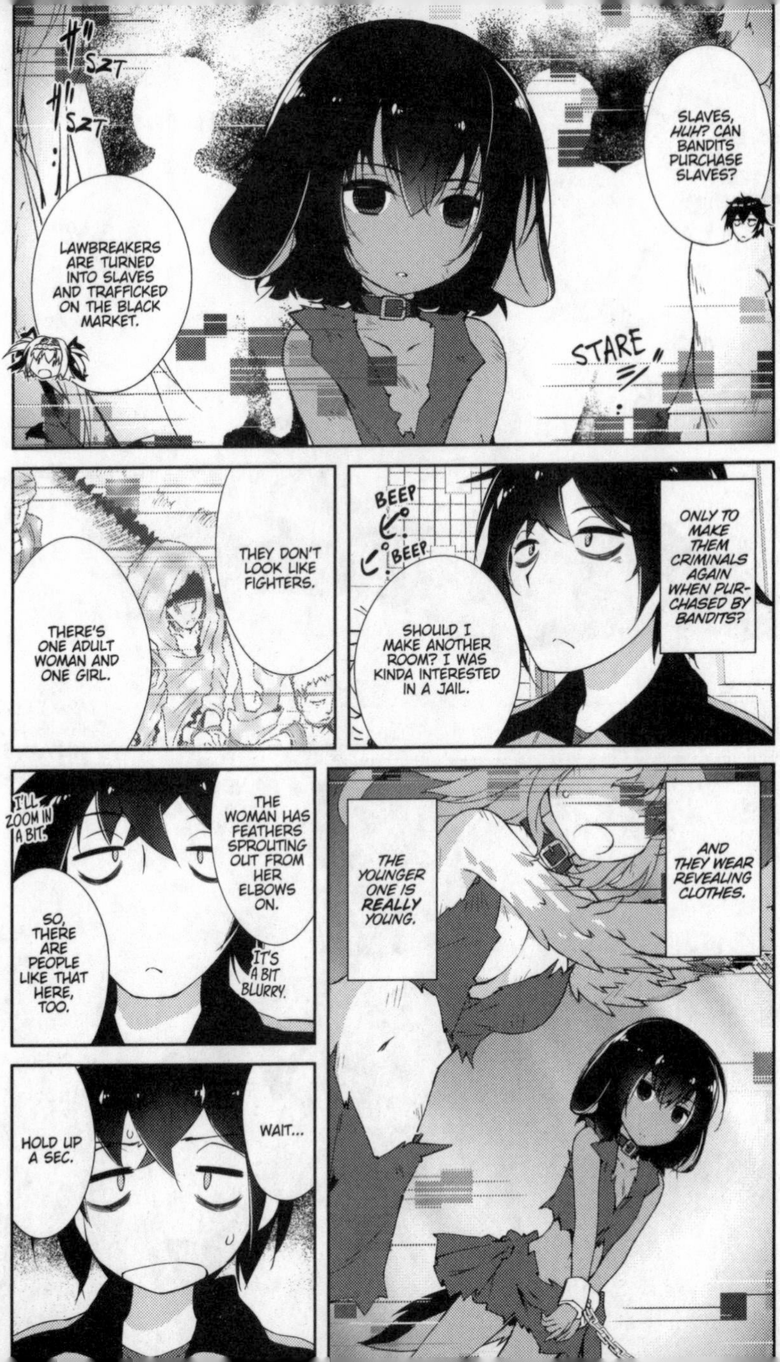

SLAVES, HUH? CAN BANDITS PURCHASE SLAVES?
SZT
SZT
LAWBREAKERS ARE TURNED INTO SLAVES AND TRAFFICKED ON THE BLACK MARKET.
STARE
ONLY TO MAKE THEM CRIMINALS AGAIN WHEN PURCHASED BY BANDITS?
BEEP
BEEP
SHOULD I MAKE ANOTHER ROOM? I WAS KINDA INTERESTED IN A JAIL.
THEY DON'T LOOK LIKE FIGHTERS.
THERE'S ONE ADULT WOMAN AND ONE GIRL.
AND THEY WEAR REVEALING CLOTHES.
THE YOUNGER ONE IS REALLY YOUNG.
THE WOMAN HAS FEATHERS SPROUTING OUT FROM HER ELBOWS ON.
I'LL ZOOM IN A BIT.
IT'S A BIT BLURRY.
SO, THERE ARE PEOPLE LIKE THAT HERE, TOO.
WAIT...
HOLD UP A SEC.

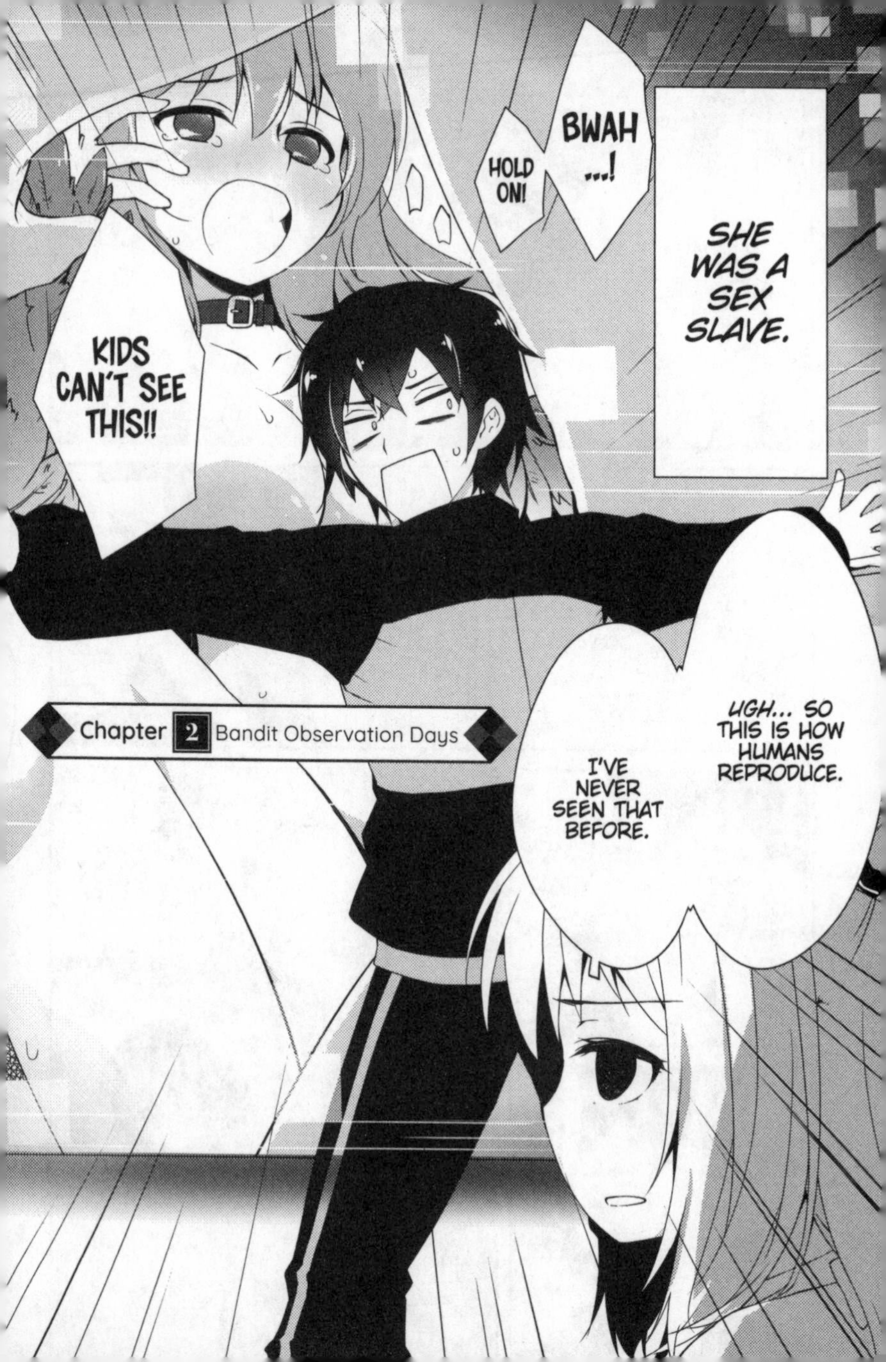
SHE WAS A SEX SLAVE.
BWAH ...!
HOLD ON!
KIDS CAN'T SEE THIS!!
Chapter 2 Bandit Observation Days
UGH... SO THIS IS HOW HUMANS REPRODUCE.
I'VE NEVER SEEN THAT BEFORE.

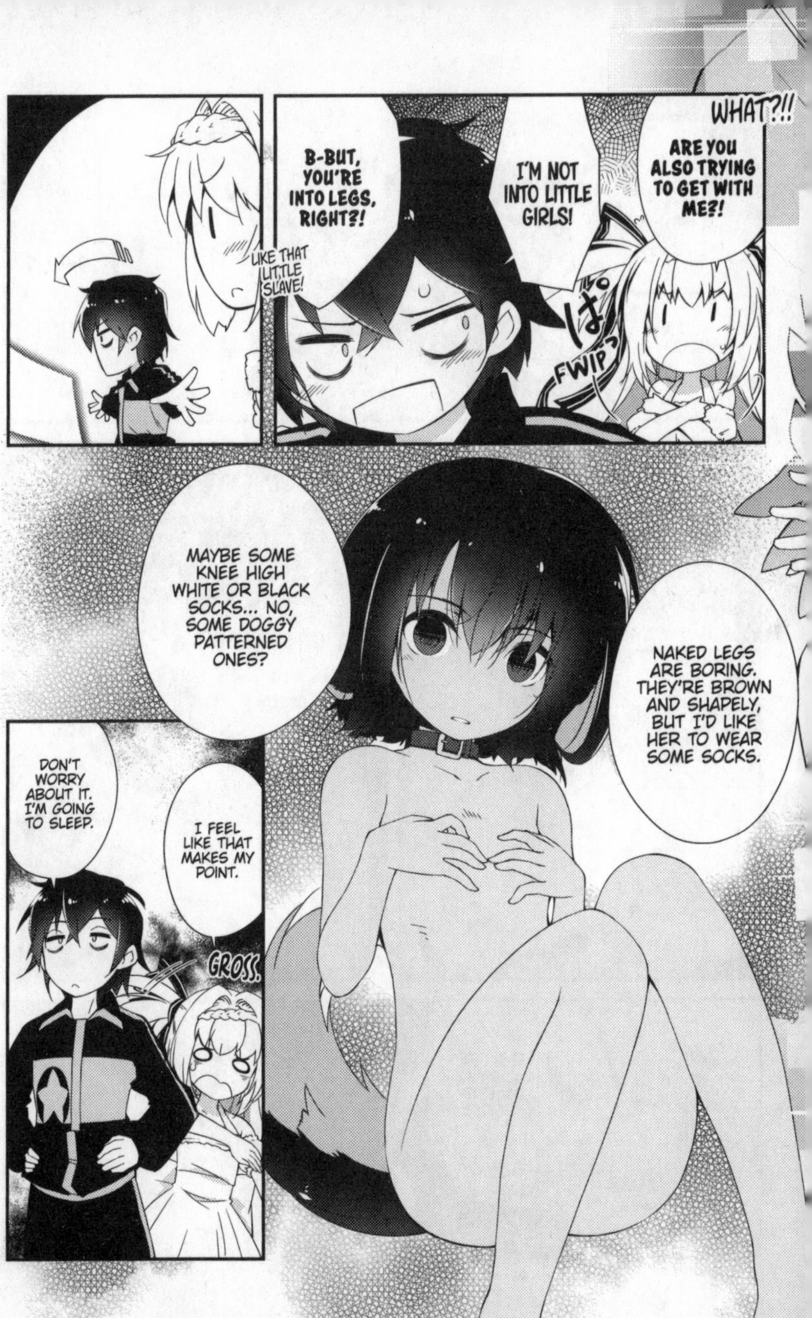
WHAT?!!
ARE YOU ALSO TRYING TO GET WITH ME?!
ぱっ
FWIP
I'M NOT INTO LITTLE GIRLS!
B-BUT, YOU'RE INTO LEGS, RIGHT?!
LIKE THAT LITTLE SLAVE!
NAKED LEGS ARE BORING. THEY'RE BROWN AND SHAPELY, BUT I'D LIKE HER TO WEAR SOME SOCKS.
MAYBE SOME KNEE HIGH WHITE OR BLACK SOCKS... NO, SOME DOGGY PATTERNED ONES?
I FEEL LIKE THAT MAKES MY POINT.
DON'T WORRY ABOUT IT. I'M GOING TO SLEEP.
GROSS.

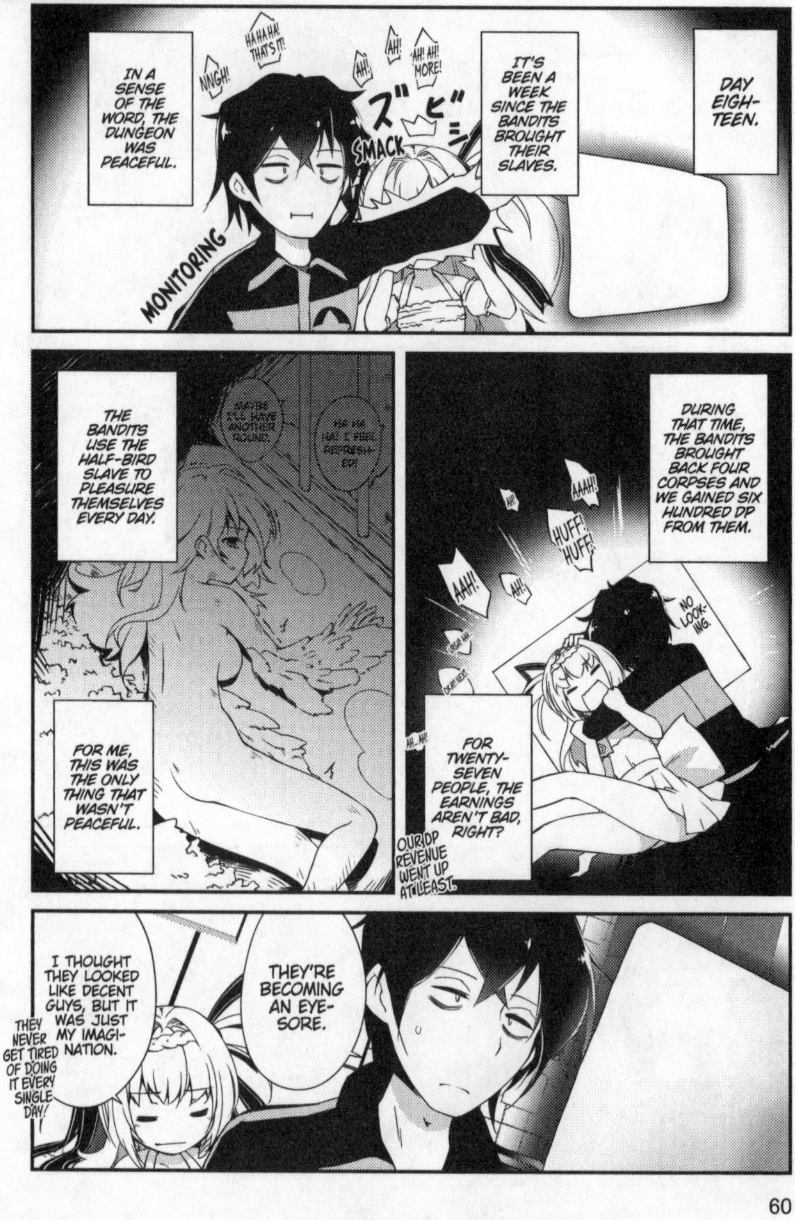
DAY EIGHTEEN.
IT'S BEEN A WEEK SINCE THE BANDITS BROUGHT THEIR SLAVES.
AH! AH! MORE!
AH!
AH!
HA HA HA! THAT'S IT!
NNGH!
ズビシ
SMACK
IN A SENSE OF THE WORD, THE DUNGEON WAS PEACEFUL.
MONITORING
DURING THAT TIME, THE BANDITS BROUGHT BACK FOUR CORPSES AND WE GAINED SIX HUNDRED DP FROM THEM.
AAAH!
AH!
HUFF! HUFF!
AH!
AH!
NO LOOKING.
FOR TWENTY-SEVEN PEOPLE, THE EARNINGS AREN'T BAD, RIGHT?
OUR DP REVENUE WENT UP AT LEAST.
THE BANDITS USE THE HALF-BIRD SLAVE TO PLEASURE THEMSELVES EVERY DAY.
HA HA HA! I FEEL REFRESHED!
MAYBE I'LL HAVE ANOTHER ROUND.
FOR ME, THIS WAS THE ONLY THING THAT WASN'T PEACEFUL.
THEY'RE BECOMING AN EYESORE.
I THOUGHT THEY LOOKED LIKE DECENT GUYS, BUT IT WAS JUST MY IMAGINATION.
THEY NEVER GET TIRED OF DOING IT EVERY SINGLE DAY!

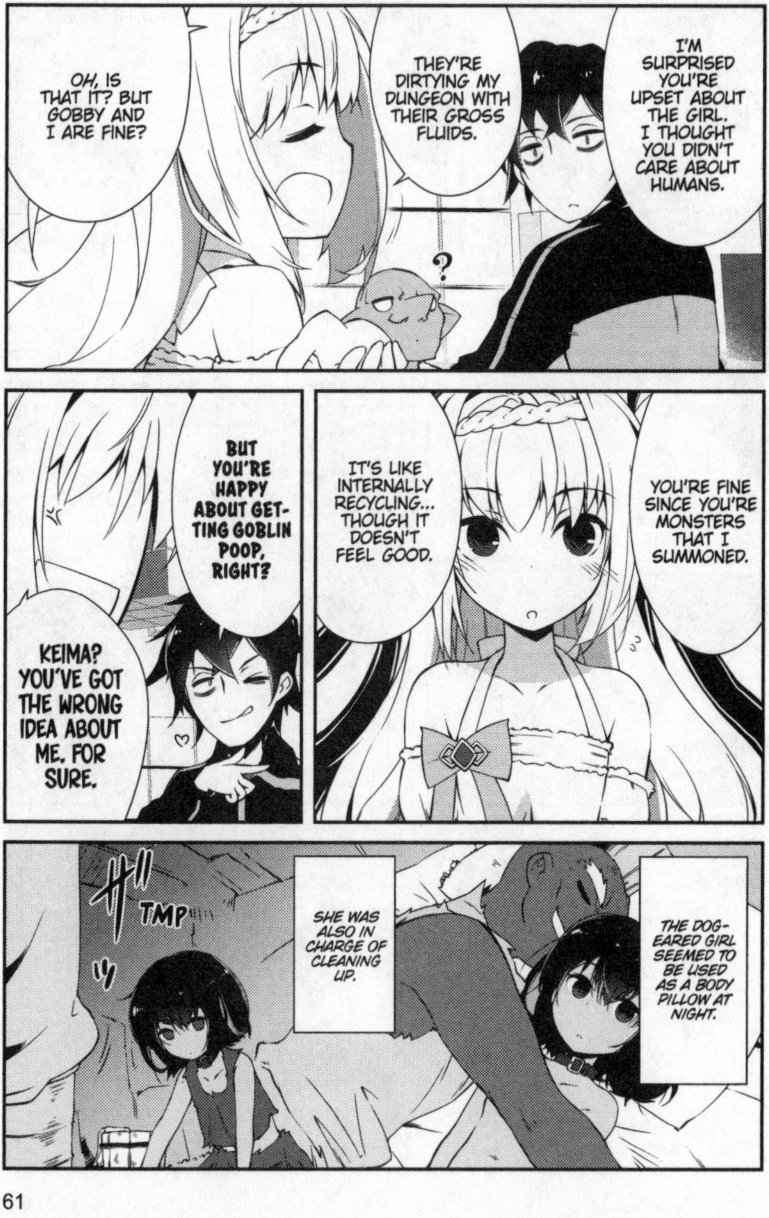
I'M SURPRISED YOU'RE UPSET ABOUT THE GIRL. I THOUGHT YOU DIDN'T CARE ABOUT HUMANS.
THEY'RE DIRTYING MY DUNGEON WITH THEIR GROSS FLUIDS.
OH, IS THAT IT? BUT GOBBY AND I ARE FINE?
YOU'RE FINE SINCE YOU'RE MONSTERS THAT I SUMMONED.
IT'S LIKE INTERNALLY RECYCLING... THOUGH IT DOESN'T FEEL GOOD.
BUT YOU'RE HAPPY ABOUT GET-TING GOBLIN POOP, RIGHT?
KEIMA? YOU'VE GOT THE WRONG IDEA ABOUT ME. FOR SURE.
THE DOG-EARED GIRL SEEMED TO BE USED AS A BODY PILLOW AT NIGHT.
SHE WAS ALSO IN CHARGE OF CLEANING UP.
TMP

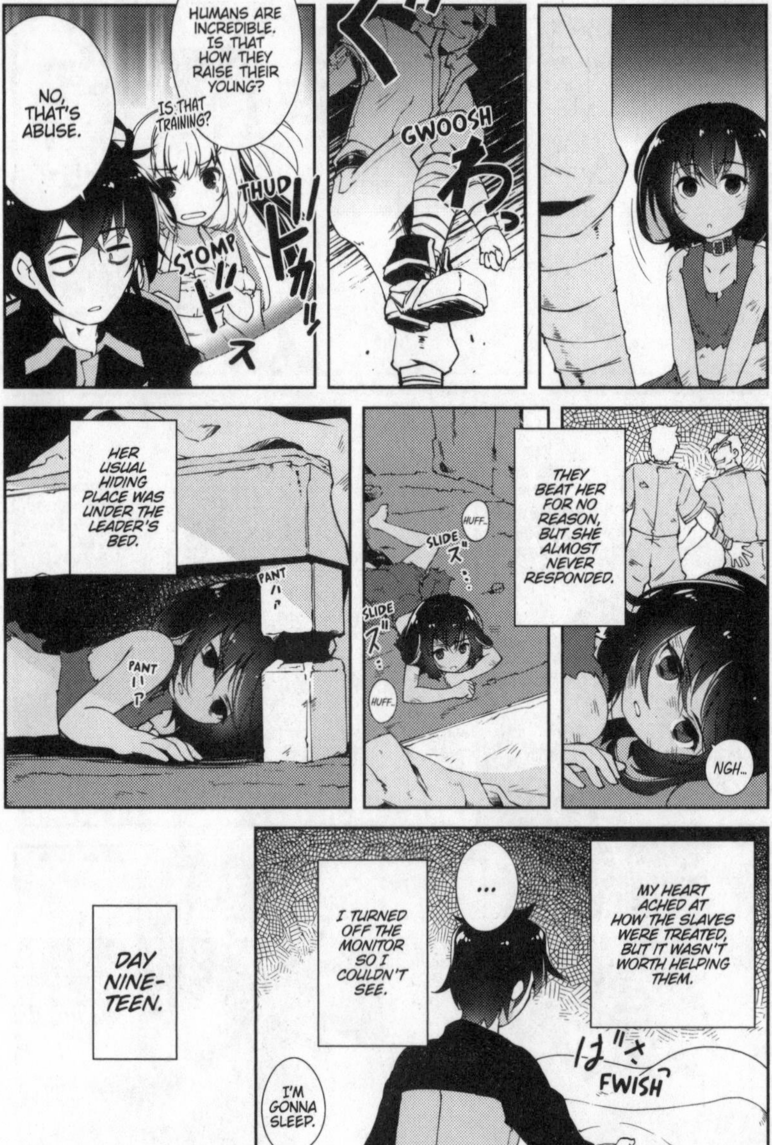
GWOOSH
HUMANS ARE INCREDIBLE. IS THAT HOW THEY RAISE THEIR YOUNG?
IS THAT TRAINING?
NO, THAT'S ABUSE.
THUD
STOMP
THEY BEAT HER FOR NO REASON, BUT SHE ALMOST NEVER RESPONDED.
NGH...
HUFF...
SLIDE
SLIDE
HUFF...
HER USUAL HIDING PLACE WAS UNDER THE LEADER'S BED.
PANT
PANT
MY HEART ACHED AT HOW THE SLAVES WERE TREATED, BUT IT WASN'T WORTH HELPING THEM.
...
I TURNED OFF THE MONITOR SO I COULDN'T SEE.
FWISH
I'M GONNA SLEEP.
DAY NINETEEN.

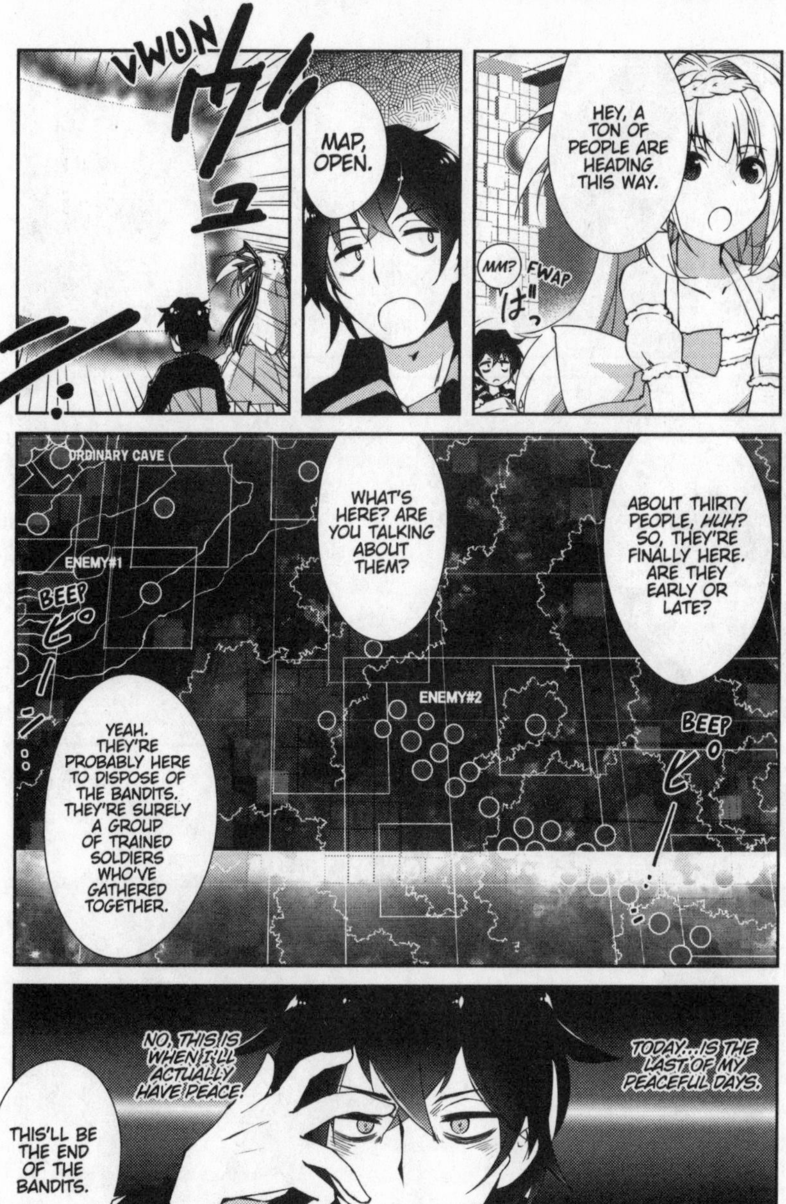
HEY, A TON OF PEOPLE ARE HEADING THIS WAY.
MM?
FWAP
ばっ
MAP, OPEN.
VWUN
ABOUT THIRTY PEOPLE, *HUH*? SO, THEY'RE FINALLY HERE. ARE THEY EARLY OR LATE?
WHAT'S HERE? ARE YOU TALKING ABOUT THEM?
ORDINARY CAVE
ENEMY#1
ENEMY#2
BEEP
BEEP
YEAH. THEY'RE PROBABLY HERE TO DISPOSE OF THE BANDITS. THEY'RE SURELY A GROUP OF TRAINED SOLDIERS WHO'VE GATHERED TOGETHER.
TODAY...IS THE LAST OF MY PEACEFUL DAYS.
NO, THIS IS WHEN I'LL ACTUALLY HAVE PEACE.
THIS'LL BE THE END OF THE BANDITS.

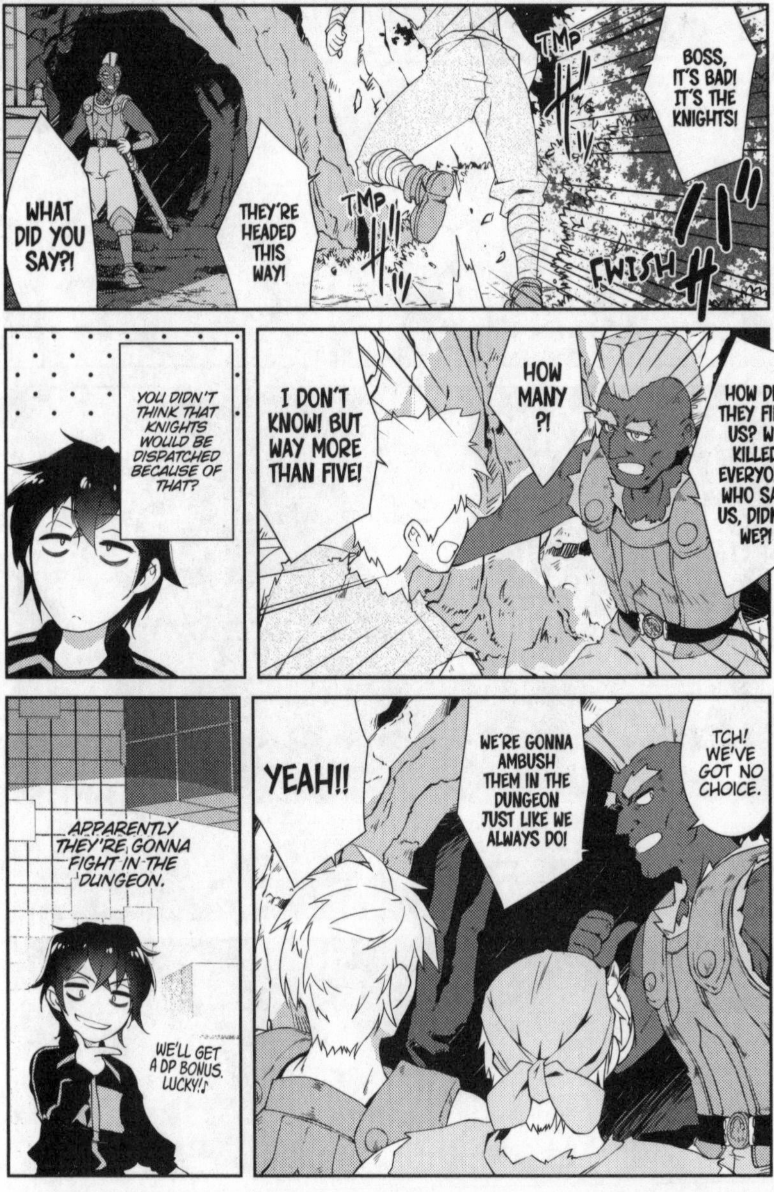
BOSS, IT'S BAD! IT'S THE KNIGHTS!
FWISH
TMP
THEY'RE HEADED THIS WAY!
TMP
WHAT DID YOU SAY?!
HOW DID THEY FIND US? WE KILLED EVERYONE WHO SAW US, DIDN'T WE?!
HOW MANY ?!
I DON'T KNOW! BUT WAY MORE THAN FIVE!
YOU DIDN'T THINK THAT KNIGHTS WOULD BE DISPATCHED BECAUSE OF THAT?
TCH! WE'VE GOT NO CHOICE.
WE'RE GONNA AMBUSH THEM IN THE DUNGEON JUST LIKE WE ALWAYS DO!
YEAH!!
APPARENTLY THEY'RE GONNA FIGHT IN THE DUNGEON.
WE'LL GET A DP BONUS. LUCKY!♪

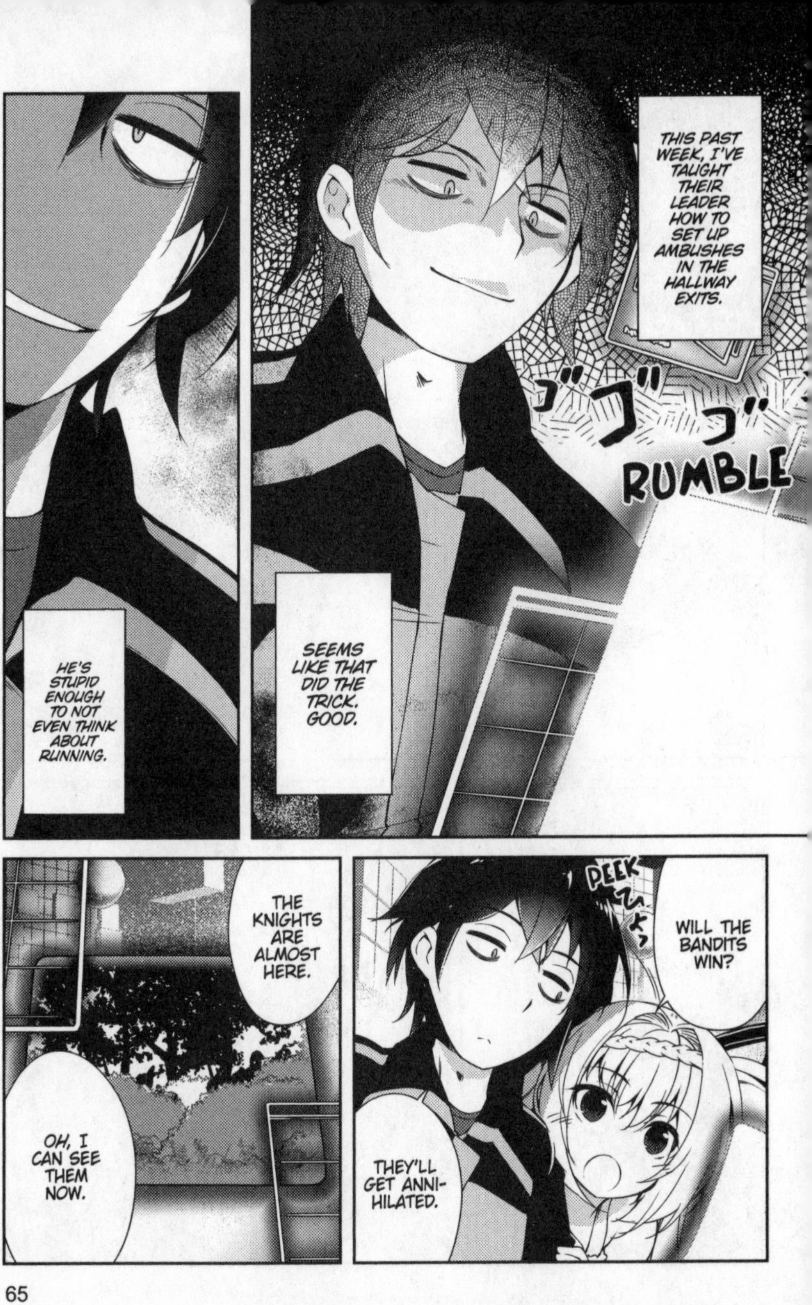
THIS PAST WEEK, I'VE TAUGHT THEIR LEADER HOW TO SET UP AMBUSHES IN THE HALLWAY EXITS.
ゴゴゴ
RUMBLE
SEEMS LIKE THAT DID THE TRICK. GOOD.
HE'S STUPID ENOUGH TO NOT EVEN THINK ABOUT RUNNING.
PEEK
ひょっ
WILL THE BANDITS WIN?
THEY'LL GET ANNI-HILATED.
THE KNIGHTS ARE ALMOST HERE.
OH, I CAN SEE THEM NOW.

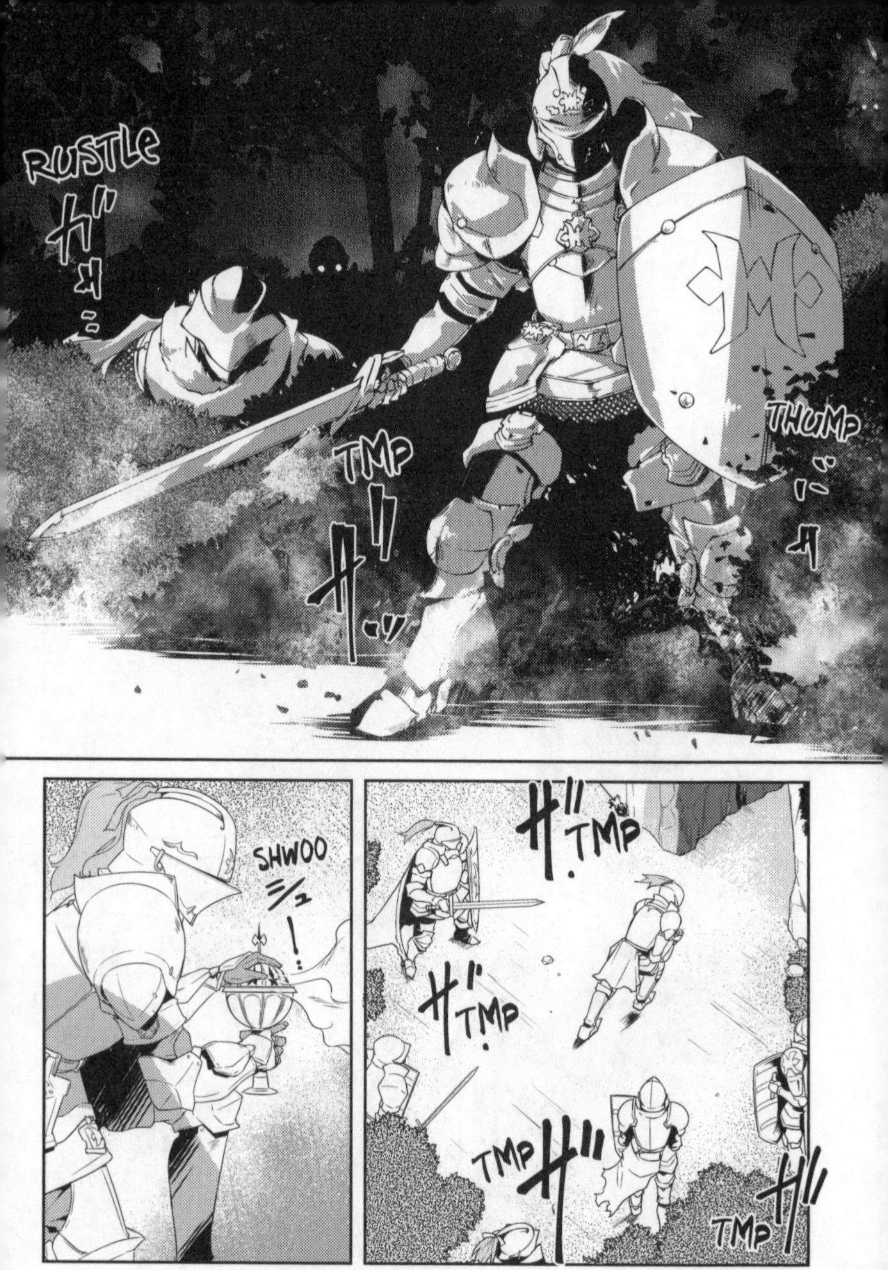
RUSTLE
TMP
THUMP
TMP
TMP
TMP
TMP
SHWOO

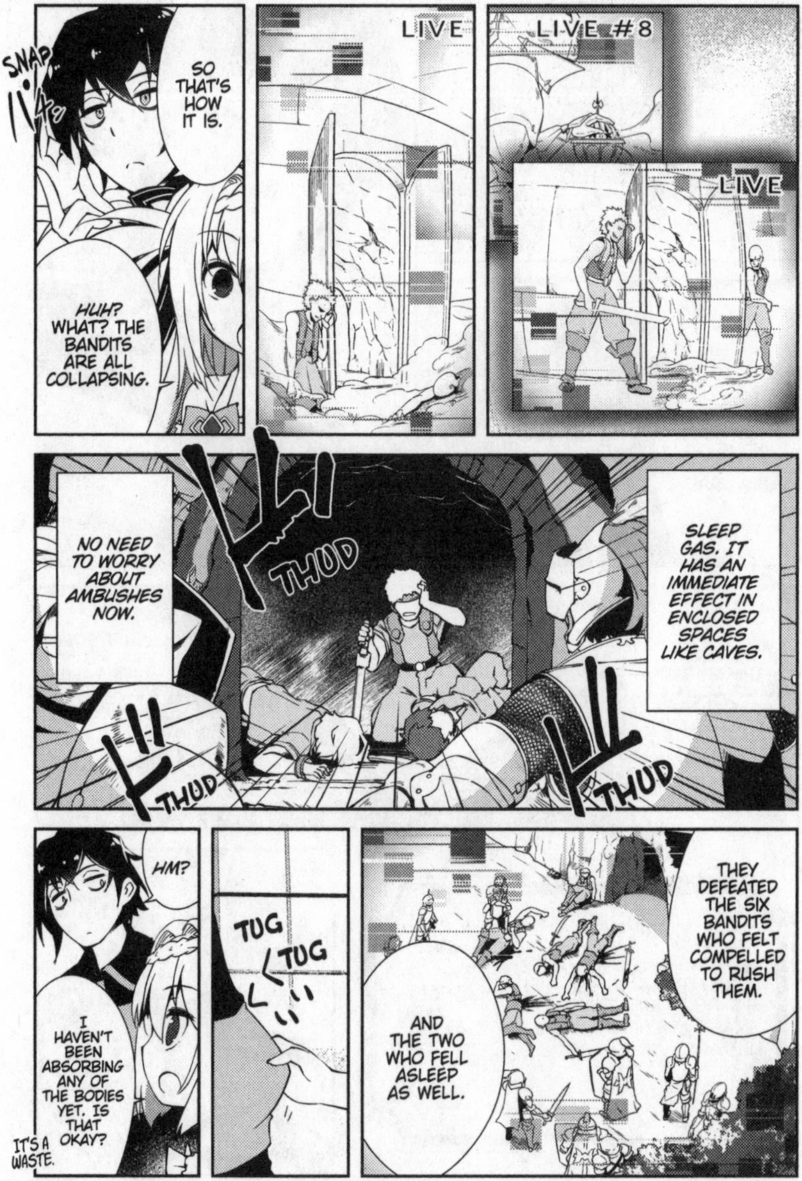
LIVE #8
LIVE
LIVE
SO THAT'S HOW IT IS.
SNAP
HUH? WHAT? THE BANDITS ARE ALL COLLAPSING.
SLEEP GAS. IT HAS AN IMMEDIATE EFFECT IN ENCLOSED SPACES LIKE CAVES.
THUD
NO NEED TO WORRY ABOUT AMBUSHES NOW.
THUD
THUD
THEY DEFEATED THE SIX BANDITS WHO FELT COMPELLED TO RUSH THEM.
AND THE TWO WHO FELL ASLEEP AS WELL.
TUG
TUG
HM?
I HAVEN'T BEEN ABSORBING ANY OF THE BODIES YET. IS THAT OKAY?
IT'S A WASTE.

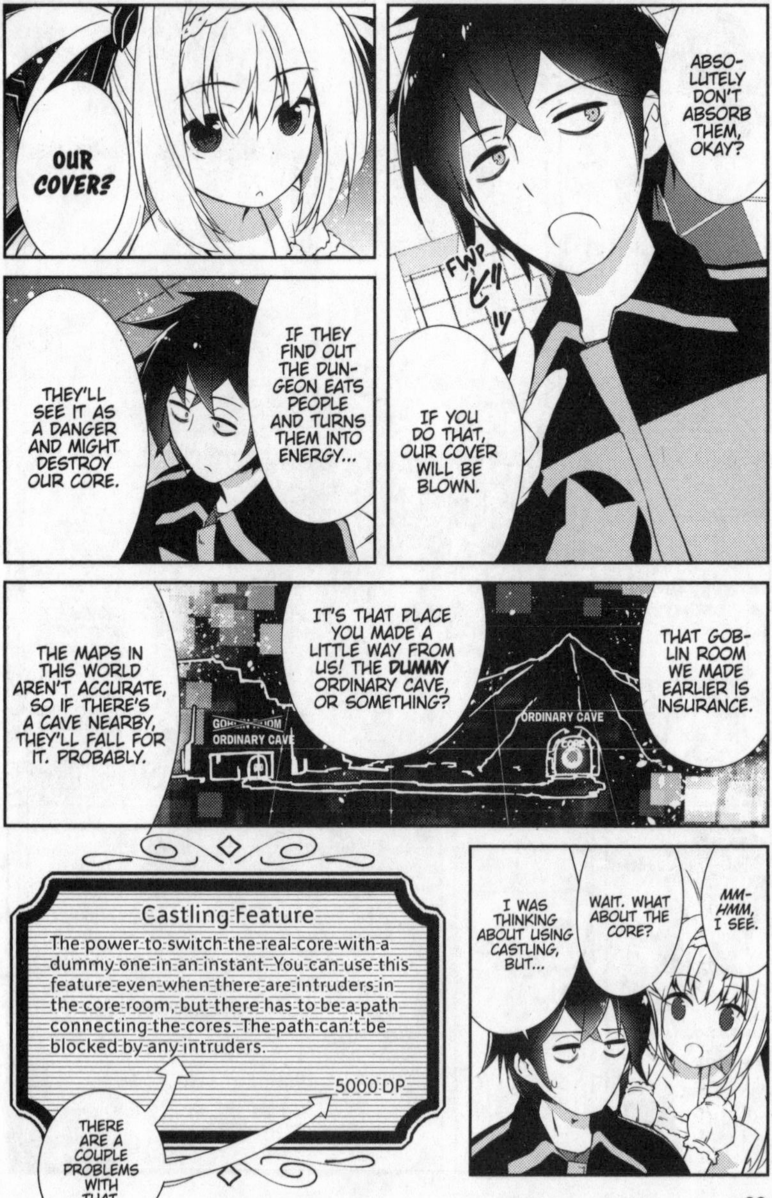
ABSO-LUTELY DON'T ABSORB THEM, OKAY?
FWP
IF YOU DO THAT, OUR COVER WILL BE BLOWN.
OUR COVER?
IF THEY FIND OUT THE DUN-GEON EATS PEOPLE AND TURNS THEM INTO ENERGY...
THEY'LL SEE IT AS A DANGER AND MIGHT DESTROY OUR CORE.
THAT GOB-LIN ROOM WE MADE EARLIER IS INSURANCE.
ORDINARY CAVE
CORE
IT'S THAT PLACE YOU MADE A LITTLE WAY FROM US! THE DUMMY ORDINARY CAVE, OR SOMETHING?
ORDINARY CAVE
THE MAPS IN THIS WORLD AREN'T ACCURATE, SO IF THERE'S A CAVE NEARBY, THEY'LL FALL FOR IT. PROBABLY.
MM-HMM, I SEE.
WAIT. WHAT ABOUT THE CORE?
I WAS THINKING ABOUT USING CASTLING, BUT...
Castling Feature
The power to switch the real core with a dummy one in an instant. You can use this feature even when there are intruders in the core room, but there has to be a path connecting the cores. The path can't be blocked by any intruders.
5000 DP
THERE ARE A COUPLE PROBLEMS WITH THAT.

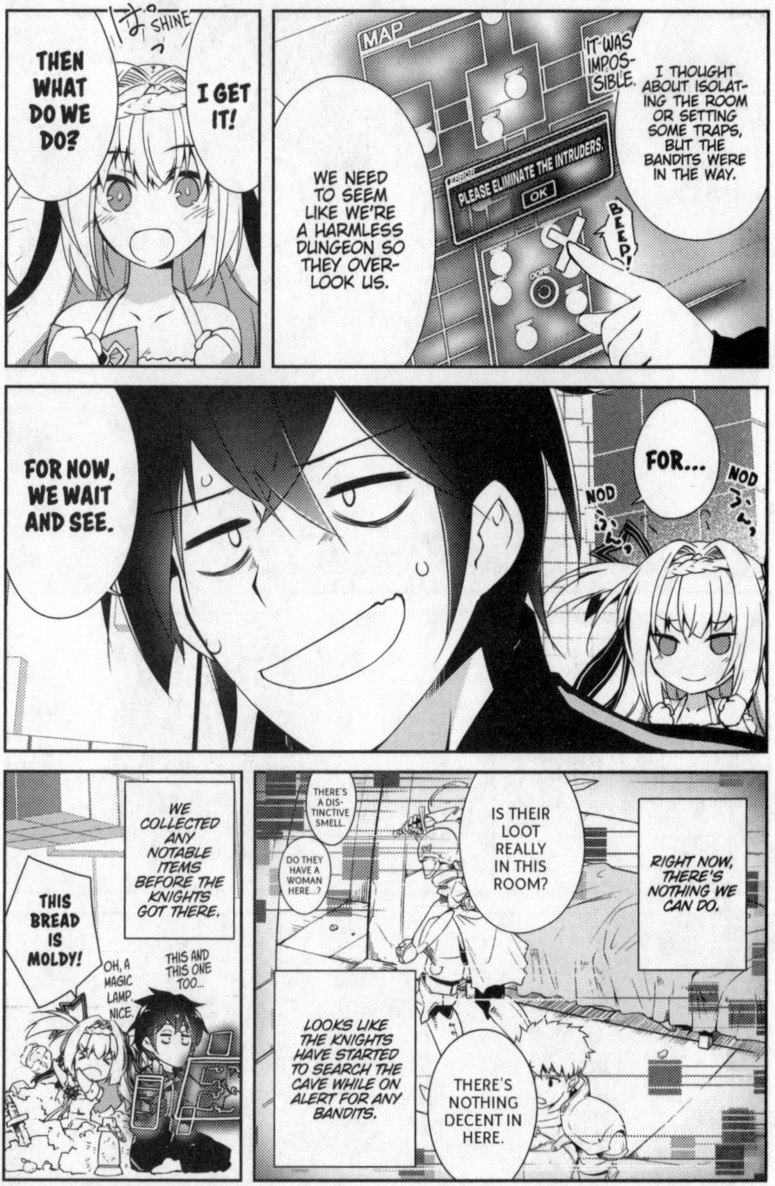
I THOUGHT ABOUT ISOLATING THE ROOM OR SETTING SOME TRAPS, BUT THE BANDITS WERE IN THE WAY.
IT WAS IMPOSSIBLE.
MAP
ERROR
PLEASE ELIMINATE THE INTRUDERS.
OK
BEEP!
WE NEED TO SEEM LIKE WE'RE A HARMLESS DUNGEON SO THEY OVERLOOK US.
I GET IT!
SHINE
THEN WHAT DO WE DO?
FOR...
NOD
NOD
FOR NOW, WE WAIT AND SEE.
RIGHT NOW, THERE'S NOTHING WE CAN DO.
IS THEIR LOOT REALLY IN THIS ROOM?
THERE'S A DISTINCTIVE SMELL.
DO THEY HAVE A WOMAN HERE...?
THERE'S NOTHING DECENT IN HERE.
LOOKS LIKE THE KNIGHTS HAVE STARTED TO SEARCH THE CAVE WHILE ON ALERT FOR ANY BANDITS.
WE COLLECTED ANY NOTABLE ITEMS BEFORE THE KNIGHTS GOT THERE.
THIS AND THIS ONE TOO...
OH, A MAGIC LAMP. NICE.
THIS BREAD IS MOLDY!

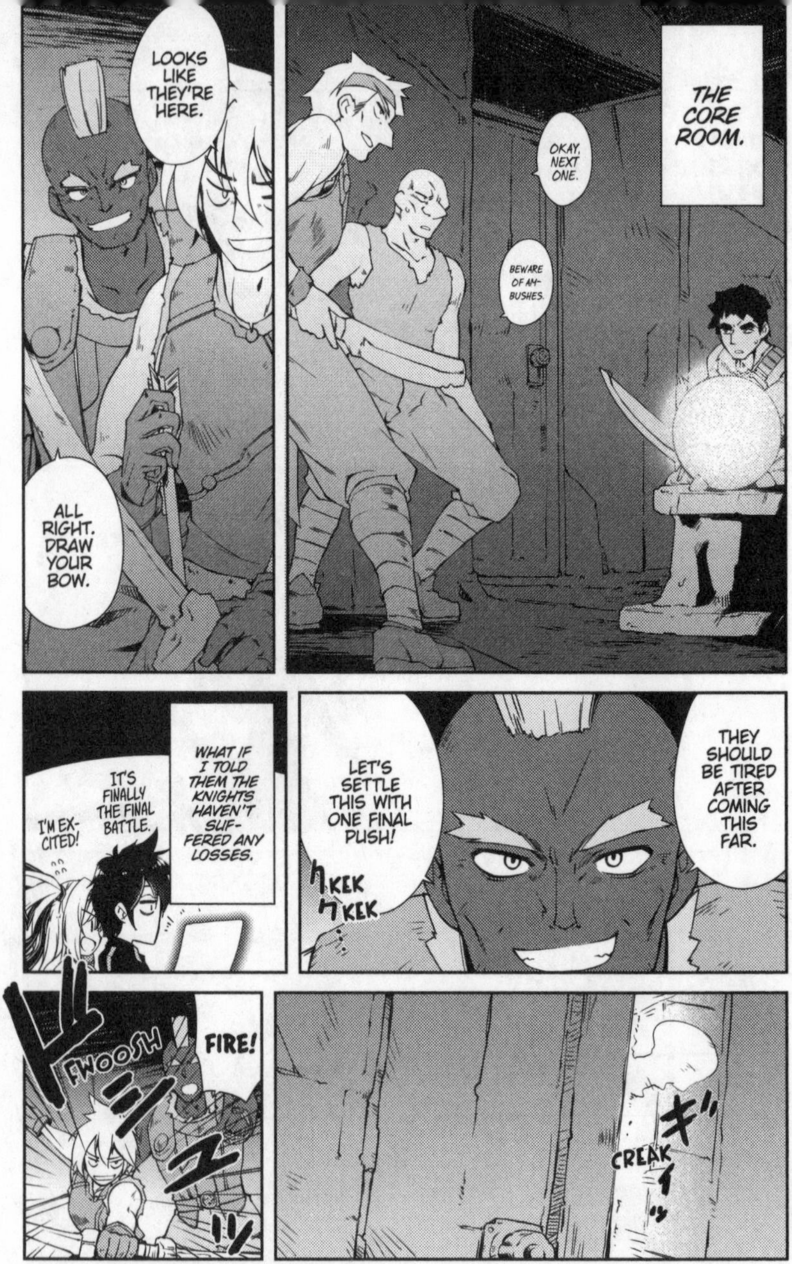
THE CORE ROOM.
OKAY, NEXT ONE.
BEWARE OF AMBUSHES.
LOOKS LIKE THEY'RE HERE.
ALL RIGHT. DRAW YOUR BOW.
THEY SHOULD BE TIRED AFTER COMING THIS FAR.
LET'S SETTLE THIS WITH ONE FINAL PUSH!
KEK KEK
WHAT IF I TOLD THEM THE KNIGHTS HAVEN'T SUFFERED ANY LOSSES.
IT'S FINALLY THE FINAL BATTLE.
I'M EXCITED!
CREAK
FIRE!
FWOOSH

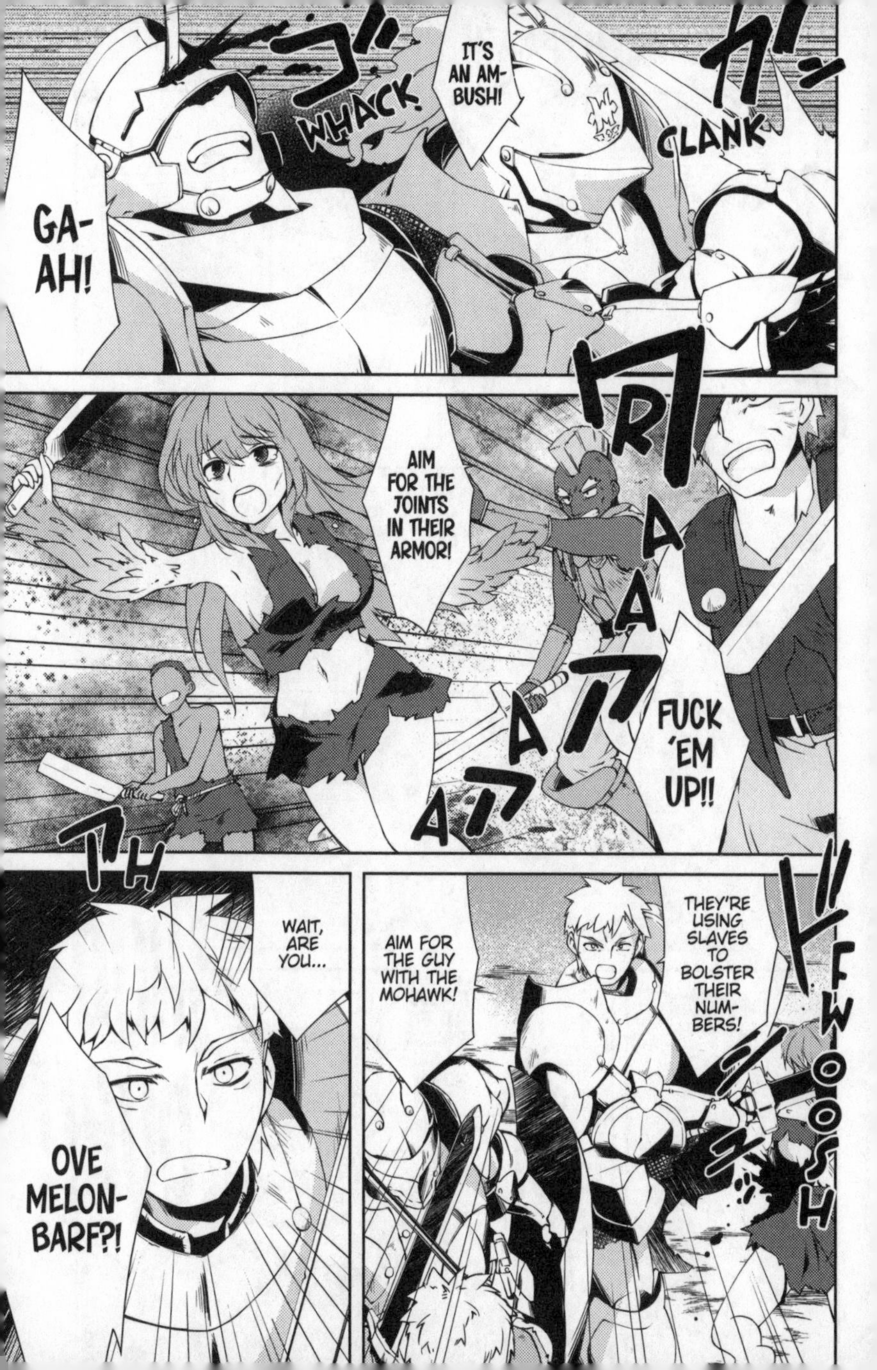
CLANK
IT'S AN AM-BUSH!
WHACK
GA-AH!
RAAAA
FUCK 'EM UP!!
AIM FOR THE JOINTS IN THEIR ARMOR!
TH
FWOOSH
THEY'RE USING SLAVES TO BOLSTER THEIR NUM-BERS!
AIM FOR THE GUY WITH THE MOHAWK!
WAIT, ARE YOU...
OVE MELON-BARF?!

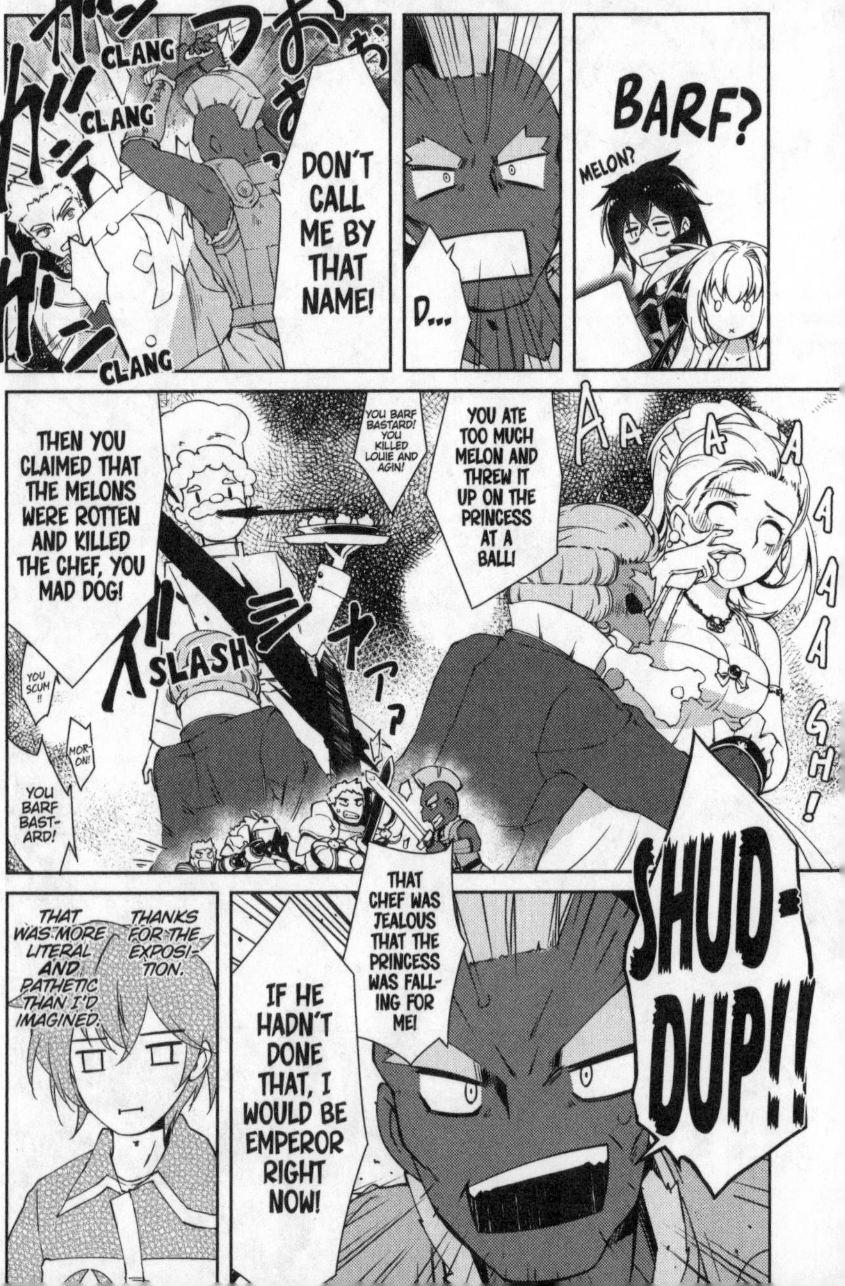
BARF?
MELON?
D...
HYAAAH!
DON'T CALL ME BY THAT NAME!
CLANG
CLANG
CLANG
AAAAAAAAAAGH!
YOU ATE TOO MUCH MELON AND THREW IT UP ON THE PRINCESS AT A BALL!
YOU BARF BASTARD! YOU KILLED LOUIE AND AGIN!
THEN YOU CLAIMED THAT THE MELONS WERE ROTTEN AND KILLED THE CHEF, YOU MAD DOG!
SLASH
YOU SCUM!!
MOR-ON!
YOU BARF BAST-ARD!
SHUD-DUP!!
THAT CHEF WAS JEALOUS THAT THE PRINCESS WAS FALL-ING FOR ME!
IF HE HADN'T DONE THAT, I WOULD BE EMPEROR RIGHT NOW!
THANKS FOR THE EXPOSI-TION.
THAT WAS MORE LITERAL AND PATHETIC THAN I'D IMAGINED.

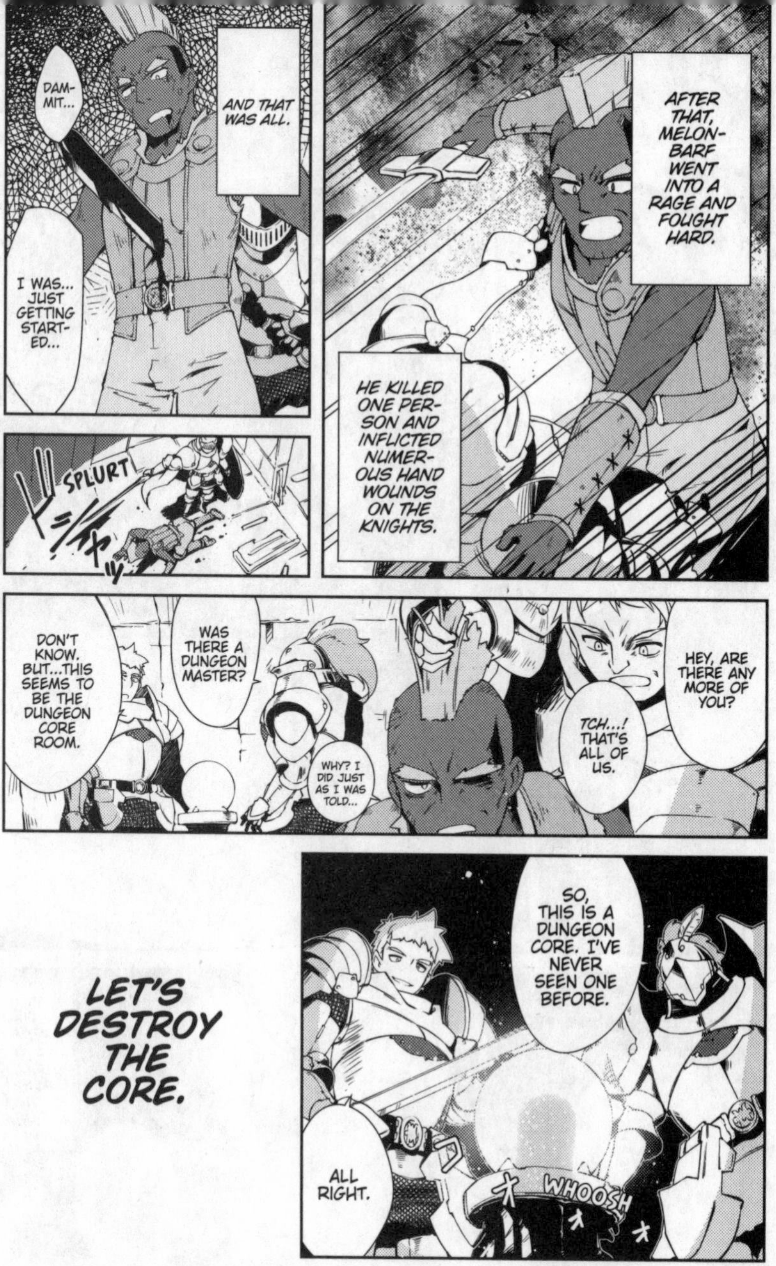
AFTER THAT, MELON-BARF WENT INTO A RAGE AND FOUGHT HARD.
HE KILLED ONE PERSON AND INFLICTED NUMEROUS HAND WOUNDS ON THE KNIGHTS.
AND THAT WAS ALL.
DAM-MIT...
I WAS... JUST GETTING START-ED...
SPLURT
HEY, ARE THERE ANY MORE OF YOU?
TCH...! THAT'S ALL OF US.
WHY? I DID JUST AS I WAS TOLD...
WAS THERE A DUNGEON MASTER?
DON'T KNOW. BUT...THIS SEEMS TO BE THE DUNGEON CORE ROOM.
SO, THIS IS A DUNGEON CORE. I'VE NEVER SEEN ONE BEFORE.
LET'S DESTROY THE CORE.
ALL RIGHT.
WHOOSH

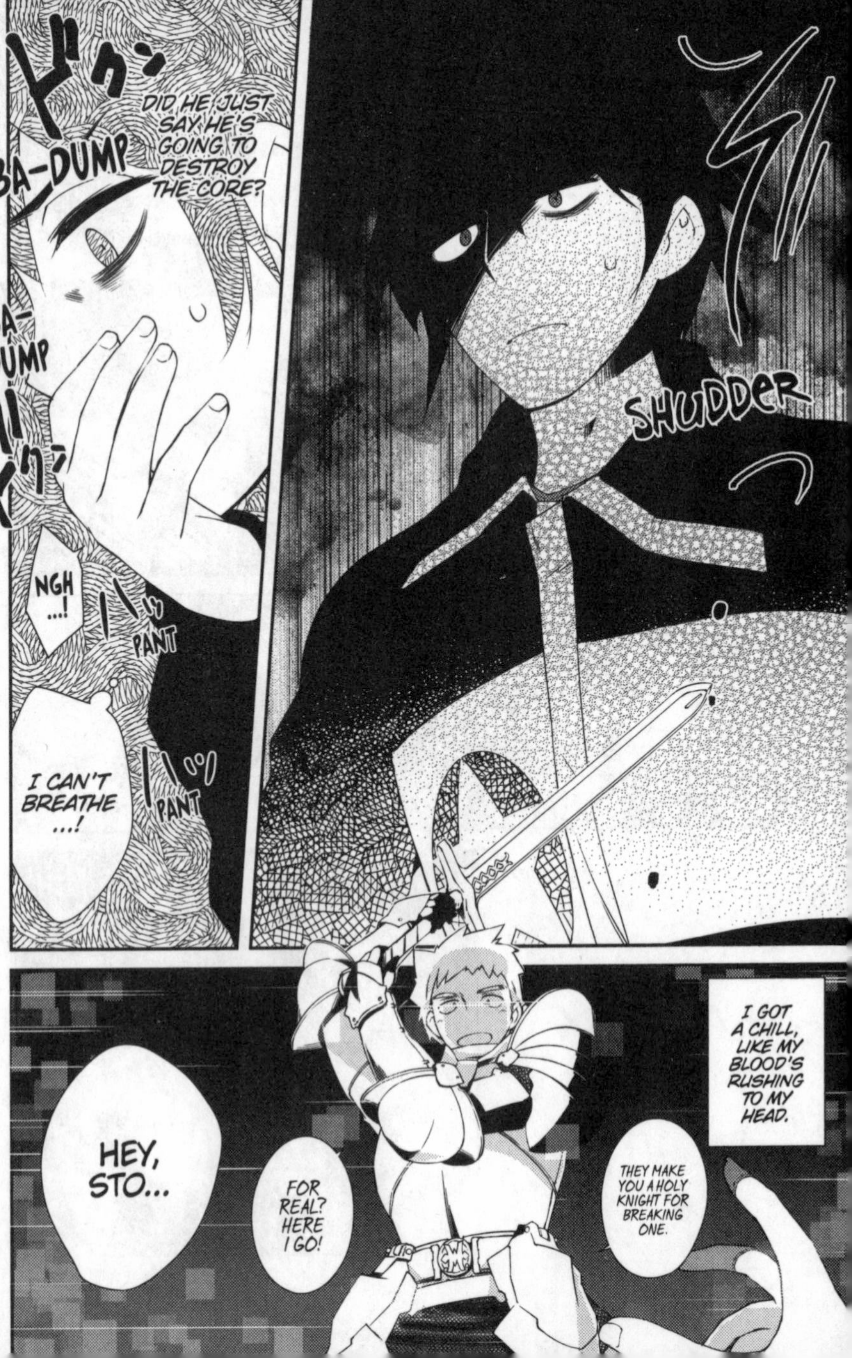
SHUDDER
BA-DUMP
DID HE JUST SAY HE'S GOING TO DESTROY THE CORE?
BA-DUMP
NGH ...!
PANT
PANT
I CAN'T BREATHE ...!
I GOT A CHILL, LIKE MY BLOOD'S RUSHING TO MY HEAD.
THEY MAKE YOU A HOLY KNIGHT FOR BREAKING ONE.
FOR REAL? HERE I GO!
HEY, STO...

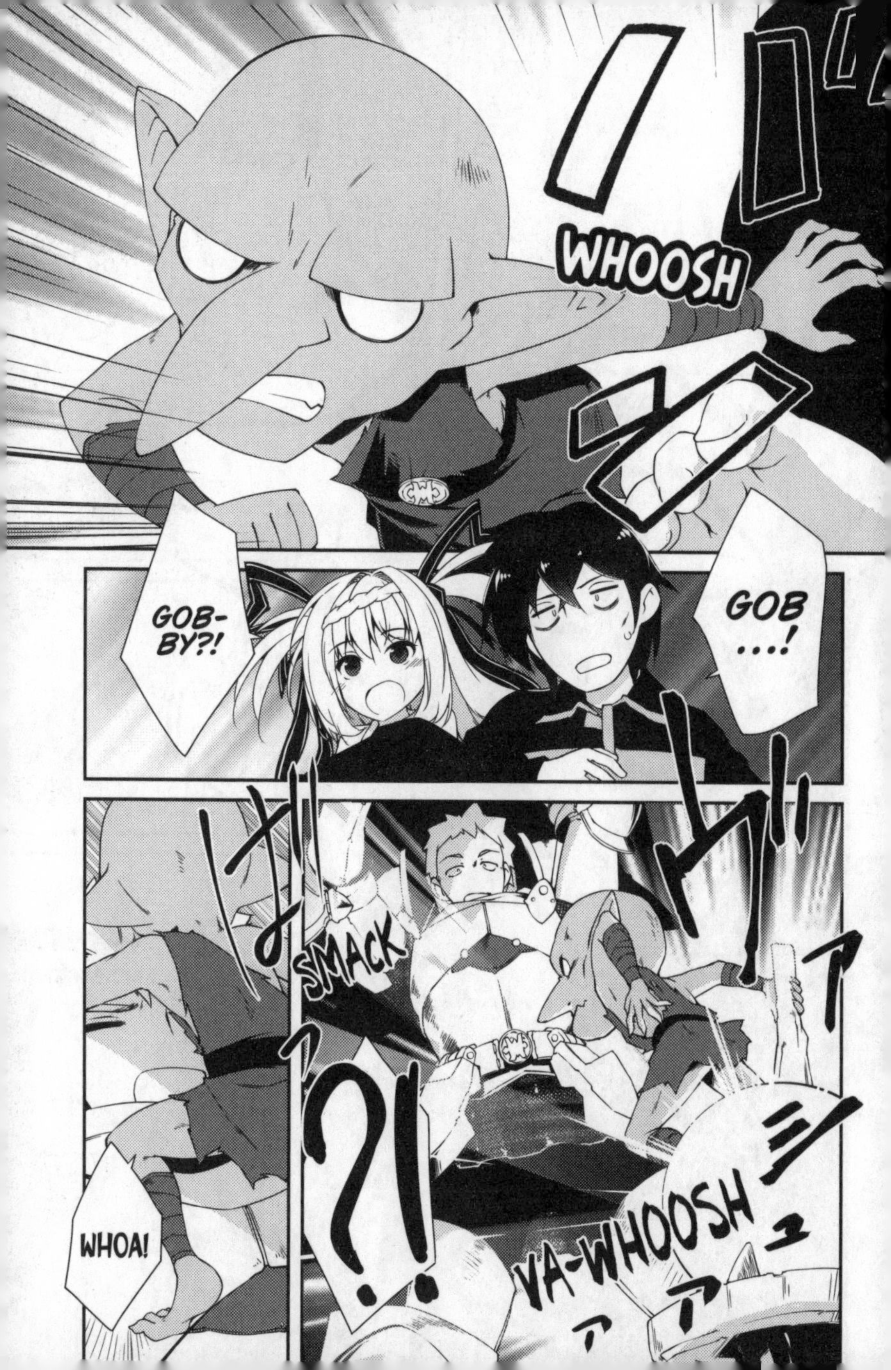
WHOOSH
GOB ...!
GOB-BY?!
SMACK
?!
VA-WHOOSH
WHOA!

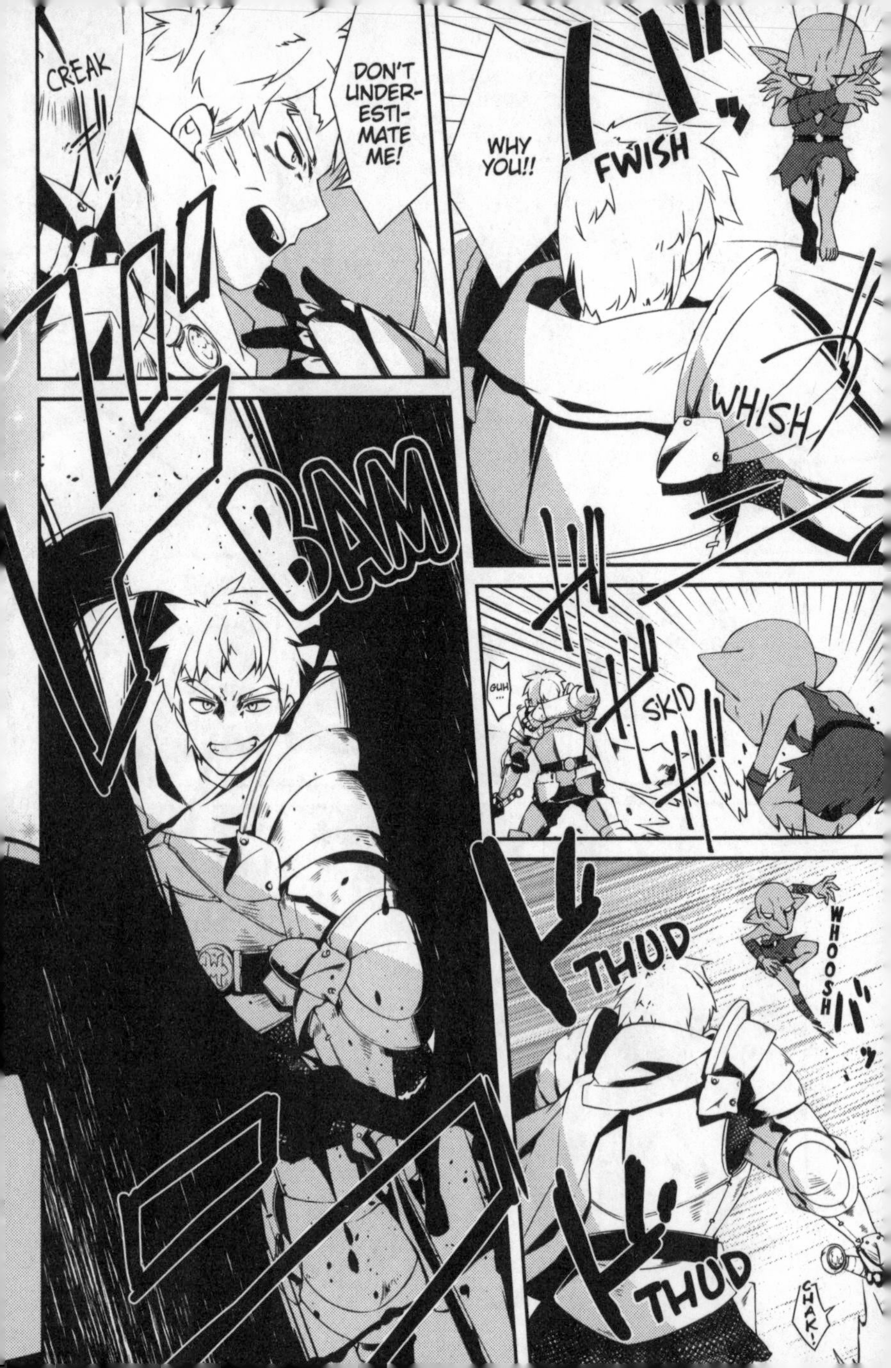
FWISH
WHY YOU!!
WHISH
DON'T UNDER-ESTI-MATE ME!
CREAK
GUH...
SKID
WHOOSH
THUD
THUD
CHAK!
BAM

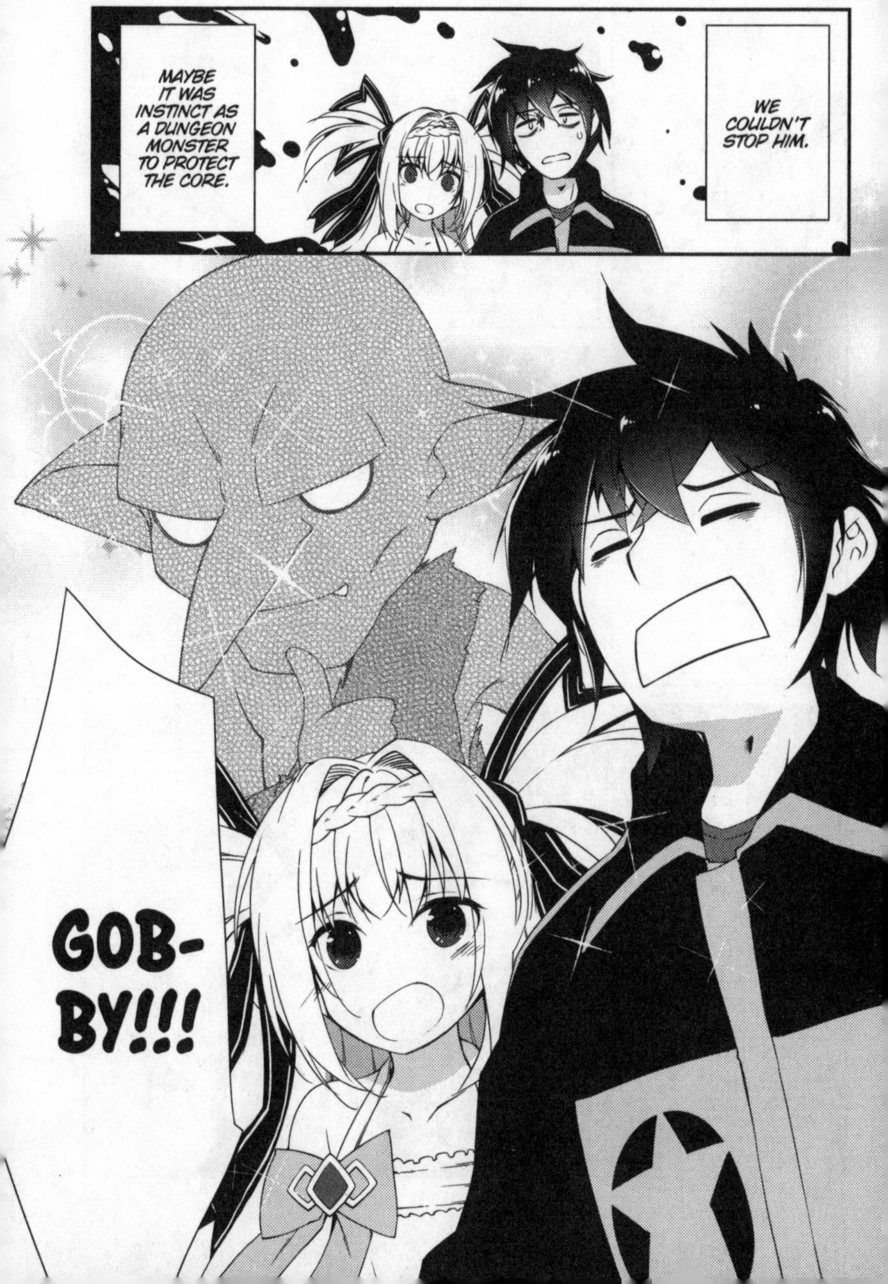
WE COULDN'T STOP HIM.
MAYBE IT WAS INSTINCT AS A DUNGEON MONSTER TO PROTECT THE CORE.
GOB-BY!!!

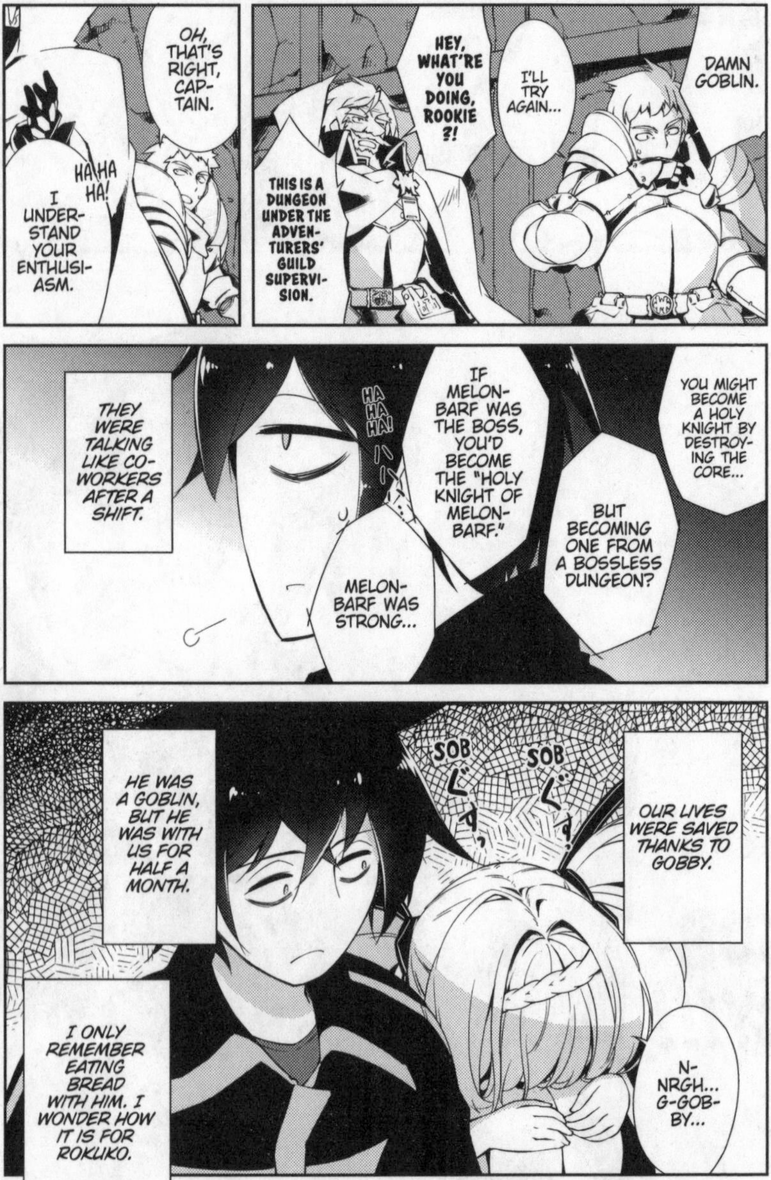
DAMN GOBLIN.
I'LL TRY AGAIN...
HEY, WHAT'RE YOU DOING, ROOKIE?!
THIS IS A DUNGEON UNDER THE ADVENTURERS' GUILD SUPERVISION.
OH, THAT'S RIGHT, CAPTAIN.
HA HA HA!
I UNDERSTAND YOUR ENTHUSIASM.
YOU MIGHT BECOME A HOLY KNIGHT BY DESTROYING THE CORE...
BUT BECOMING ONE FROM A BOSSLESS DUNGEON?
IF MELON-BARF WAS THE BOSS, YOU'D BECOME THE "HOLY KNIGHT OF MELON-BARF."
HA HA HA!
MELON-BARF WAS STRONG...
THEY WERE TALKING LIKE CO-WORKERS AFTER A SHIFT.
OUR LIVES WERE SAVED THANKS TO GOBBY.
SOB
SOB
N-NRGH... G-GOBBY...
HE WAS A GOBLIN, BUT HE WAS WITH US FOR HALF A MONTH.
I ONLY REMEMBER EATING BREAD WITH HIM. I WONDER HOW IT IS FOR ROKUKO.

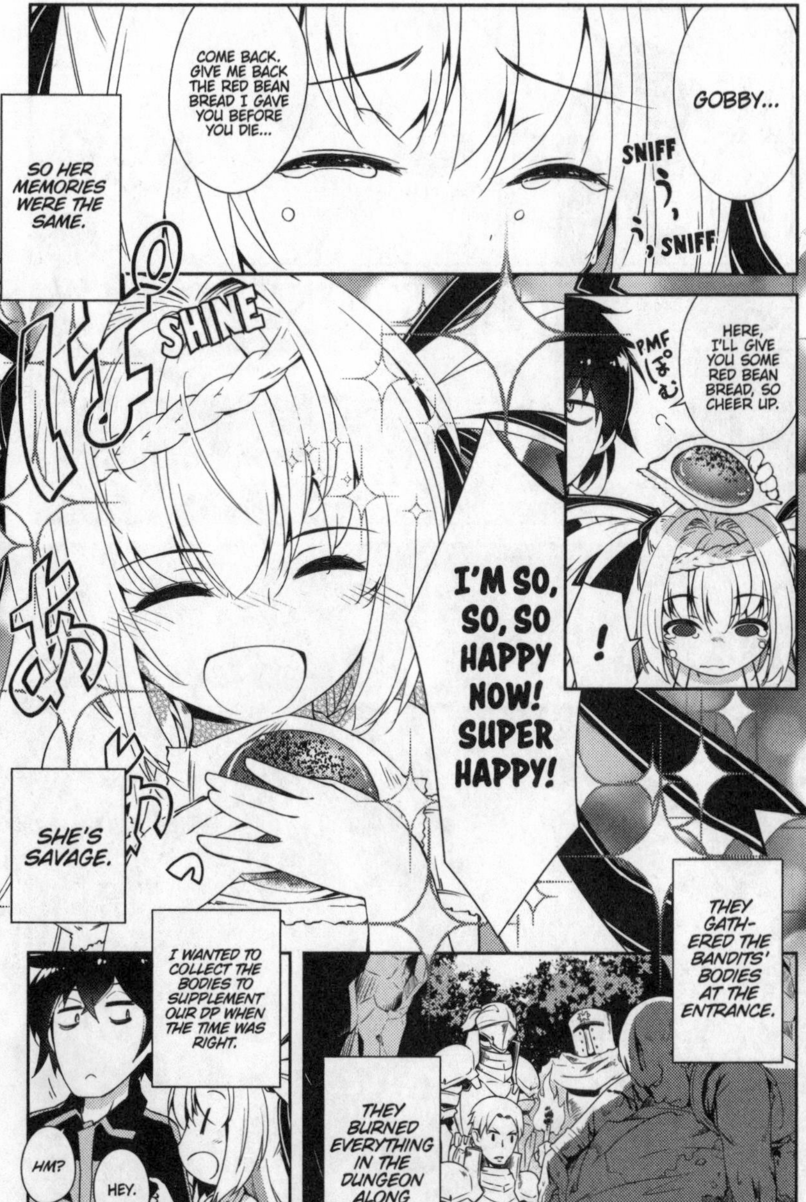
GOBBY...
SNIFF
う, う, SNIFF
COME BACK. GIVE ME BACK THE RED BEAN BREAD I GAVE YOU BEFORE YOU DIE...
SO HER MEMORIES WERE THE SAME.
PMF ぽむ
HERE, I'LL GIVE YOU SOME RED BEAN BREAD, SO CHEER UP.
!
I'M SO, SO, SO HAPPY NOW! SUPER HAPPY!
SHINE
SHE'S SAVAGE.
THEY GATHERED THE BANDITS' BODIES AT THE ENTRANCE.
THEY BURNED EVERYTHING IN THE DUNGEON ALONG WITH THEM.
I WANTED TO COLLECT THE BODIES TO SUPPLEMENT OUR DP WHEN THE TIME WAS RIGHT.
HEY.
HM?

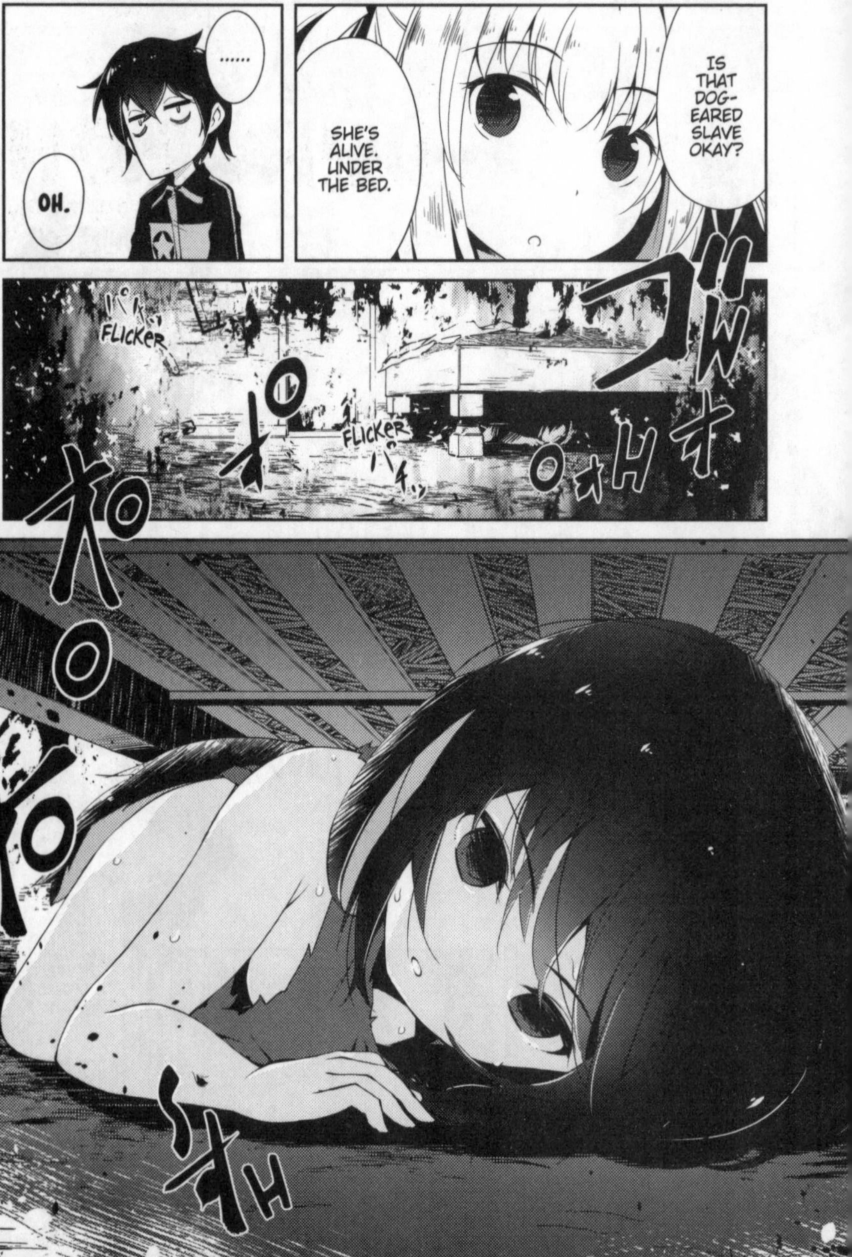
IS THAT DOG-EARED SLAVE OKAY?
SHE'S ALIVE. UNDER THE BED.
......
OH.
FLICKER
FLICKER

LAZY
DUNGEON
MASTER

RED
BEAN
BREAD! ♡

LAZY
DUNGEON
MASTER

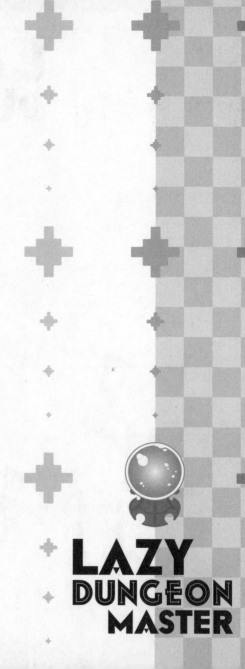

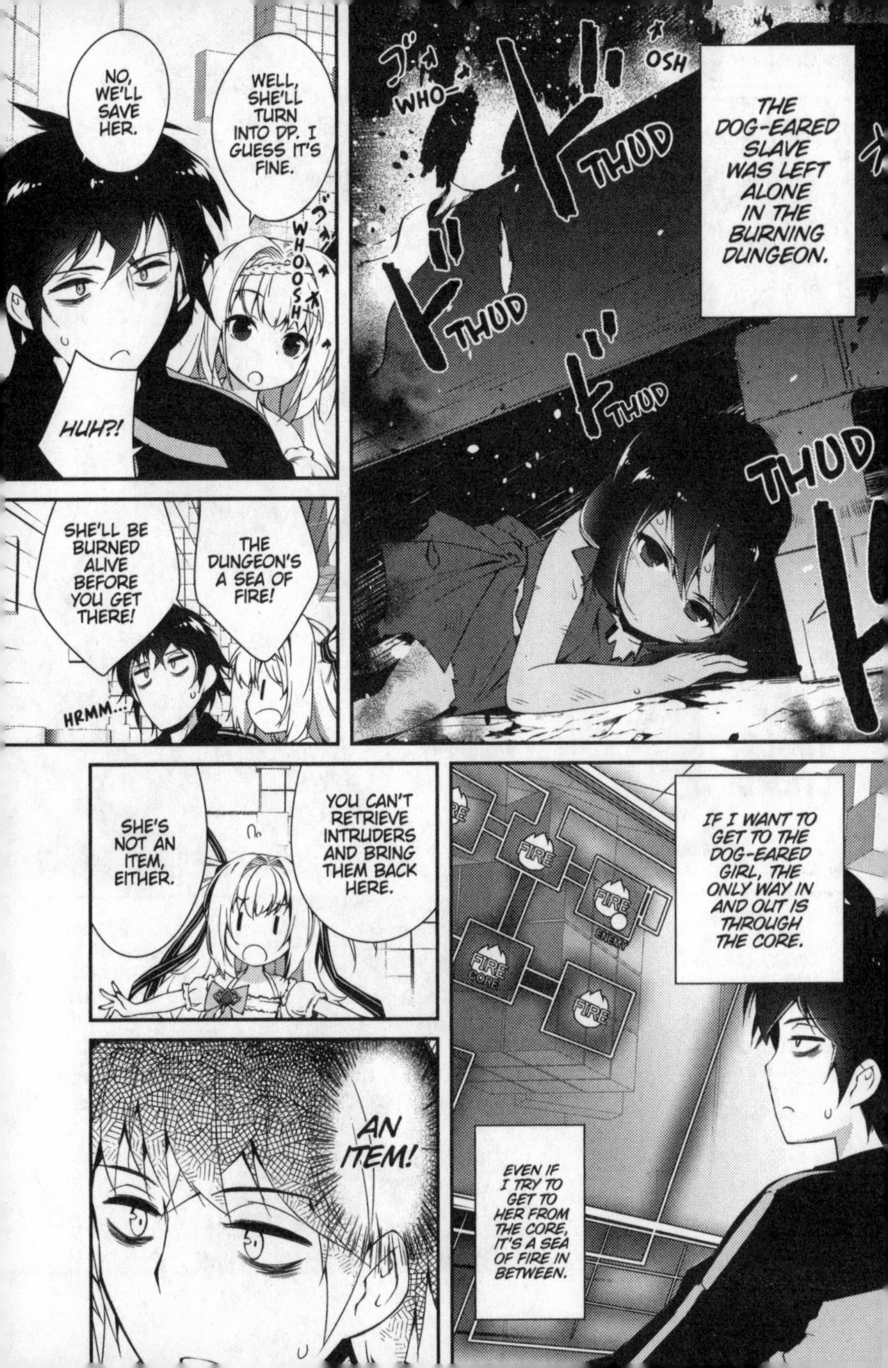
THE DOG-EARED SLAVE WAS LEFT ALONE IN THE BURNING DUNGEON.
WHO-OSH
THUD
THUD
THUD
THUD
WELL, SHE'LL TURN INTO DP. I GUESS IT'S FINE.
WHOOSH
NO, WE'LL SAVE HER.
HUH?!
THE DUNGEON'S A SEA OF FIRE!
SHE'LL BE BURNED ALIVE BEFORE YOU GET THERE!
HRMM...
IF I WANT TO GET TO THE DOG-EARED GIRL, THE ONLY WAY IN AND OUT IS THROUGH THE CORE.
FIRE
FIRE
FIRE
ENEMY
FIRE
CORE
FIRE
EVEN IF I TRY TO GET TO HER FROM THE CORE, IT'S A SEA OF FIRE IN BETWEEN.
YOU CAN'T RETRIEVE INTRUDERS AND BRING THEM BACK HERE.
SHE'S NOT AN ITEM, EITHER.
AN ITEM!

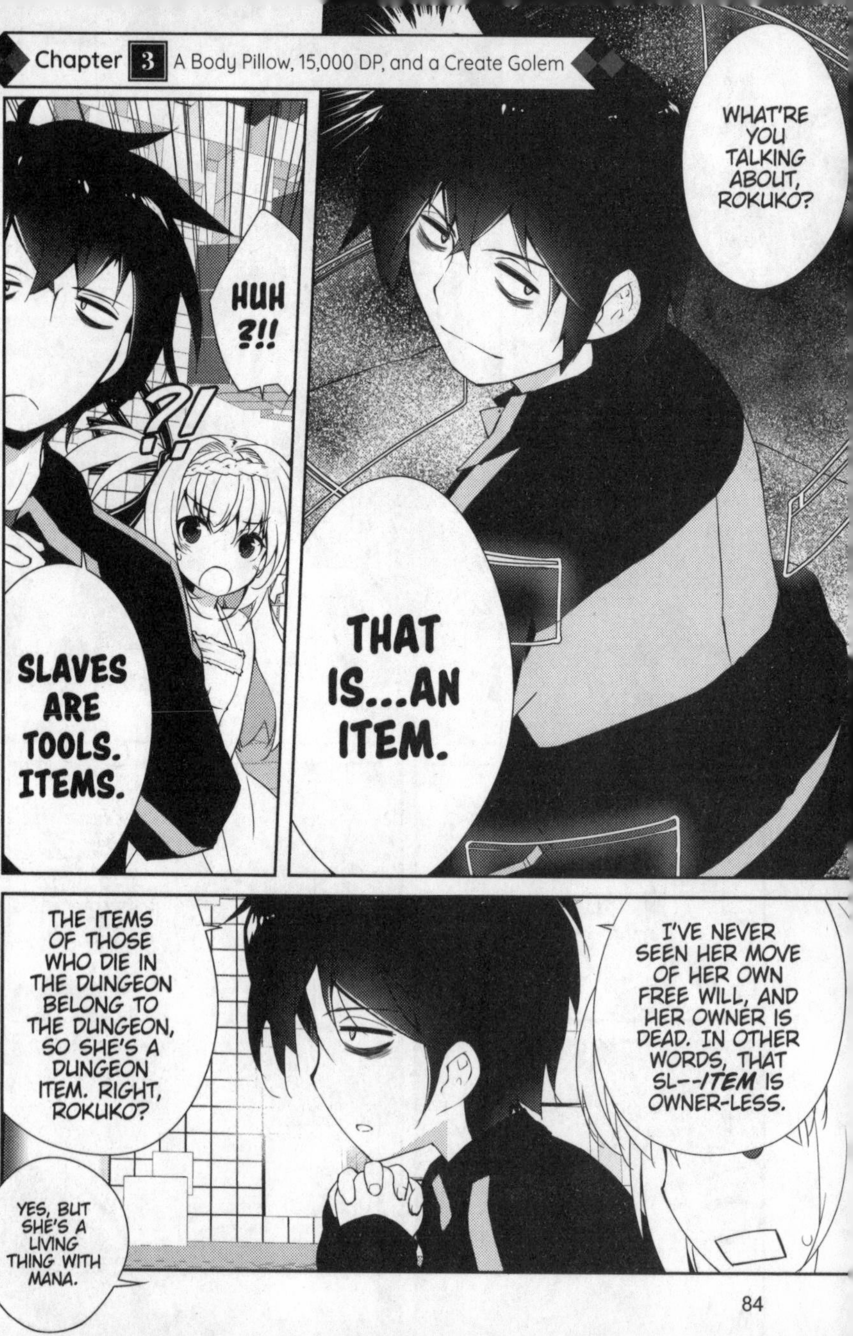
WHAT'RE YOU TALKING ABOUT, ROKUKO?
THAT IS...AN ITEM.
HUH ?!!
?!
SLAVES ARE TOOLS. ITEMS.
I'VE NEVER SEEN HER MOVE OF HER OWN FREE WILL, AND HER OWNER IS DEAD. IN OTHER WORDS, THAT SL--*ITEM* IS OWNER-LESS.
THE ITEMS OF THOSE WHO DIE IN THE DUNGEON BELONG TO THE DUNGEON, SO SHE'S A DUNGEON ITEM. RIGHT, ROKUKO?
YES, BUT SHE'S A LIVING THING WITH MANA.

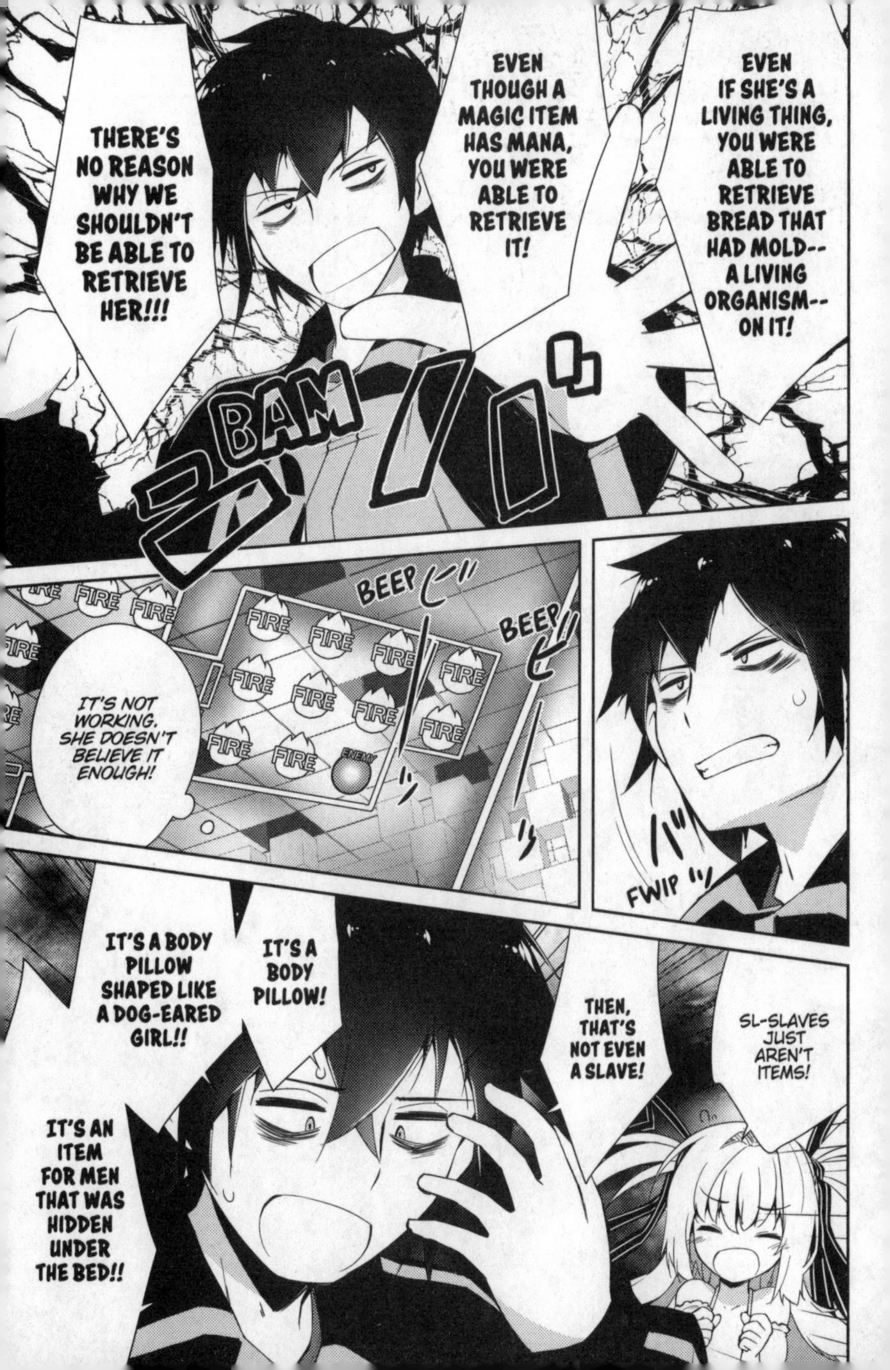
EVEN IF SHE'S A LIVING THING, YOU WERE ABLE TO RETRIEVE BREAD THAT HAD MOLD-- A LIVING ORGANISM-- ON IT!
EVEN THOUGH A MAGIC ITEM HAS MANA, YOU WERE ABLE TO RETRIEVE IT!
THERE'S NO REASON WHY WE SHOULDN'T BE ABLE TO RETRIEVE HER!!!
BAM
FWIP
BEEP
BEEP
FIRE
ENEMY
IT'S NOT WORKING. SHE DOESN'T BELIEVE IT ENOUGH!
SL-SLAVES JUST AREN'T ITEMS!
THEN, THAT'S NOT EVEN A SLAVE!
IT'S A BODY PILLOW!
IT'S A BODY PILLOW SHAPED LIKE A DOG-EARED GIRL!!
IT'S AN ITEM FOR MEN THAT WAS HIDDEN UNDER THE BED!!

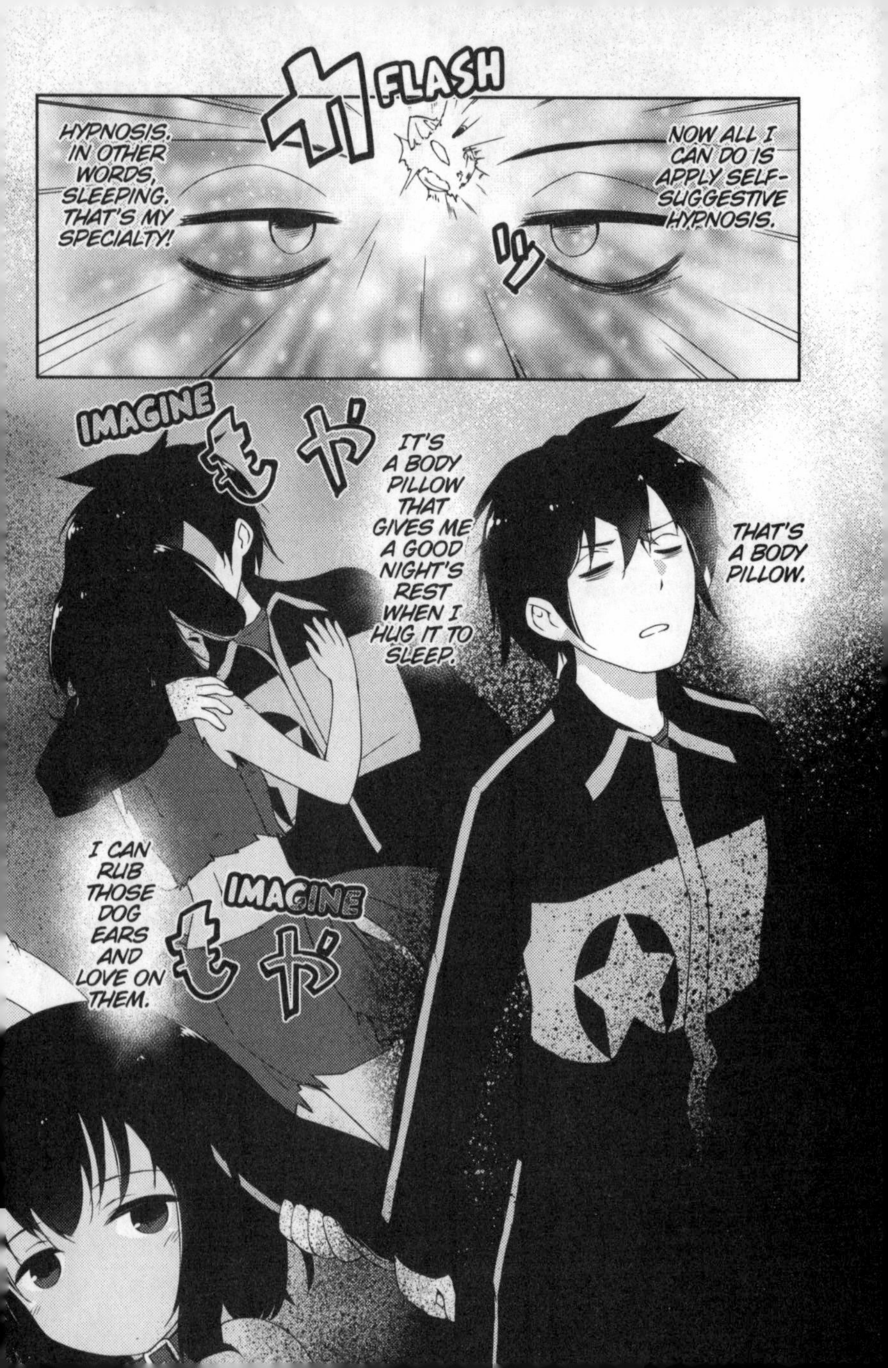
FLASH
NOW ALL I CAN DO IS APPLY SELF-SUGGESTIVE HYPNOSIS.
HYPNOSIS. IN OTHER WORDS, SLEEPING. THAT'S MY SPECIALTY!
THAT'S A BODY PILLOW.
IT'S A BODY PILLOW THAT GIVES ME A GOOD NIGHT'S REST WHEN I HUG IT TO SLEEP.
IMAGINE
IMAGINE
I CAN RUB THOSE DOG EARS AND LOVE ON THEM.

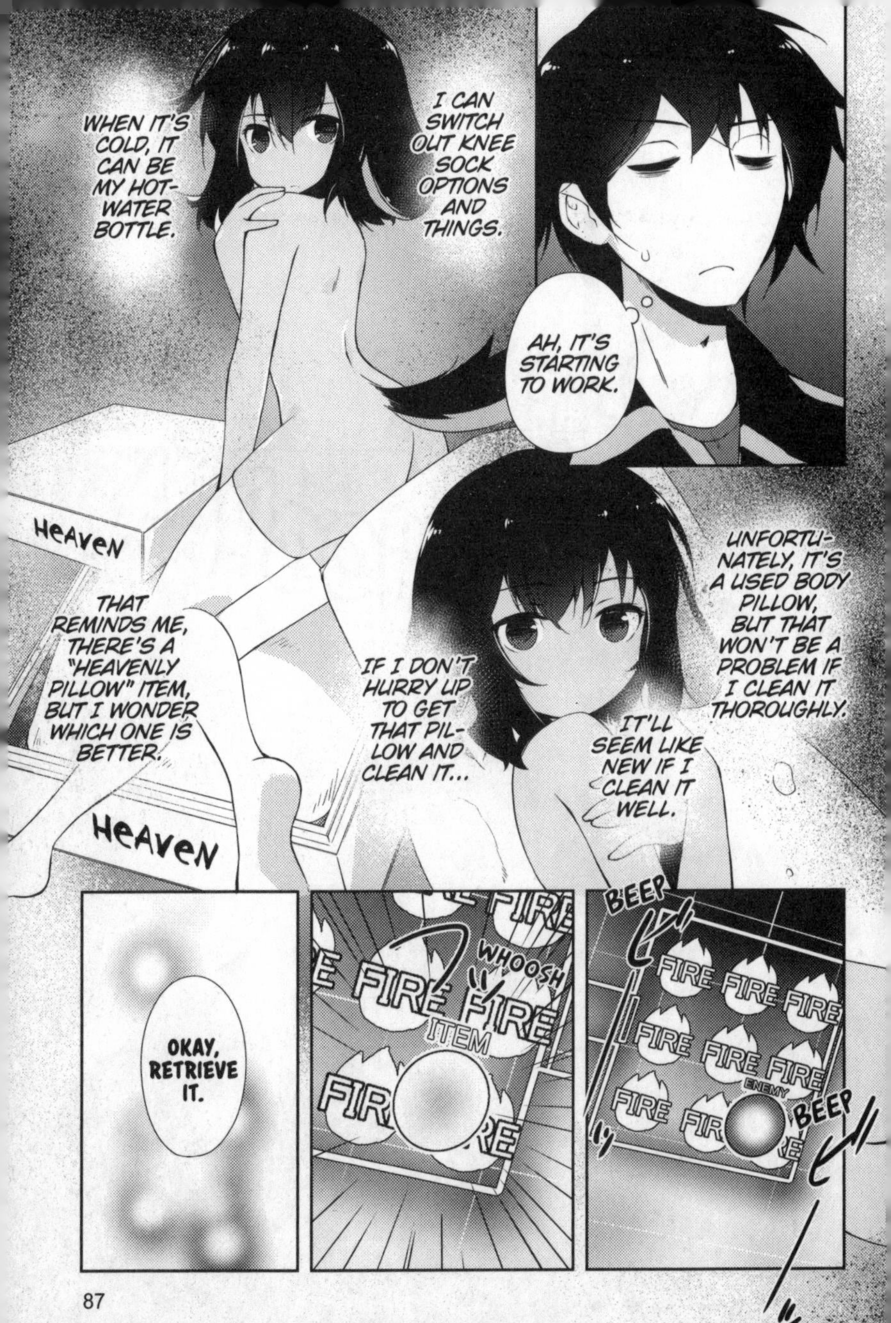
AH, IT'S STARTING TO WORK.
I CAN SWITCH OUT KNEE SOCK OPTIONS AND THINGS.
WHEN IT'S COLD, IT CAN BE MY HOT-WATER BOTTLE.
UNFORTU-NATELY, IT'S A USED BODY PILLOW, BUT THAT WON'T BE A PROBLEM IF I CLEAN IT THOROUGHLY.
IT'LL SEEM LIKE NEW IF I CLEAN IT WELL.
IF I DON'T HURRY UP TO GET THAT PIL-LOW AND CLEAN IT...
THAT REMINDS ME, THERE'S A "HEAVENLY PILLOW" ITEM, BUT I WONDER WHICH ONE IS BETTER.
HEAVEN
HEAVEN
BEEP
FIRE FIRE FIRE
FIRE FIRE FIRE
FIRE
ENEMY
BEEP
WHOOSH
FIRE FIRE
ITEM
OKAY, RETRIEVE IT.

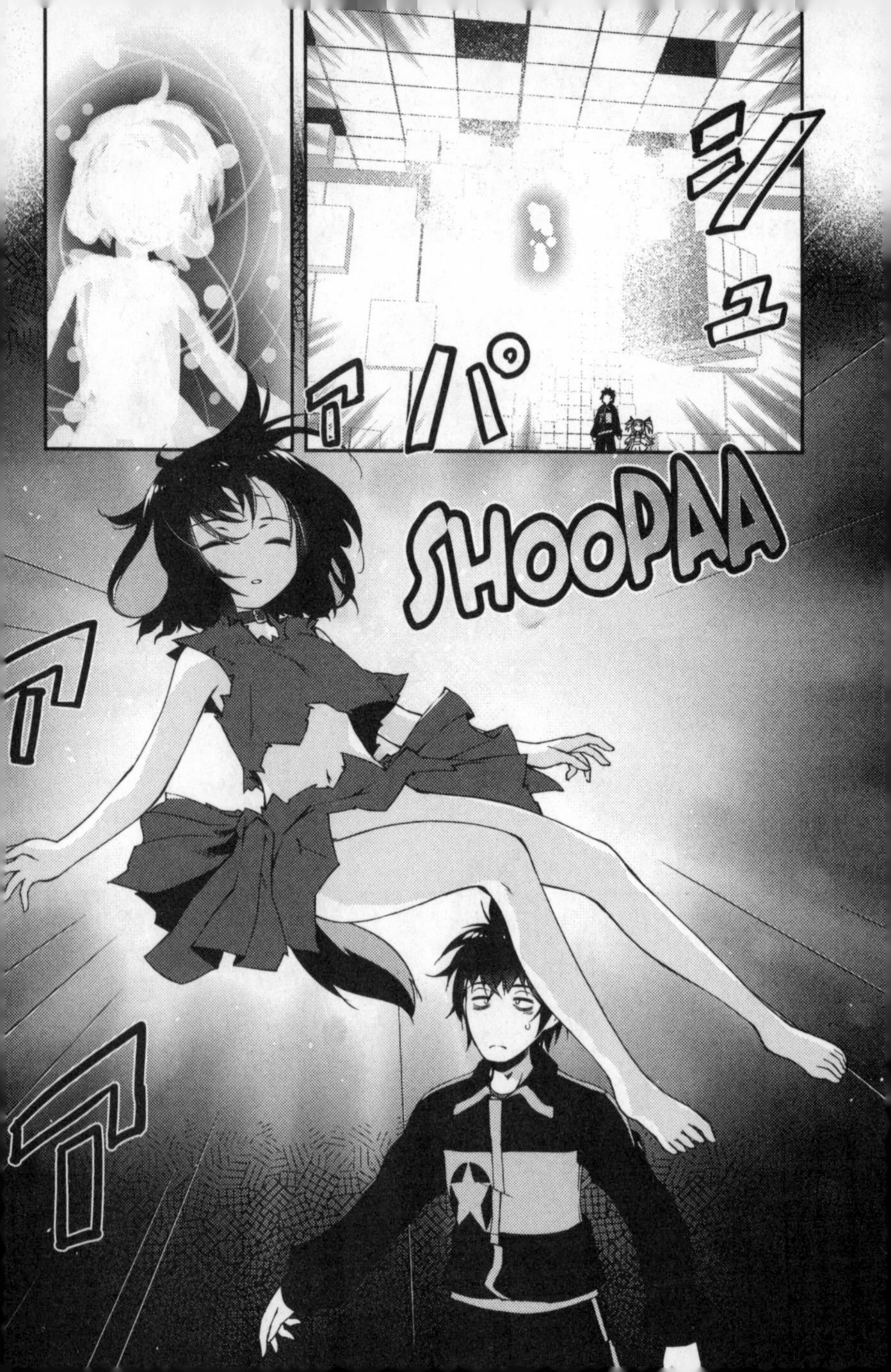
シュ
パ
ア
SHOOPAA
ア
ア

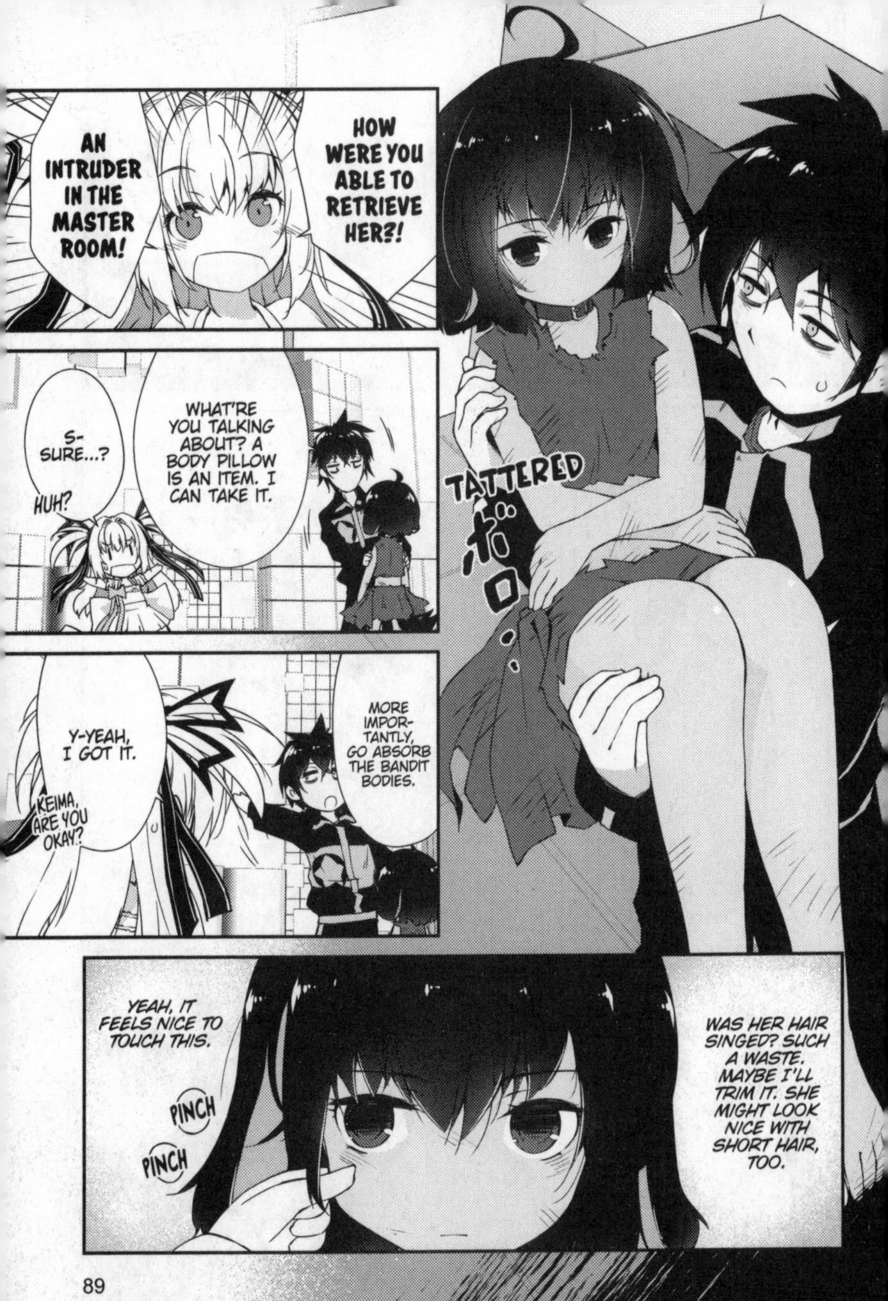
TATTERED
ボロ
HOW WERE YOU ABLE TO RETRIEVE HER?!
AN INTRUDER IN THE MASTER ROOM!
WHAT'RE YOU TALKING ABOUT? A BODY PILLOW IS AN ITEM. I CAN TAKE IT.
S-SURE...?
HUH?
MORE IMPORTANTLY, GO ABSORB THE BANDIT BODIES.
Y-YEAH, I GOT IT.
KEIMA, ARE YOU OKAY?
WAS HER HAIR SINGED? SUCH A WASTE. MAYBE I'LL TRIM IT. SHE MIGHT LOOK NICE WITH SHORT HAIR, TOO.
YEAH, IT FEELS NICE TO TOUCH THIS.
PINCH
PINCH

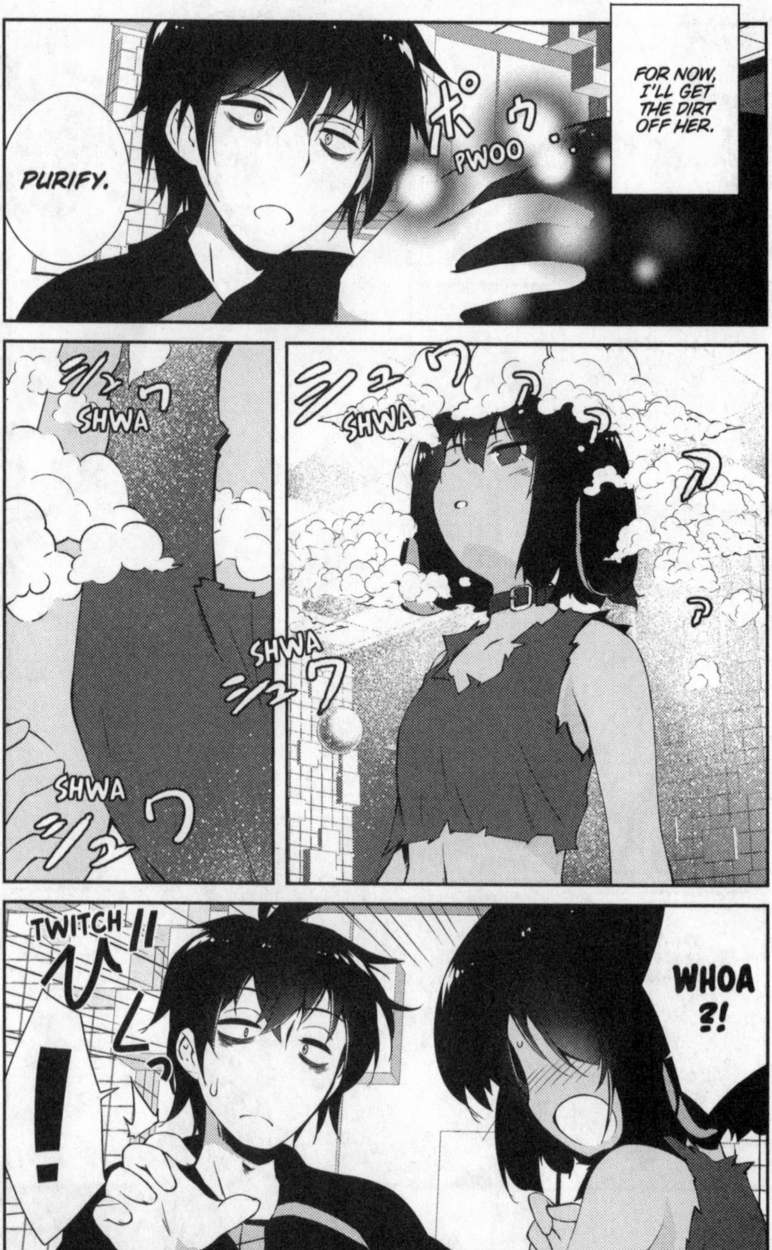
FOR NOW, I'LL GET THE DIRT OFF HER.
ポゥ
PWOO
PURIFY.
シュワ
SHWA
シュワ
SHWA
シュワ
SHWA
シュワ
SHWA
WHOA ?!
TWITCH
びくっ
!

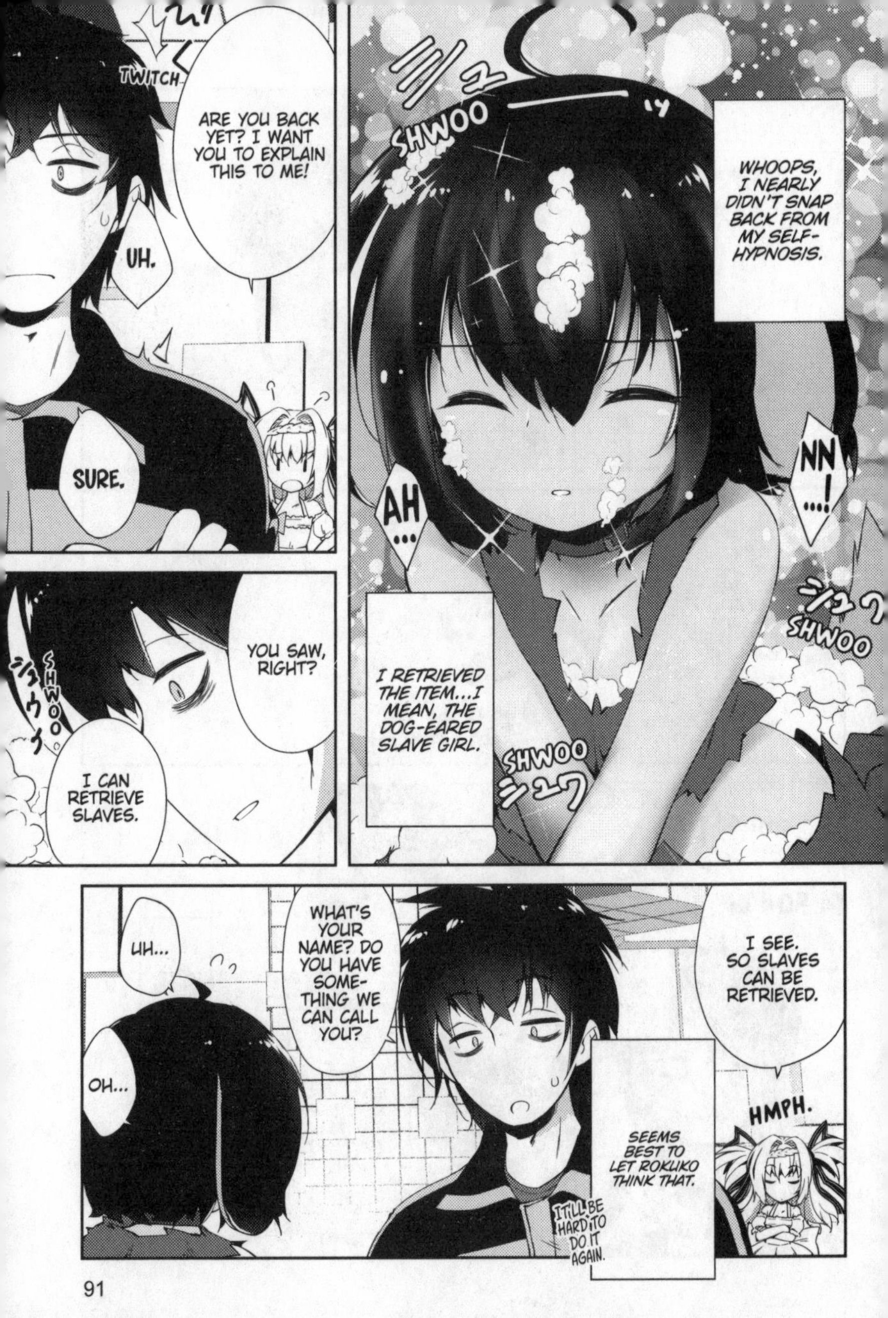
SHWOO
WHOOPS, I NEARLY DIDN'T SNAP BACK FROM MY SELF-HYPNOSIS.
NN ...!
AH ...
SHWOO
I RETRIEVED THE ITEM...I MEAN, THE DOG-EARED SLAVE GIRL.
SHWOO
TWITCH
ARE YOU BACK YET? I WANT YOU TO EXPLAIN THIS TO ME!
UH.
SURE.
YOU SAW, RIGHT?
SHWOO
I CAN RETRIEVE SLAVES.
I SEE. SO SLAVES CAN BE RETRIEVED.
WHAT'S YOUR NAME? DO YOU HAVE SOME-THING WE CAN CALL YOU?
UH...
HMPH.
SEEMS BEST TO LET ROKUKO THINK THAT.
IT'LL BE HARD TO DO IT AGAIN.
OH...

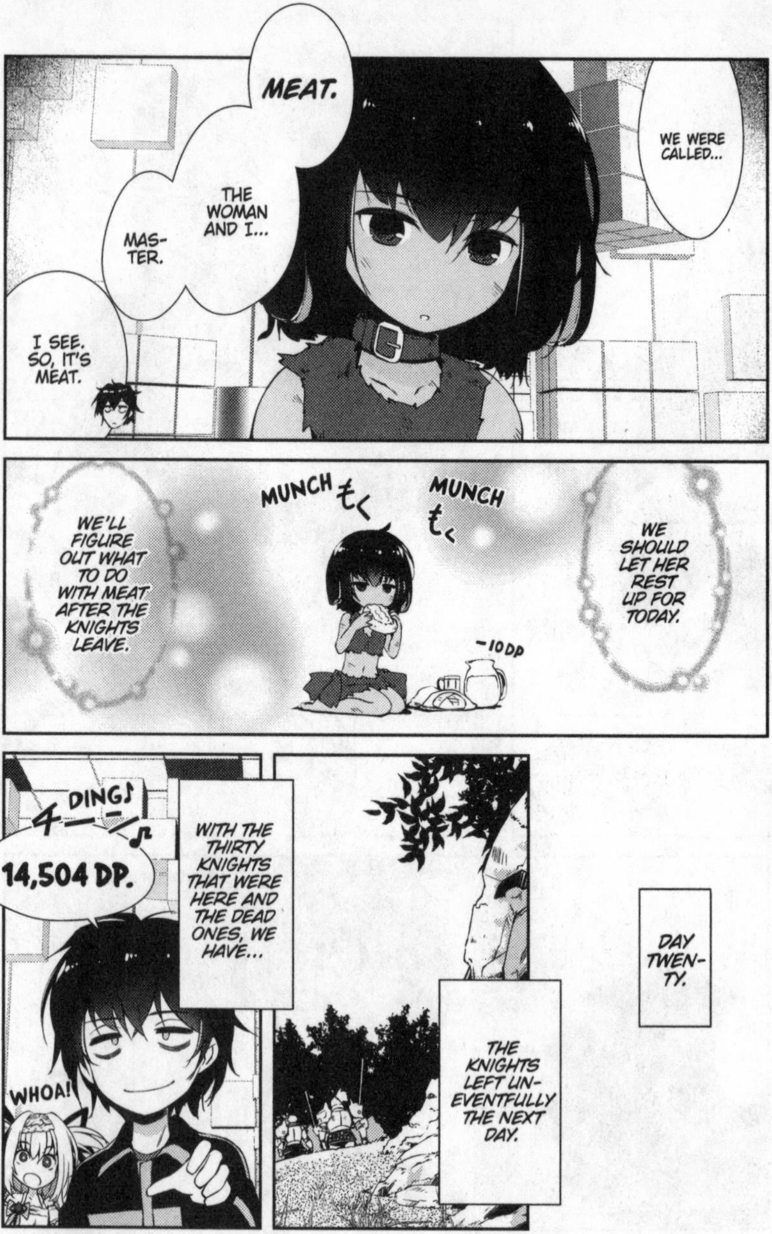
WE WERE CALLED...
MEAT.
THE WOMAN AND I...
MASTER.
I SEE. SO, IT'S MEAT.
WE SHOULD LET HER REST UP FOR TODAY.
MUNCH もく
MUNCH もく
-10DP
WE'LL FIGURE OUT WHAT TO DO WITH MEAT AFTER THE KNIGHTS LEAVE.
DAY TWENTY.
THE KNIGHTS LEFT UNEVENTFULLY THE NEXT DAY.
WITH THE THIRTY KNIGHTS THAT WERE HERE AND THE DEAD ONES, WE HAVE...
DING♪ チーン♪
14,504 DP.
WHOA!

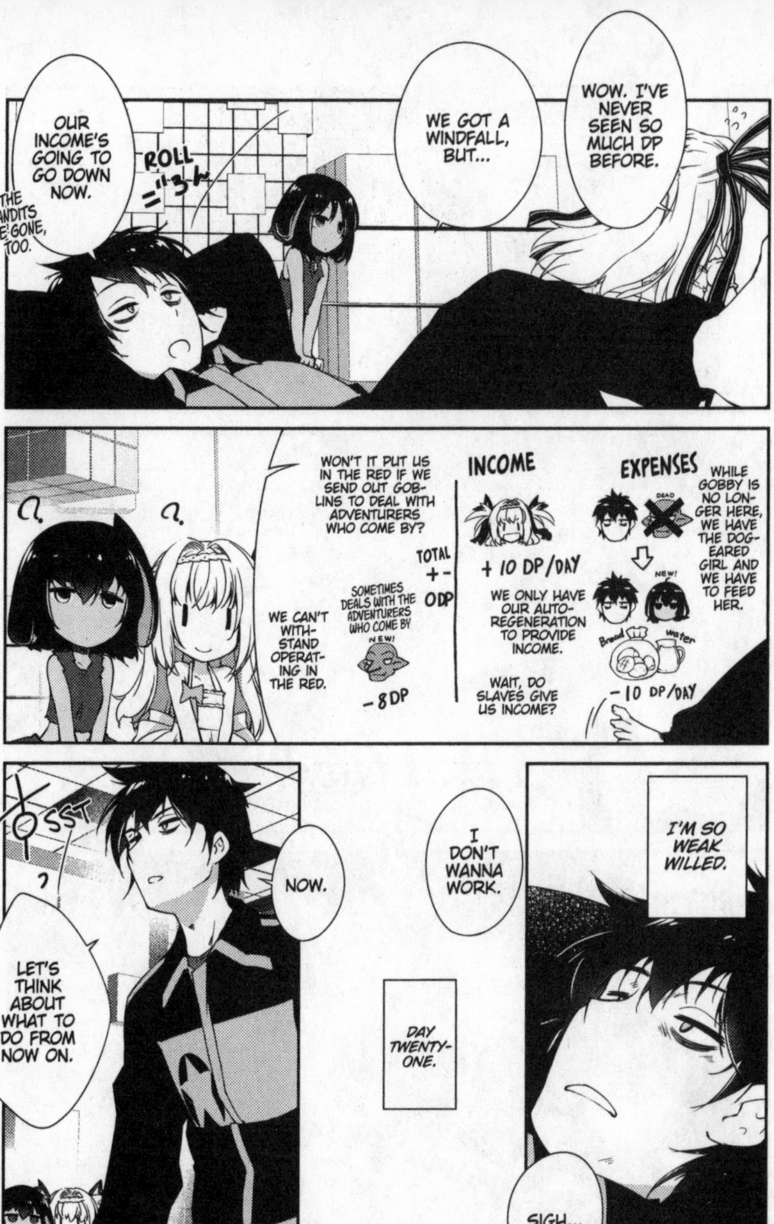
WOW. I'VE NEVER SEEN SO MUCH DP BEFORE.
WE GOT A WINDFALL, BUT...
ROLL
OUR INCOME'S GOING TO GO DOWN NOW.
THE BANDITS ARE GONE, TOO.
WHILE GOBBY IS NO LONGER HERE, WE HAVE THE DOG-EARED GIRL AND WE HAVE TO FEED HER.
EXPENSES
DEAD
NEW!
Bread
water
-10 DP/DAY
INCOME
+10 DP/DAY
WE ONLY HAVE OUR AUTO-REGENERATION TO PROVIDE INCOME.
WAIT, DO SLAVES GIVE US INCOME?
TOTAL
+-
0DP
WON'T IT PUT US IN THE RED IF WE SEND OUT GOB-LINS TO DEAL WITH ADVENTURERS WHO COME BY?
SOMETIMES DEALS WITH THE ADVENTURERS WHO COME BY
NEW!
-8DP
WE CAN'T WITH-STAND OPERAT-ING IN THE RED.
I'M SO WEAK WILLED.
SIGH...
DAY TWENTY-ONE.
I DON'T WANNA WORK.
NOW.
SST
LET'S THINK ABOUT WHAT TO DO FROM NOW ON.

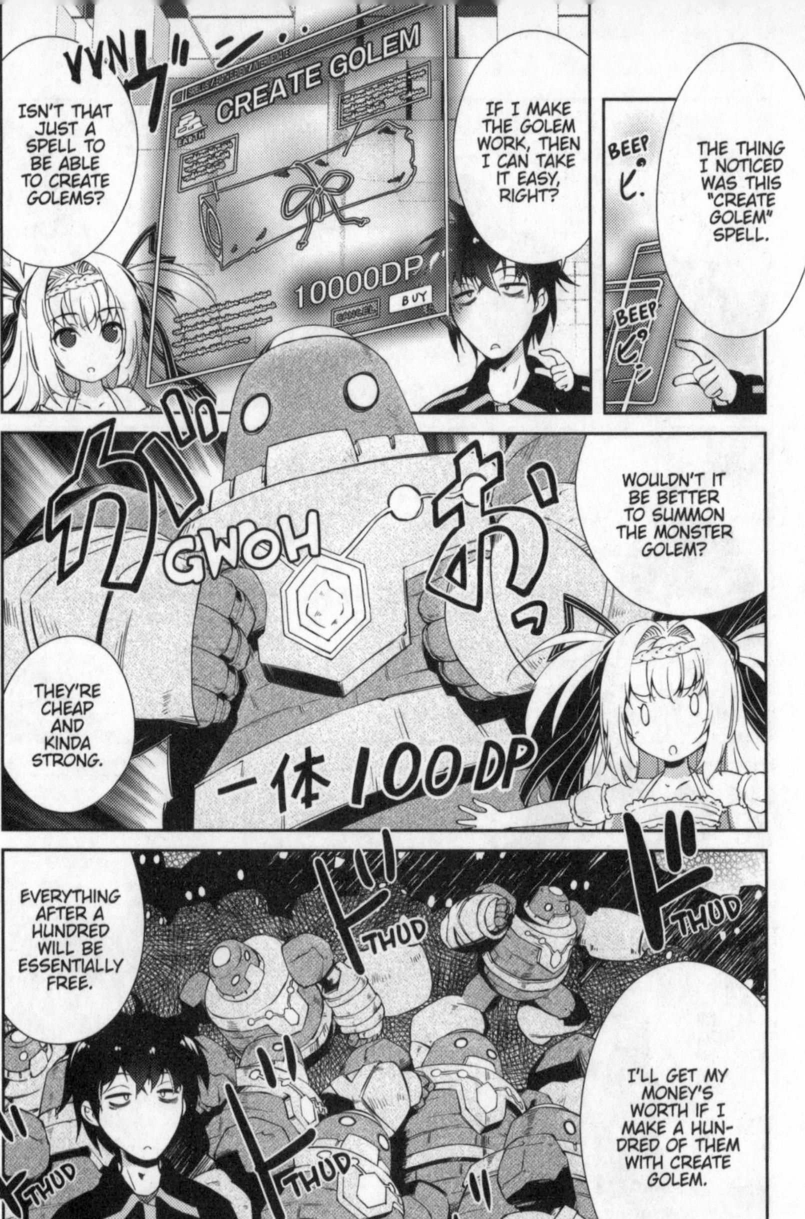
THE THING I NOTICED WAS THIS "CREATE GOLEM" SPELL.
BEEP ピ.
BEEP ピッ
IF I MAKE THE GOLEM WORK, THEN I CAN TAKE IT EASY, RIGHT?
VVN ヴン..
CREATE GOLEM
CREATE GOLEM
EARTH
10000DP
CANCEL
BUY
ISN'T THAT JUST A SPELL TO BE ABLE TO CREATE GOLEMS?
WOULDN'T IT BE BETTER TO SUMMON THE MONSTER GOLEM?
GWOH がおっ
THEY'RE CHEAP AND KINDA STRONG.
一体 100 DP
I'LL GET MY MONEY'S WORTH IF I MAKE A HUNDRED OF THEM WITH CREATE GOLEM.
THUD ド
THUD ド
EVERYTHING AFTER A HUNDRED WILL BE ESSENTIALLY FREE.
THUD ド
THUD ド
THUD ド

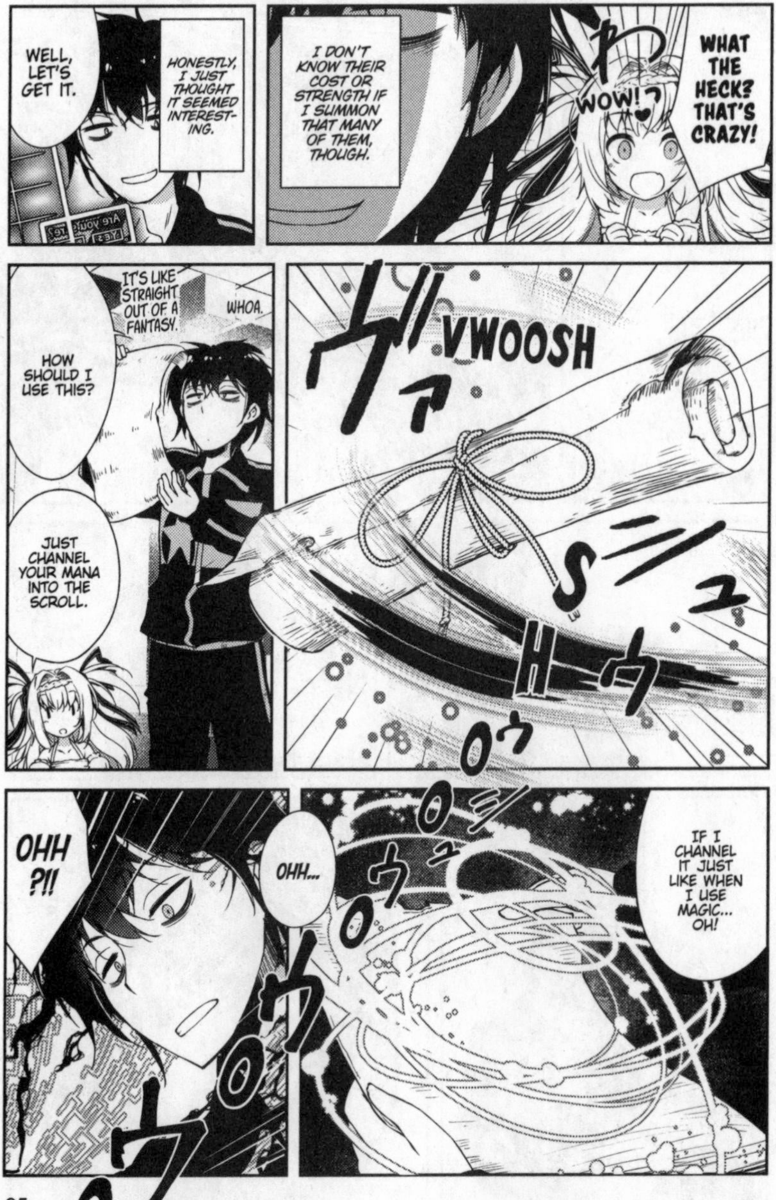
WHAT THE HECK? THAT'S CRAZY!
WOW!♥
I DON'T KNOW THEIR COST OR STRENGTH IF I SUMMON THAT MANY OF THEM, THOUGH.
HONESTLY, I JUST THOUGHT IT SEEMED INTERESTING.
WELL, LET'S GET IT.
VWOOSH
SHH
WHOA.
IT'S LIKE STRAIGHT OUT OF A FANTASY.
HOW SHOULD I USE THIS?
JUST CHANNEL YOUR MANA INTO THE SCROLL.
IF I CHANNEL IT JUST LIKE WHEN I USE MAGIC... OH!
OHH...
OHH ?!!

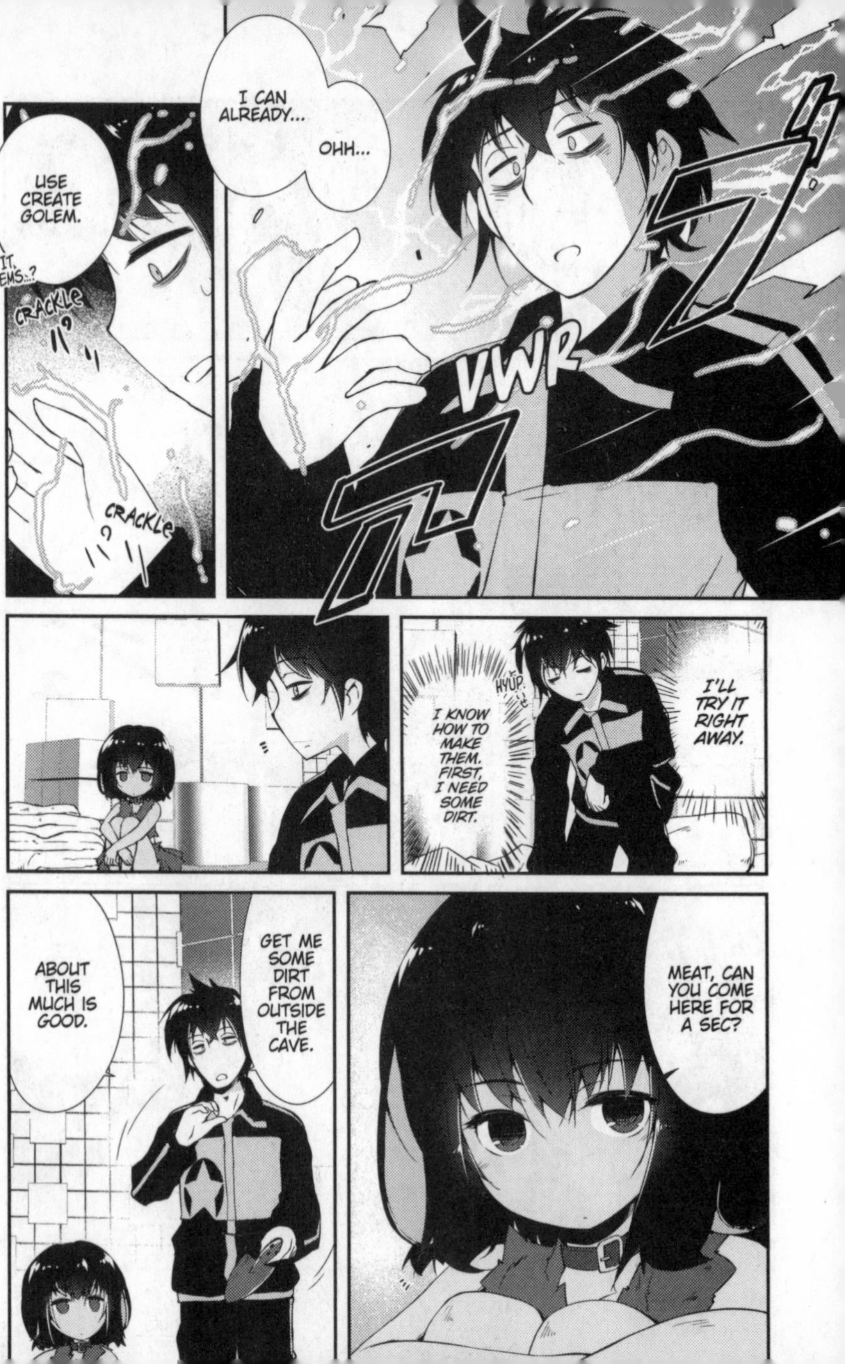
I CAN ALREADY...
OHH...
VWR
USE CREATE GOLEM.
IT SEEMS...?
CRACKLE
CRACKLE
I'LL TRY IT RIGHT AWAY.
HYUP.
I KNOW HOW TO MAKE THEM. FIRST, I NEED SOME DIRT.
MEAT, CAN YOU COME HERE FOR A SEC?
GET ME SOME DIRT FROM OUTSIDE THE CAVE.
ABOUT THIS MUCH IS GOOD.

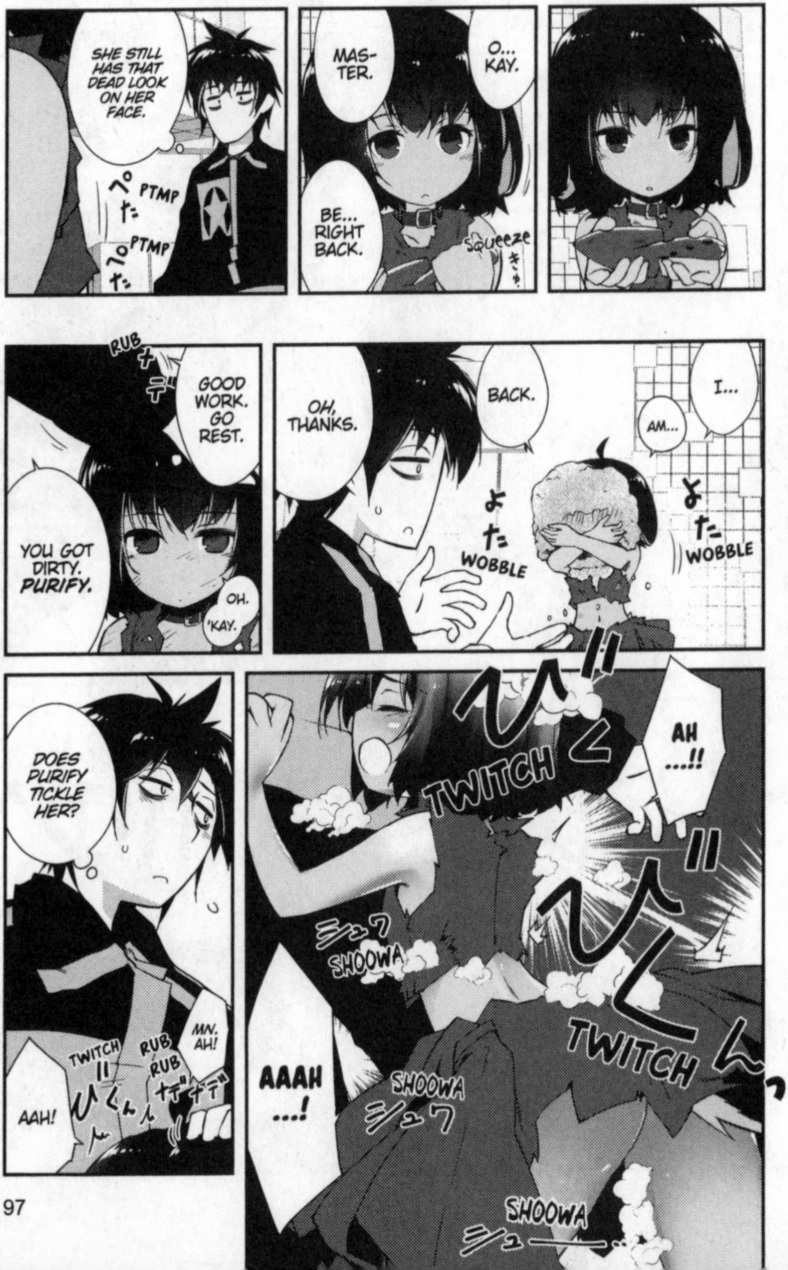
O... KAY.
MAS-TER.
BE... RIGHT BACK.
Squeeze きゅ
SHE STILL HAS THAT DEAD LOOK ON HER FACE.
ぺた PTMP
ぺた PTMP
I...
AM...
BACK.
よた WOBBLE
よた WOBBLE
OH, THANKS.
RUB ナデ
GOOD WORK. GO REST.
YOU GOT DIRTY. PURIFY.
OH. 'KAY.
AH ...!!
びく TWITCH
びくん TWITCH
シュワ SHOOWA
AAAH ...!
SHOOWA シュワ
SHOOWA シュー
DOES PURIFY TICKLE HER?
MN. AH!
RUB RUB ナデナデ
TWITCH ひくん
AAH!

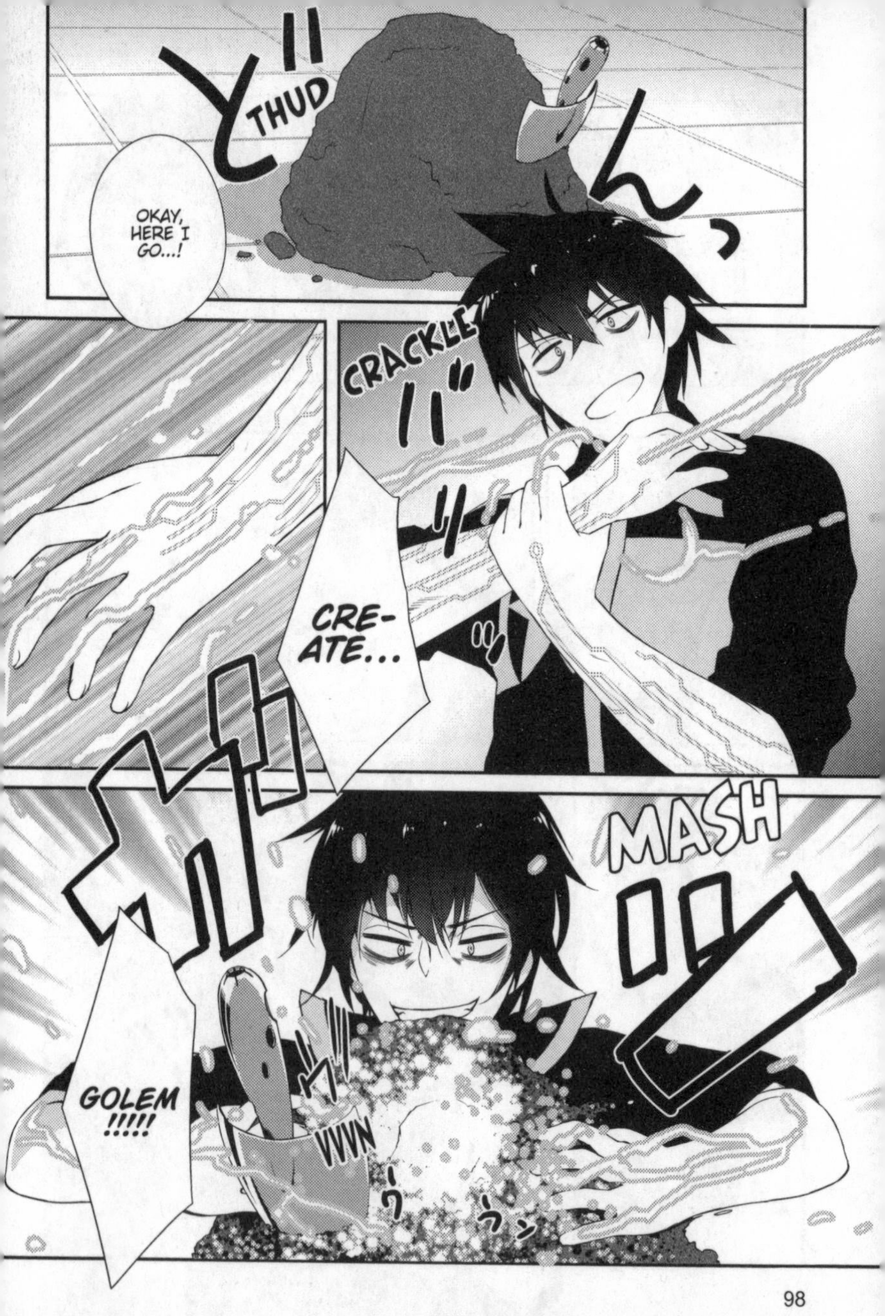
THUD
OKAY, HERE I GO...!
CRACKLE
CRE-ATE...
MASH
GOLEM!!!!!
VVVN

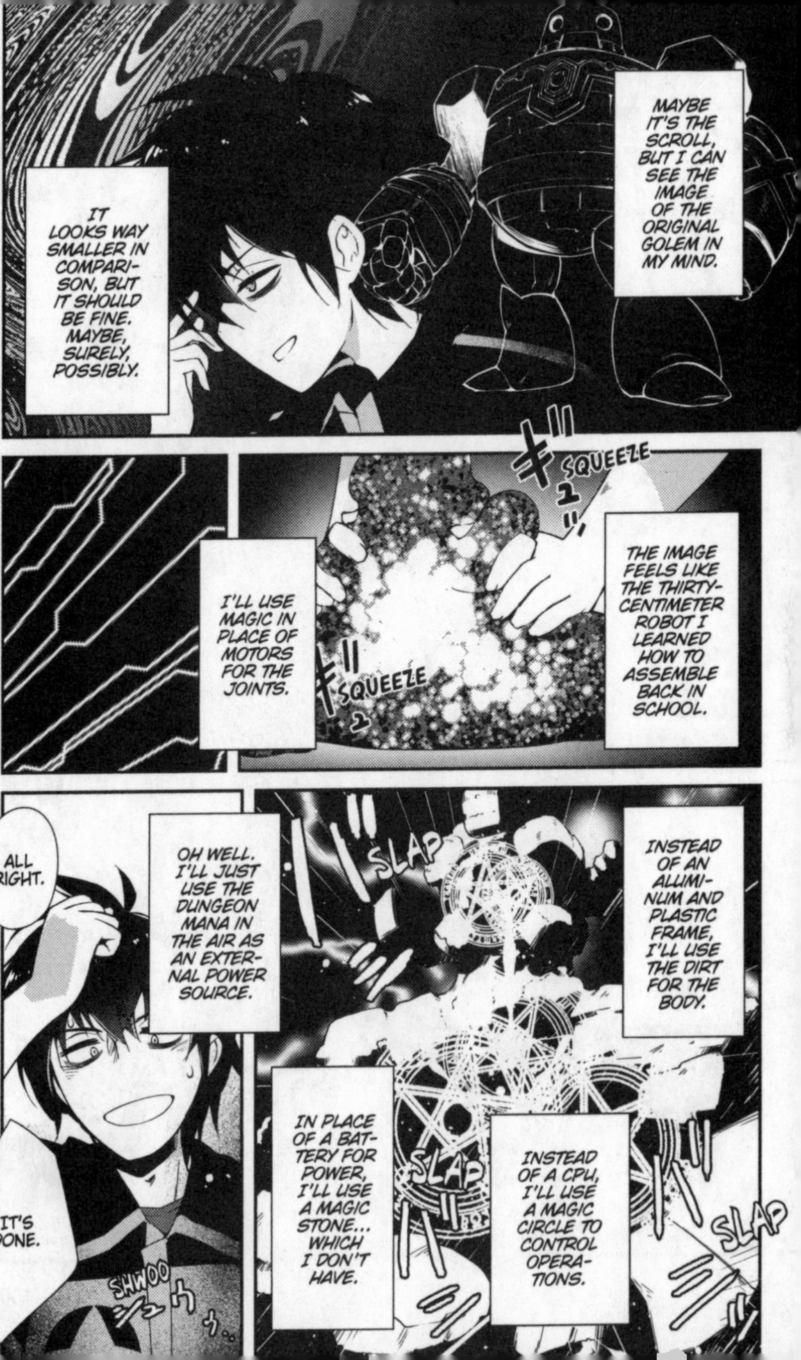
MAYBE IT'S THE SCROLL, BUT I CAN SEE THE IMAGE OF THE ORIGINAL GOLEM IN MY MIND.
IT LOOKS WAY SMALLER IN COMPARISON, BUT IT SHOULD BE FINE. MAYBE, SURELY, POSSIBLY.
SQUEEZE
THE IMAGE FEELS LIKE THE THIRTY-CENTIMETER ROBOT I LEARNED HOW TO ASSEMBLE BACK IN SCHOOL.
I'LL USE MAGIC IN PLACE OF MOTORS FOR THE JOINTS.
SQUEEZE
INSTEAD OF AN ALUMINUM AND PLASTIC FRAME, I'LL USE THE DIRT FOR THE BODY.
SLAP
INSTEAD OF A CPU, I'LL USE A MAGIC CIRCLE TO CONTROL OPERATIONS.
IN PLACE OF A BATTERY FOR POWER, I'LL USE A MAGIC STONE... WHICH I DON'T HAVE.
SLAP
SLAP
OH WELL. I'LL JUST USE THE DUNGEON MANA IN THE AIR AS AN EXTERNAL POWER SOURCE.
ALL RIGHT.
IT'S DONE.
SHWOO

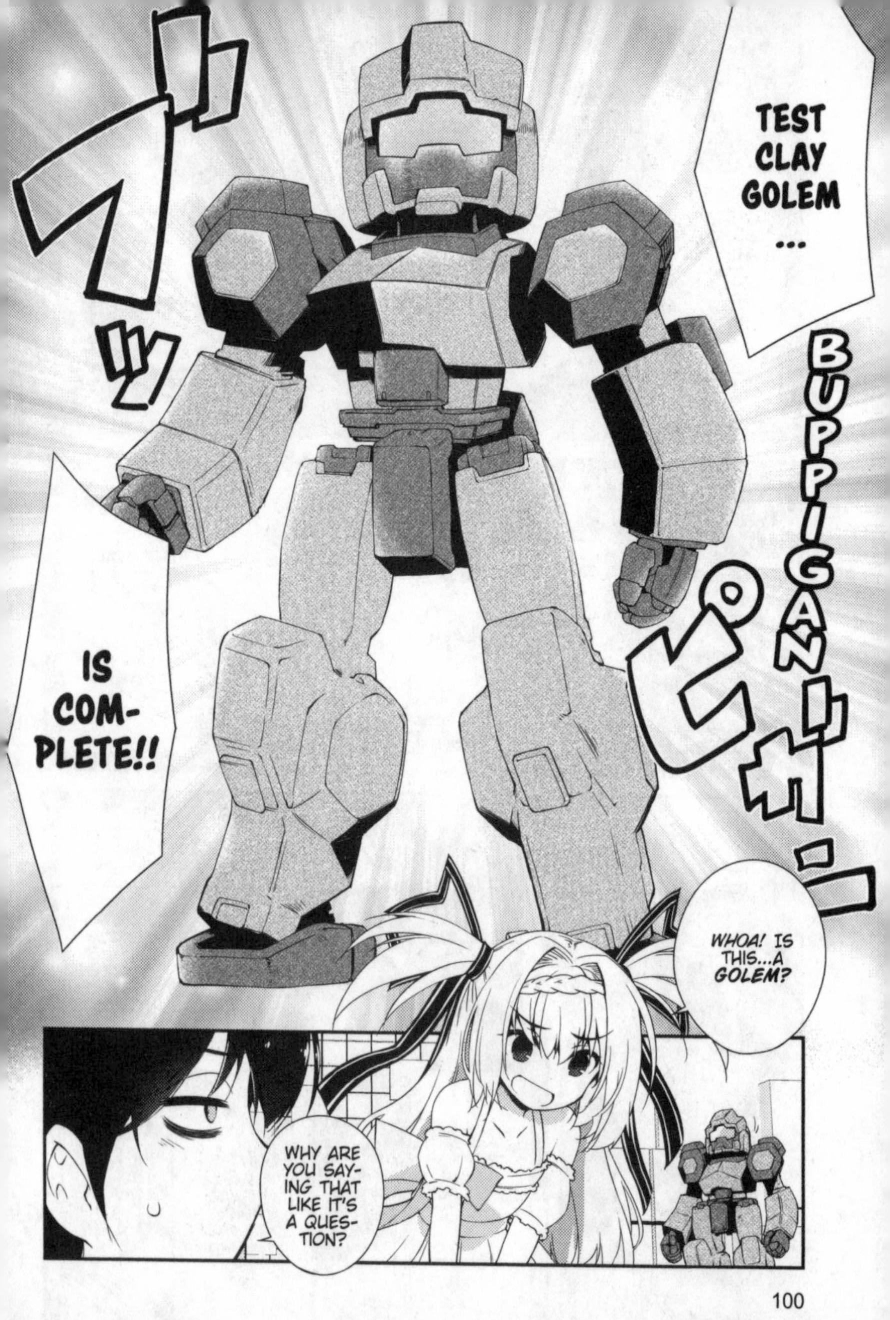
TEST CLAY GOLEM ...
IS COM-PLETE!!
BUPPIGAN!
WHOA! IS THIS...A GOLEM?
WHY ARE YOU SAY-ING THAT LIKE IT'S A QUES-TION?

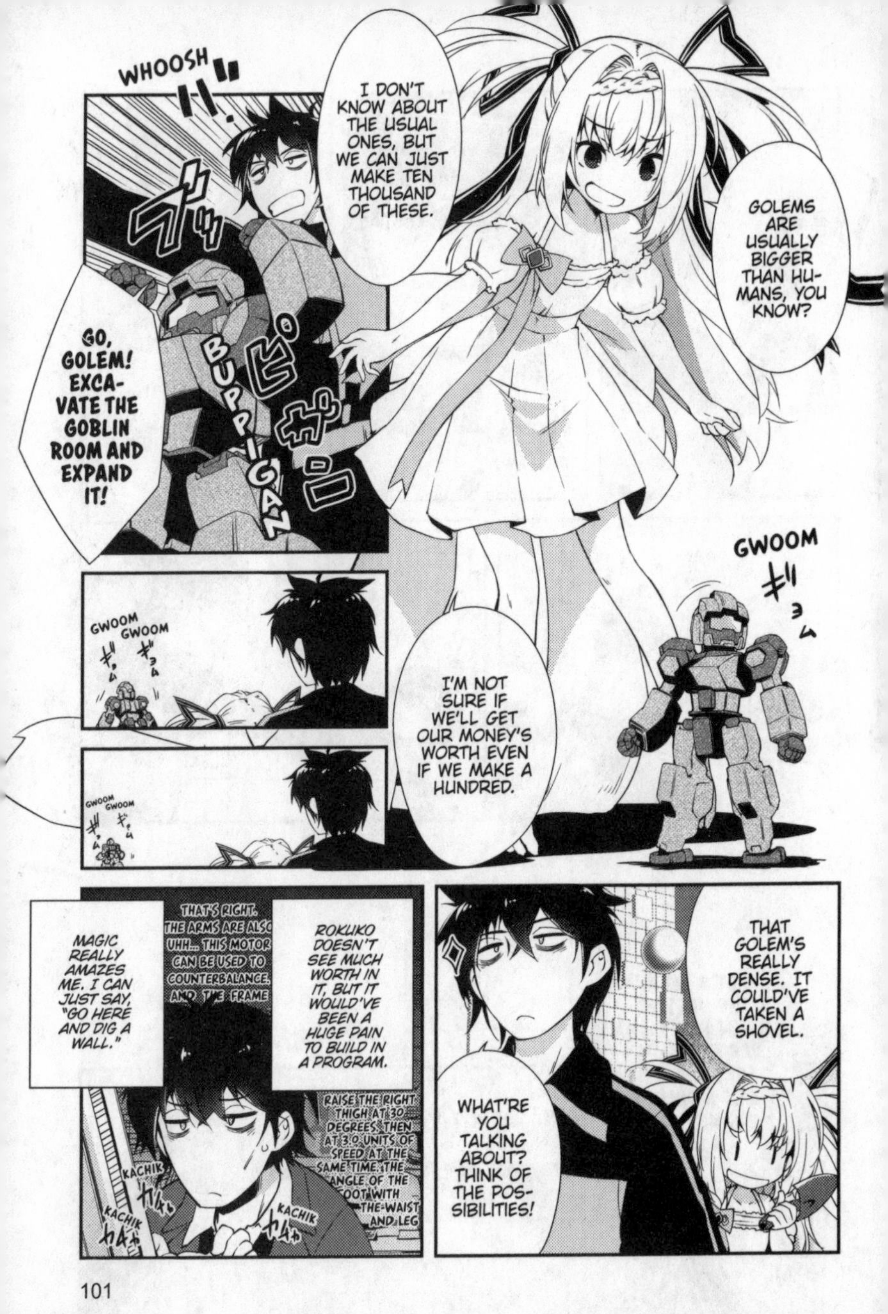

GOLEMS ARE USUALLY BIGGER THAN HU-MANS, YOU KNOW?
I DON'T KNOW ABOUT THE USUAL ONES, BUT WE CAN JUST MAKE TEN THOUSAND OF THESE.
WHOOSH
GO, GOLEM! EXCA-VATE THE GOBLIN ROOM AND EXPAND IT!
BUPPIGAN
GWOOM
I'M NOT SURE IF WE'LL GET OUR MONEY'S WORTH EVEN IF WE MAKE A HUNDRED.
GWOOM GWOOM
GWOOM GWOOM
THAT GOLEM'S REALLY DENSE. IT COULD'VE TAKEN A SHOVEL.
WHAT'RE YOU TALKING ABOUT? THINK OF THE POS-SIBILITIES!
ROKUKO DOESN'T SEE MUCH WORTH IN IT, BUT IT WOULD'VE BEEN A HUGE PAIN TO BUILD IN A PROGRAM.
THAT'S RIGHT. THE ARMS ARE ALSO UHH... THIS MOTOR CAN BE USED TO COUNTERBALANCE. AND THE FRAME
MAGIC REALLY AMAZES ME. I CAN JUST SAY, "GO HERE AND DIG A WALL."
RAISE THE RIGHT THIGH AT 30 DEGREES, THEN AT 3.0 UNITS OF SPEED AT THE SAME TIME THE ANGLE OF THE FOOT WITH THE WAIST AND LEG
KACHIK
KACHIK
KACHIK

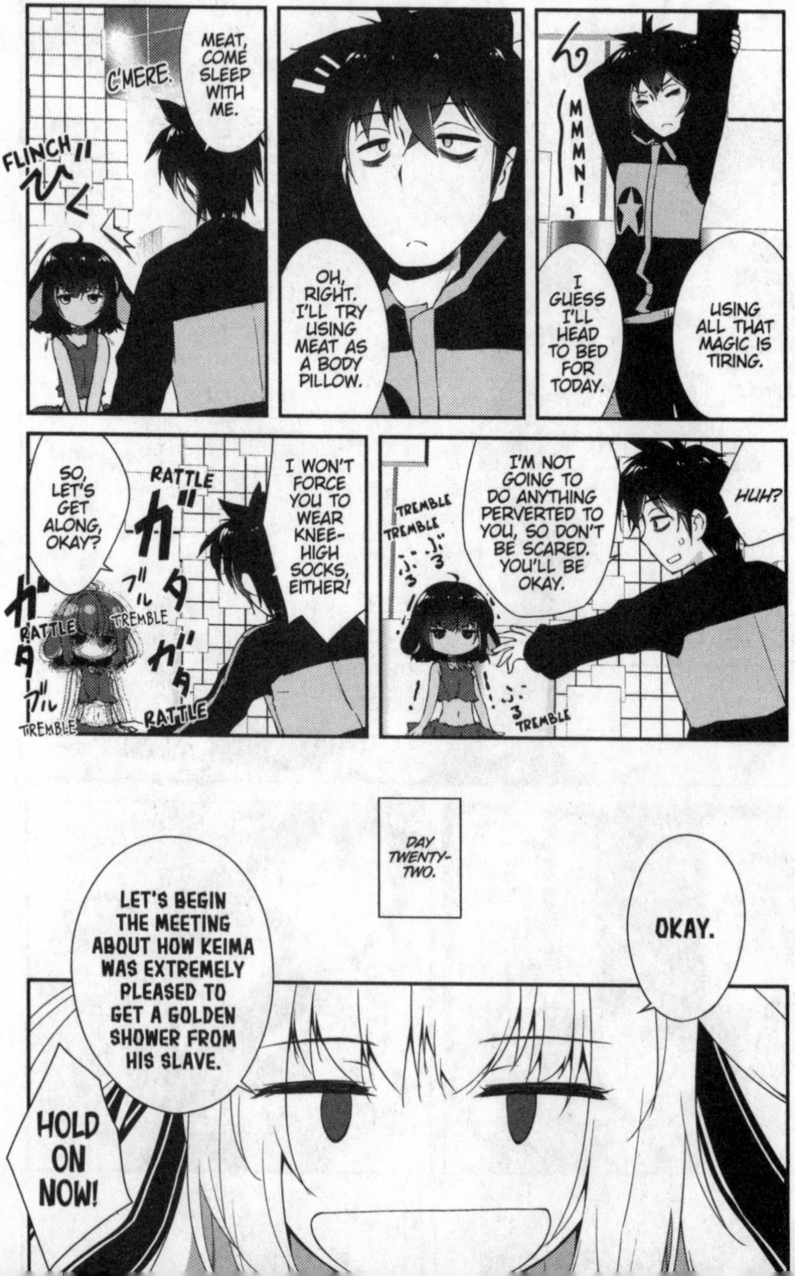
USING ALL THAT MAGIC IS TIRING.
I GUESS I'LL HEAD TO BED FOR TODAY.
MMMMN!
OH, RIGHT. I'LL TRY USING MEAT AS A BODY PILLOW.
MEAT, COME SLEEP WITH ME.
C'MERE.
FLINCH
HUH?
I'M NOT GOING TO DO ANYTHING PERVERTED TO YOU, SO DON'T BE SCARED. YOU'LL BE OKAY.
TREMBLE
TREMBLE
TREMBLE
I WON'T FORCE YOU TO WEAR KNEE-HIGH SOCKS, EITHER!
SO, LET'S GET ALONG, OKAY?
RATTLE
TREMBLE
RATTLE
RATTLE
TREMBLE
DAY TWENTY-TWO.
OKAY.
LET'S BEGIN THE MEETING ABOUT HOW KEIMA WAS EXTREMELY PLEASED TO GET A GOLDEN SHOWER FROM HIS SLAVE.
HOLD ON NOW!

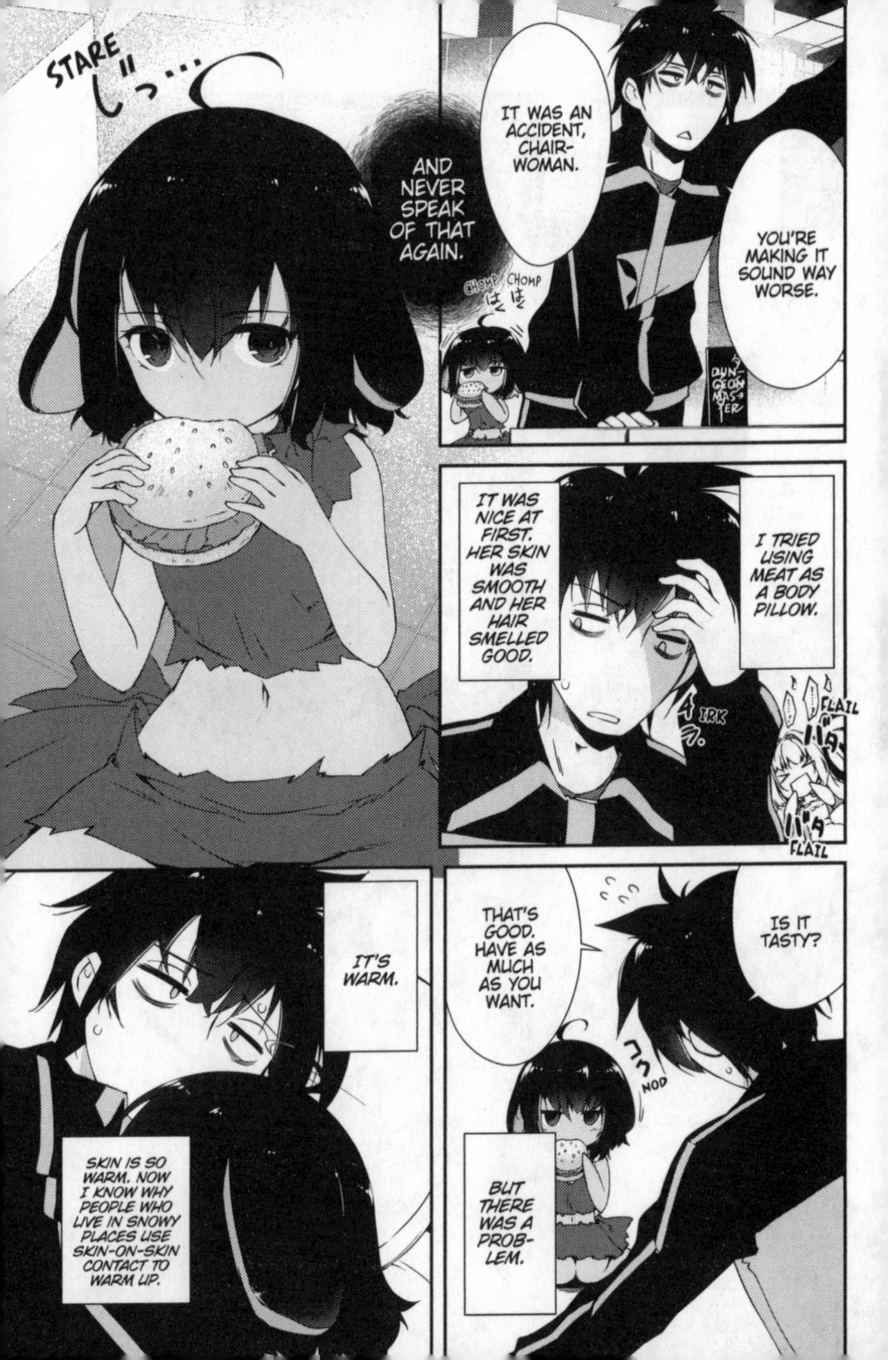
YOU'RE MAKING IT SOUND WAY WORSE.
IT WAS AN ACCIDENT, CHAIR-WOMAN.
CHOMP CHOMP
DUN-GEON MAS-TER
I TRIED USING MEAT AS A BODY PILLOW.
IT WAS NICE AT FIRST. HER SKIN WAS SMOOTH AND HER HAIR SMELLED GOOD.
IRK
FLAIL
FLAIL
STARE
じっ…
AND NEVER SPEAK OF THAT AGAIN.
IS IT TASTY?
NOD
THAT'S GOOD. HAVE AS MUCH AS YOU WANT.
BUT THERE WAS A PROB-LEM.
IT'S WARM.
SKIN IS SO WARM. NOW I KNOW WHY PEOPLE WHO LIVE IN SNOWY PLACES USE SKIN-ON-SKIN CONTACT TO WARM UP.

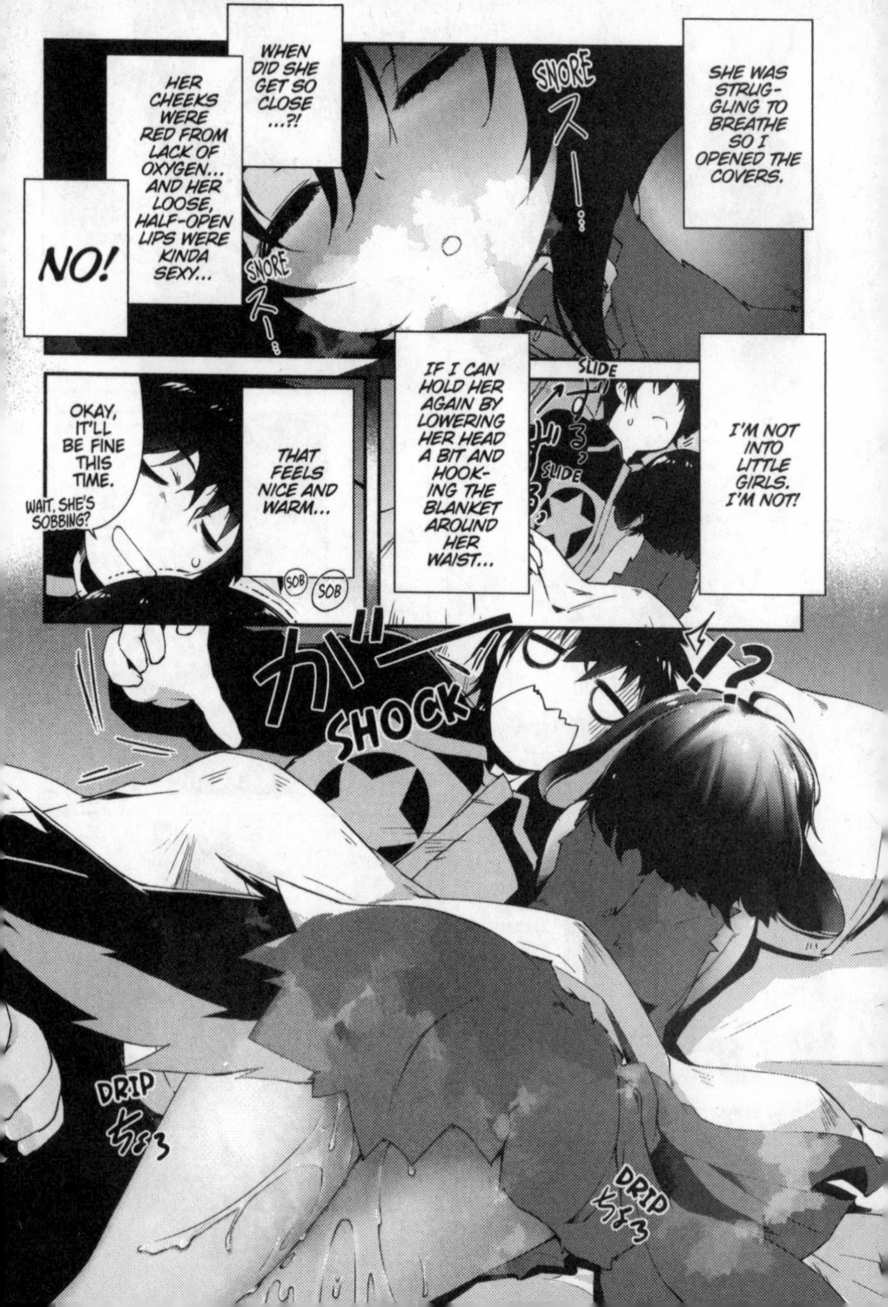
SHE WAS STRUGGLING TO BREATHE SO I OPENED THE COVERS.
SNORE
WHEN DID SHE GET SO CLOSE ...?!
HER CHEEKS WERE RED FROM LACK OF OXYGEN... AND HER LOOSE, HALF-OPEN LIPS WERE KINDA SEXY...
NO!
SNORE
I'M NOT INTO LITTLE GIRLS. I'M NOT!
SLIDE
SLIDE
IF I CAN HOLD HER AGAIN BY LOWERING HER HEAD A BIT AND HOOKING THE BLANKET AROUND HER WAIST...
THAT FEELS NICE AND WARM...
OKAY, IT'LL BE FINE THIS TIME.
WAIT, SHE'S SOBBING?
SOB
SOB
!?
SHOCK
DRIP
DRIP

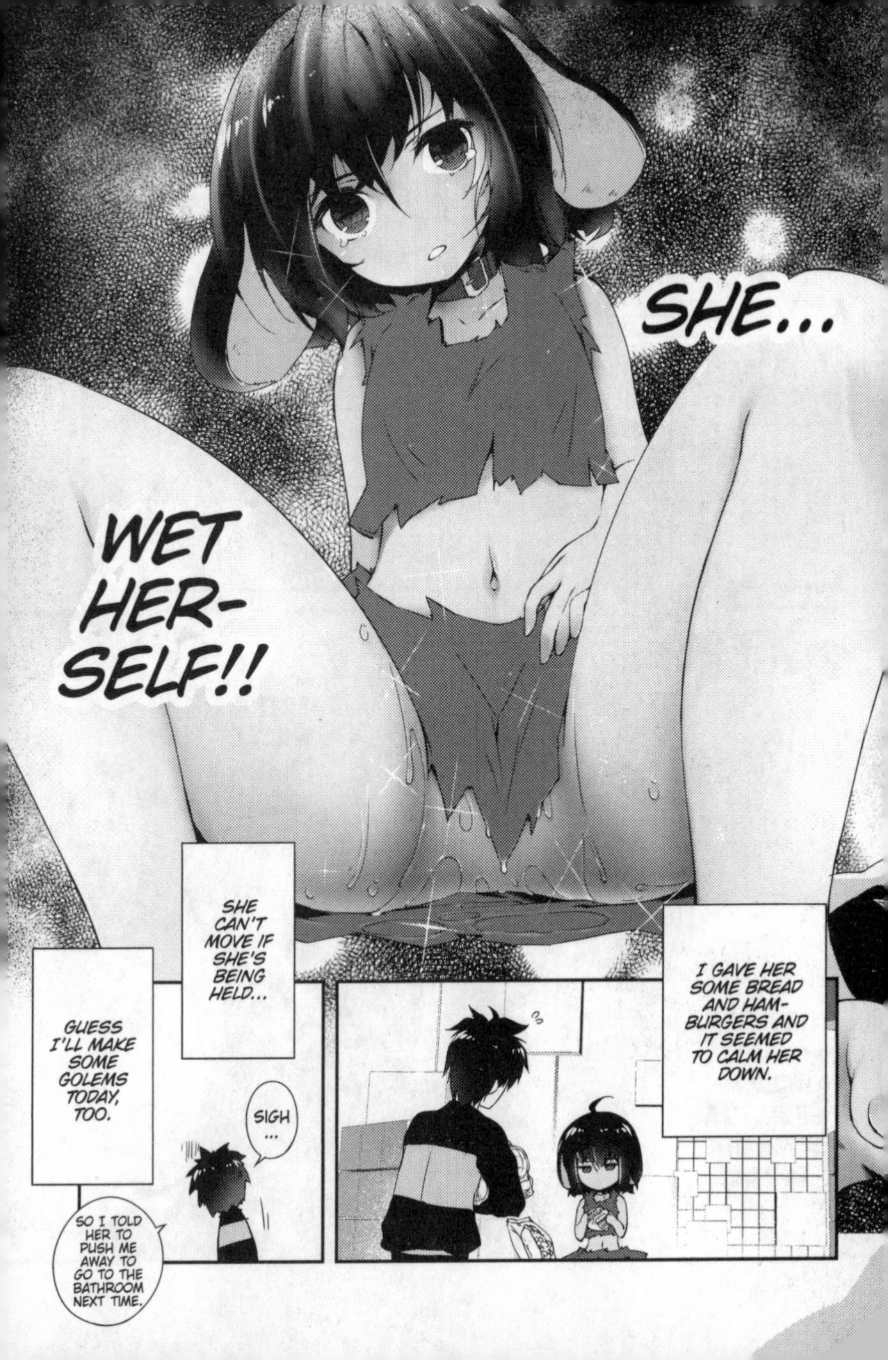
SHE...
WET HER-SELF!!
SHE CAN'T MOVE IF SHE'S BEING HELD...
I GAVE HER SOME BREAD AND HAM-BURGERS AND IT SEEMED TO CALM HER DOWN.
GUESS I'LL MAKE SOME GOLEMS TODAY, TOO.
SIGH...
SO I TOLD HER TO PUSH ME AWAY TO GO TO THE BATHROOM NEXT TIME.

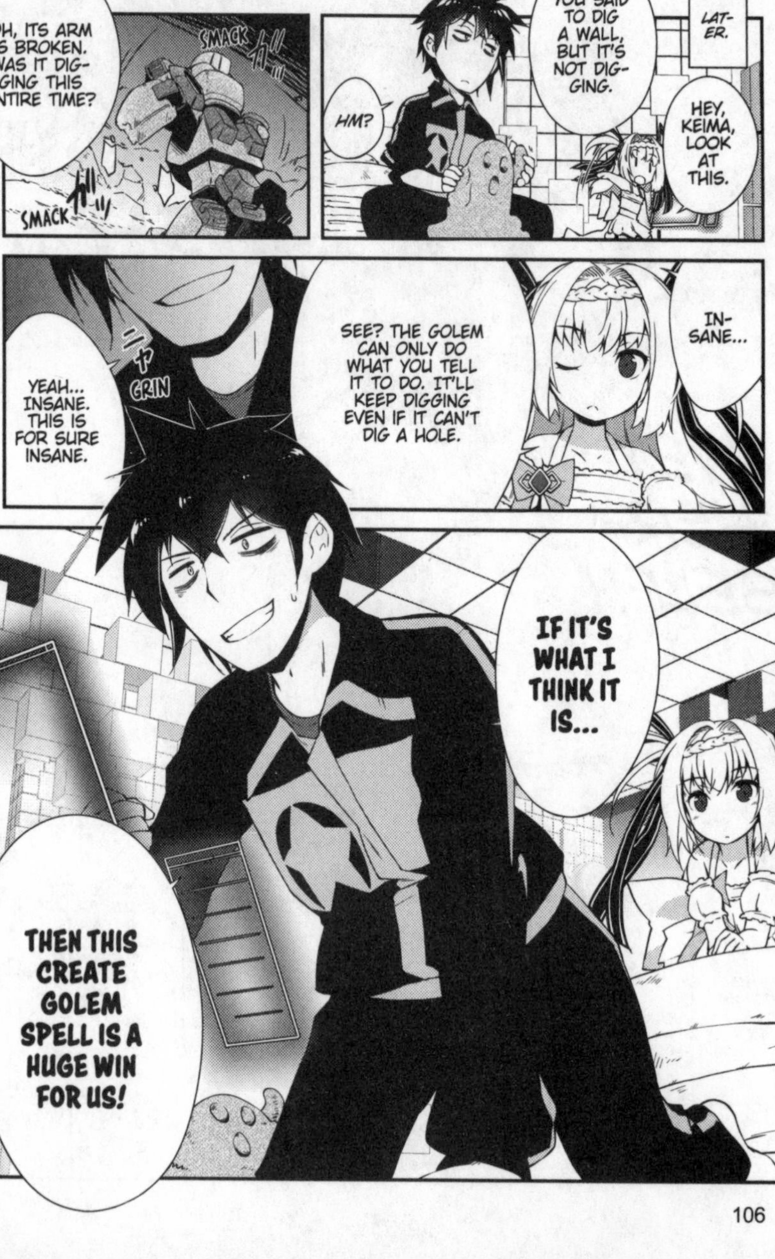
LATER.
HEY, KEIMA, LOOK AT THIS.
HM?
YOU SAID TO DIG A WALL, BUT IT'S NOT DIGGING.
SMACK
SMACK
OH, ITS ARM IS BROKEN. WAS IT DIGGING THIS ENTIRE TIME?
INSANE...
SEE? THE GOLEM CAN ONLY DO WHAT YOU TELL IT TO DO. IT'LL KEEP DIGGING EVEN IF IT CAN'T DIG A HOLE.
GRIN
YEAH... INSANE. THIS IS FOR SURE INSANE.
IF IT'S WHAT I THINK IT IS...
THEN THIS CREATE GOLEM SPELL IS A HUGE WIN FOR US!

LAZY DUNGEON MASTER

LAZY
DUNGEON
MASTER

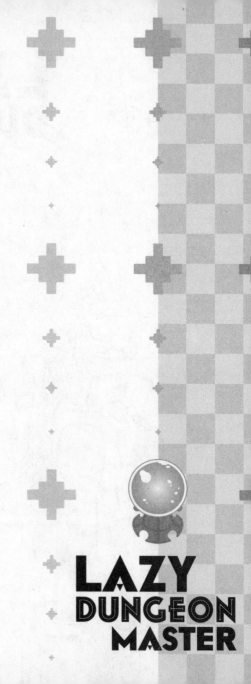

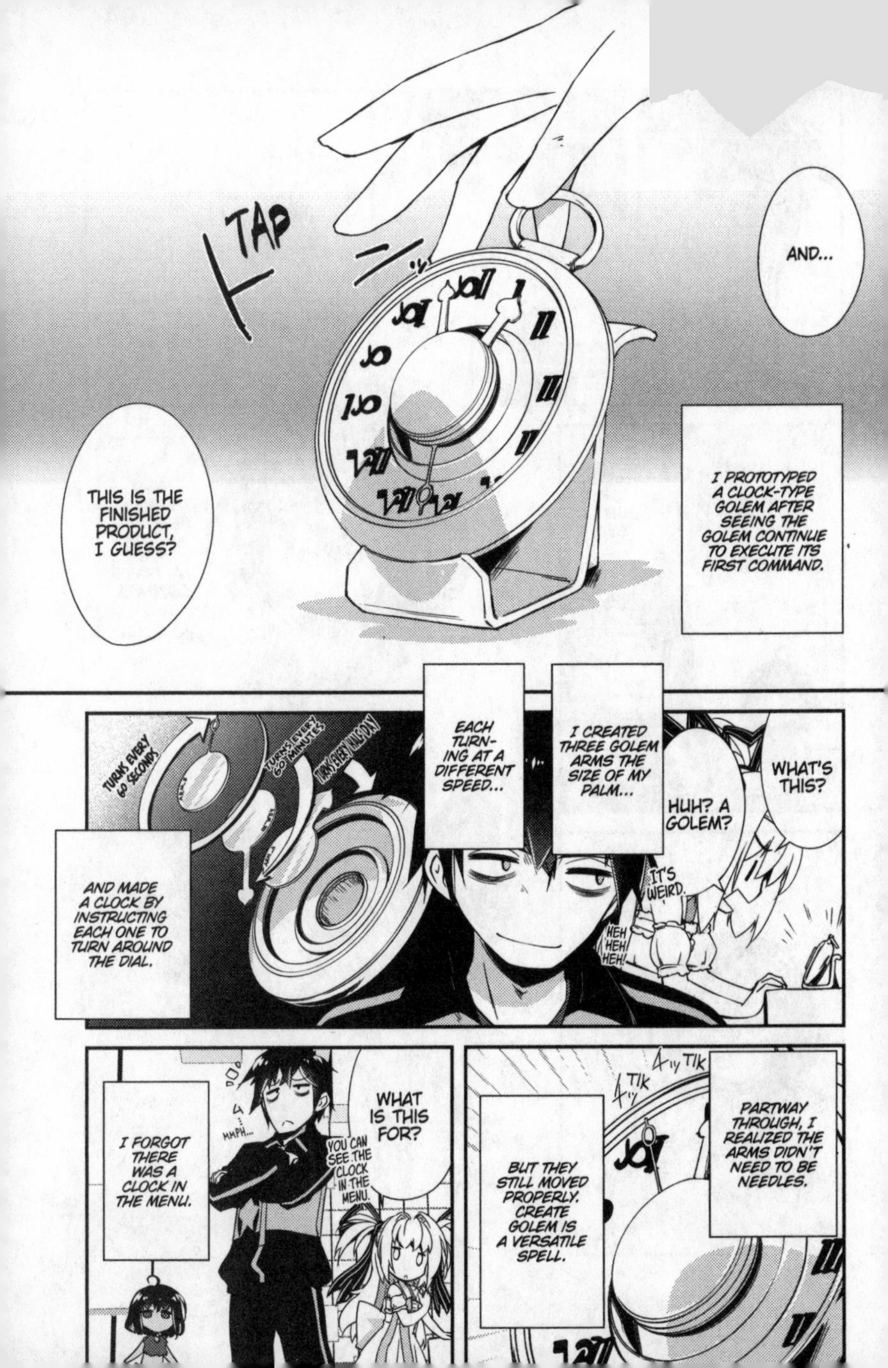
AND...
I PROTOTYPED A CLOCK-TYPE GOLEM AFTER SEEING THE GOLEM CONTINUE TO EXECUTE ITS FIRST COMMAND.
TAP
THIS IS THE FINISHED PRODUCT, I GUESS?
WHAT'S THIS?
HUH? A GOLEM?
I CREATED THREE GOLEM ARMS THE SIZE OF MY PALM...
EACH TURNING AT A DIFFERENT SPEED...
IT'S WEIRD.
HEH HEH HEH!
TURNS EVERY HALF-DAY
TURNS EVERY 60 MINUTES
TURNS EVERY 60 SECONDS
AND MADE A CLOCK BY INSTRUCTING EACH ONE TO TURN AROUND THE DIAL.
TIK
TIK
PARTWAY THROUGH, I REALIZED THE ARMS DIDN'T NEED TO BE NEEDLES.
BUT THEY STILL MOVED PROPERLY. CREATE GOLEM IS A VERSATILE SPELL.
WHAT IS THIS FOR?
YOU CAN SEE THE CLOCK IN THE MENU.
MMPH...
I FORGOT THERE WAS A CLOCK IN THE MENU.

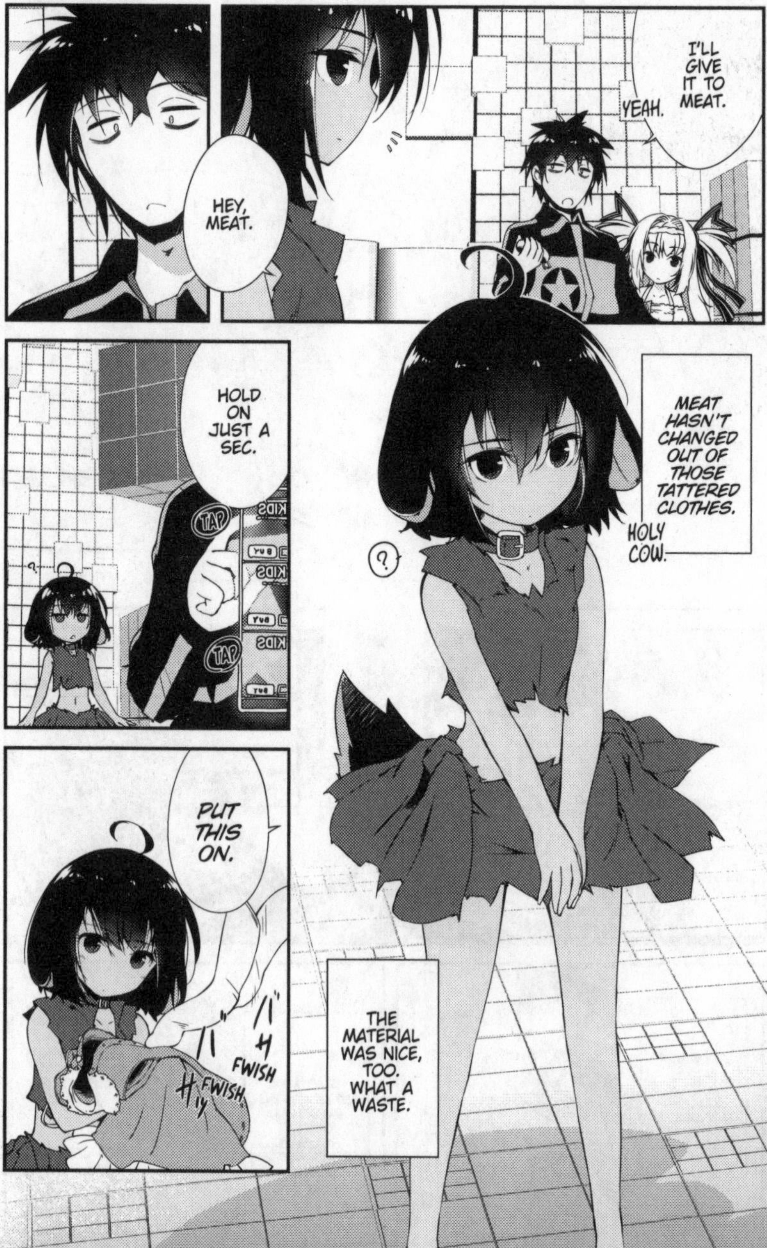
I'LL GIVE IT TO MEAT.
YEAH.
HEY, MEAT.
MEAT HASN'T CHANGED OUT OF THOSE TATTERED CLOTHES.
HOLY COW.
?
THE MATERIAL WAS NICE, TOO. WHAT A WASTE.
HOLD ON JUST A SEC.
TAP
TAP
PUT THIS ON.
FWISH
FWISH

Chapter 4 First Trip in Another World

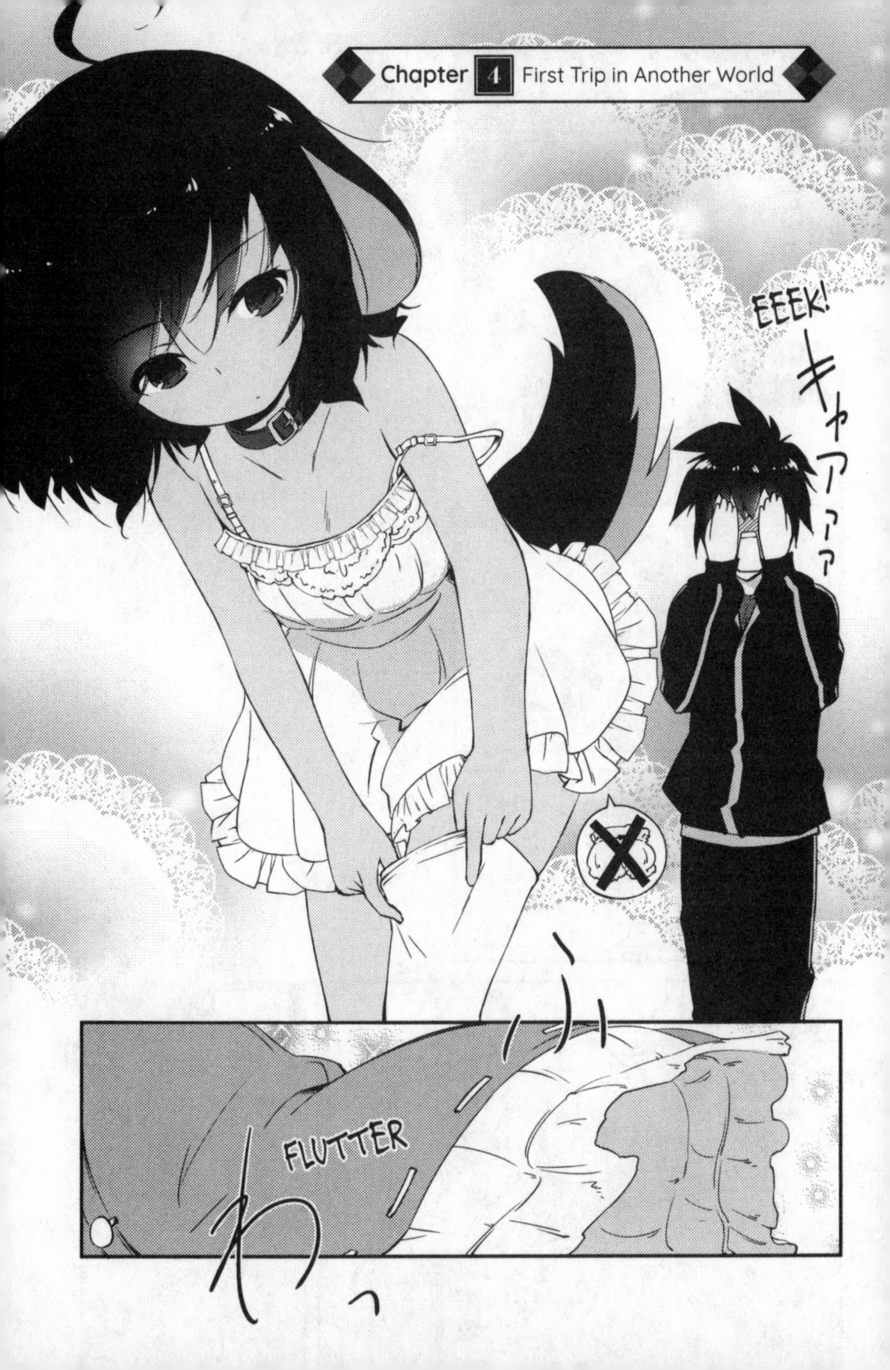
EEEK!
キャアァァァ
FLUTTER
わっ

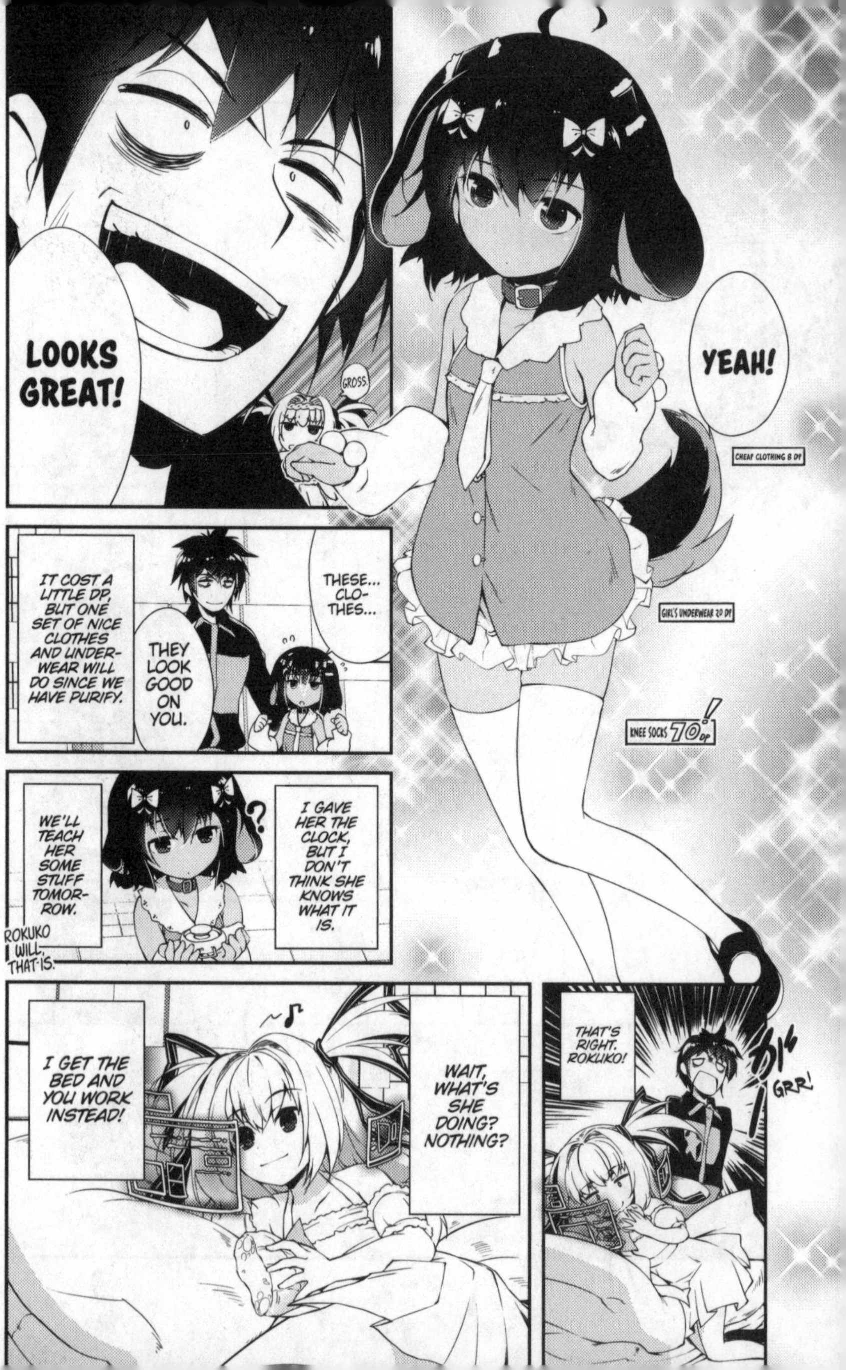
YEAH!
CHEAP CLOTHING 8 DP
GIRL'S UNDERWEAR 20 DP
KNEE SOCKS 70 DP!
LOOKS GREAT!
GROSS.
THESE... CLOTHES...
THEY LOOK GOOD ON YOU.
IT COST A LITTLE DP, BUT ONE SET OF NICE CLOTHES AND UNDERWEAR WILL DO SINCE WE HAVE PURIFY.
I GAVE HER THE CLOCK, BUT I DON'T THINK SHE KNOWS WHAT IT IS.
WE'LL TEACH HER SOME STUFF TOMORROW.
ROKUKO WILL, THAT IS.
THAT'S RIGHT. ROKUKO!
GRR!
WAIT, WHAT'S SHE DOING? NOTHING?
I GET THE BED AND YOU WORK INSTEAD!

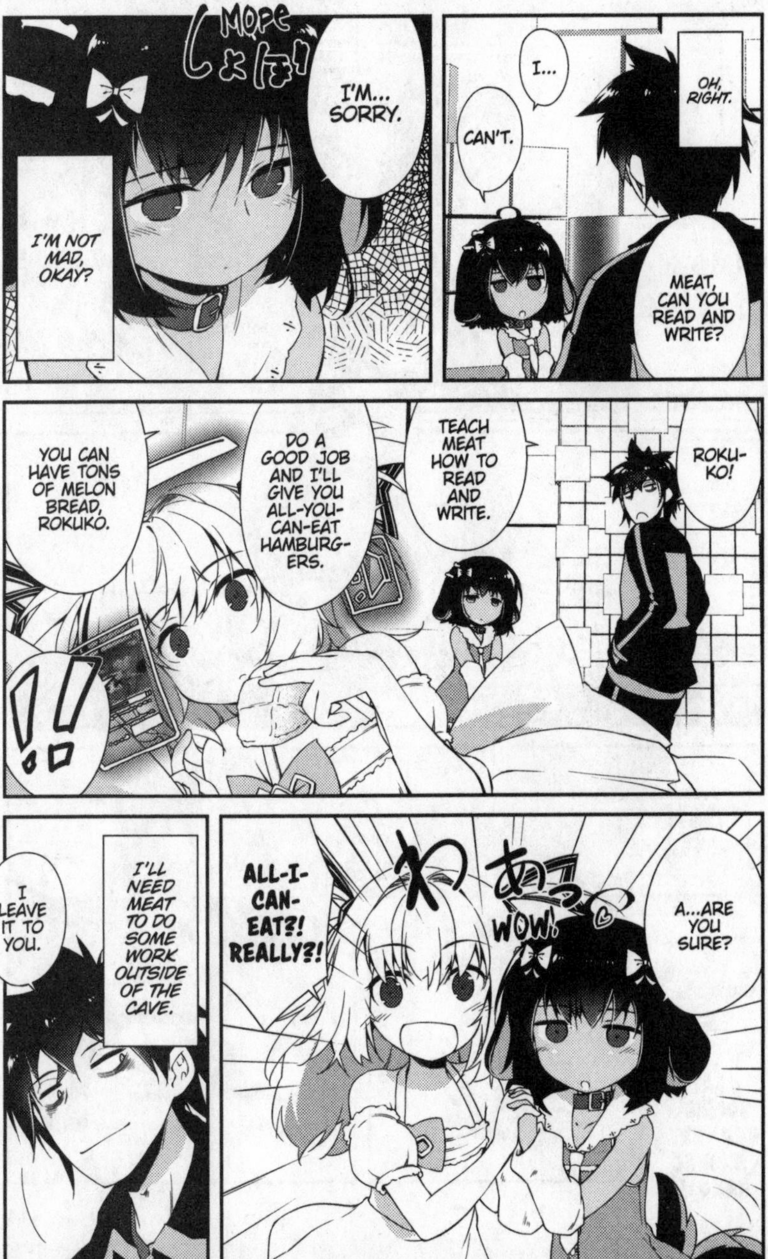
OH, RIGHT.
MEAT, CAN YOU READ AND WRITE?
I...
CAN'T.
MOPE
しょぼ
I'M... SORRY.
I'M NOT MAD, OKAY?
ROKU-KO!
TEACH MEAT HOW TO READ AND WRITE.
DO A GOOD JOB AND I'LL GIVE YOU ALL-YOU-CAN-EAT HAMBURG-ERS.
YOU CAN HAVE TONS OF MELON BREAD, ROKUKO.
!!
A...ARE YOU SURE?
わあっ
WOW!
ALL-I-CAN-EAT?! REALLY?!
I'LL NEED MEAT TO DO SOME WORK OUTSIDE OF THE CAVE.
I LEAVE IT TO YOU.

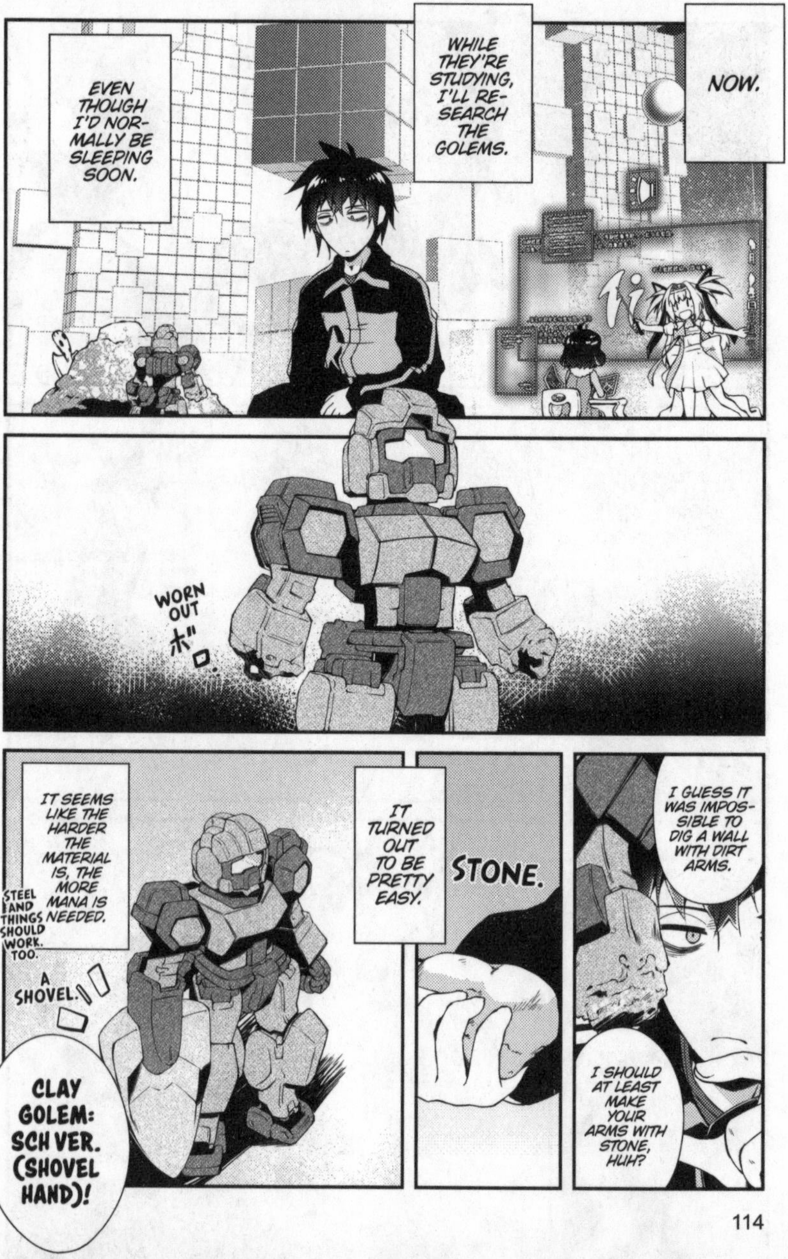
NOW.
WHILE THEY'RE STUDYING, I'LL RE-SEARCH THE GOLEMS.
EVEN THOUGH I'D NOR-MALLY BE SLEEPING SOON.
WORN OUT
ボロ
I GUESS IT WAS IMPOS-SIBLE TO DIG A WALL WITH DIRT ARMS.
I SHOULD AT LEAST MAKE YOUR ARMS WITH STONE, HUH?
STONE.
IT TURNED OUT TO BE PRETTY EASY.
IT SEEMS LIKE THE HARDER THE MATERIAL IS, THE MORE MANA IS NEEDED.
STEEL AND THINGS SHOULD WORK TOO.
A SHOVEL.
CLAY GOLEM: SCH VER. (SHOVEL HAND)!

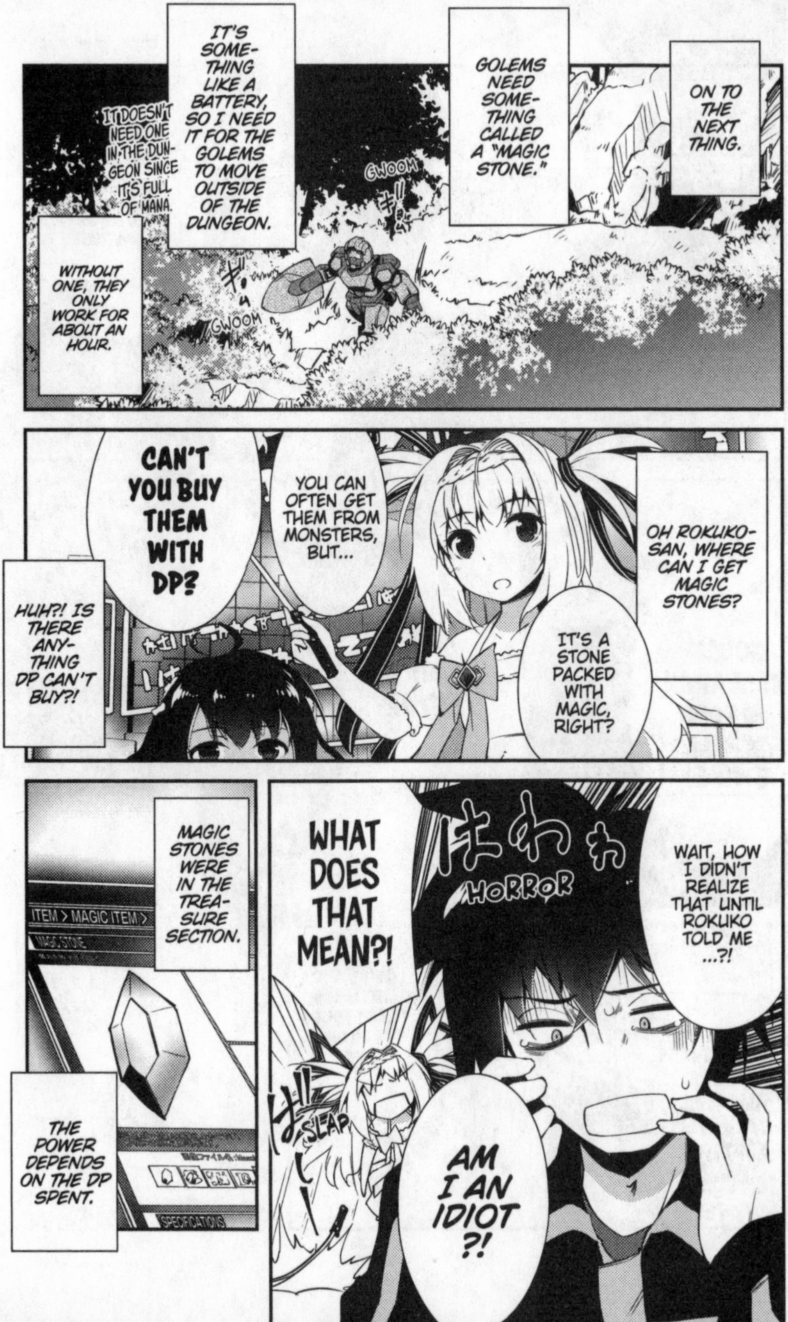
ON TO THE NEXT THING.
GOLEMS NEED SOMETHING CALLED A "MAGIC STONE."
IT'S SOMETHING LIKE A BATTERY, SO I NEED IT FOR THE GOLEMS TO MOVE OUTSIDE OF THE DUNGEON.
IT DOESN'T NEED ONE IN THE DUNGEON SINCE IT'S FULL OF MANA.
GWOOM
GWOOM
WITHOUT ONE, THEY ONLY WORK FOR ABOUT AN HOUR.
OH ROKUKO-SAN, WHERE CAN I GET MAGIC STONES?
IT'S A STONE PACKED WITH MAGIC, RIGHT?
YOU CAN OFTEN GET THEM FROM MONSTERS, BUT...
CAN'T YOU BUY THEM WITH DP?
HUH?! IS THERE ANYTHING DP CAN'T BUY?!
WAIT, HOW I DIDN'T REALIZE THAT UNTIL ROKUKO TOLD ME ...?!
HORROR
WHAT DOES THAT MEAN?!
SLAP
AM I AN IDIOT?!
MAGIC STONES WERE IN THE TREASURE SECTION.
ITEM > MAGIC ITEM >
MAGIC STONE
SPECIFICATIONS
THE POWER DEPENDS ON THE DP SPENT.

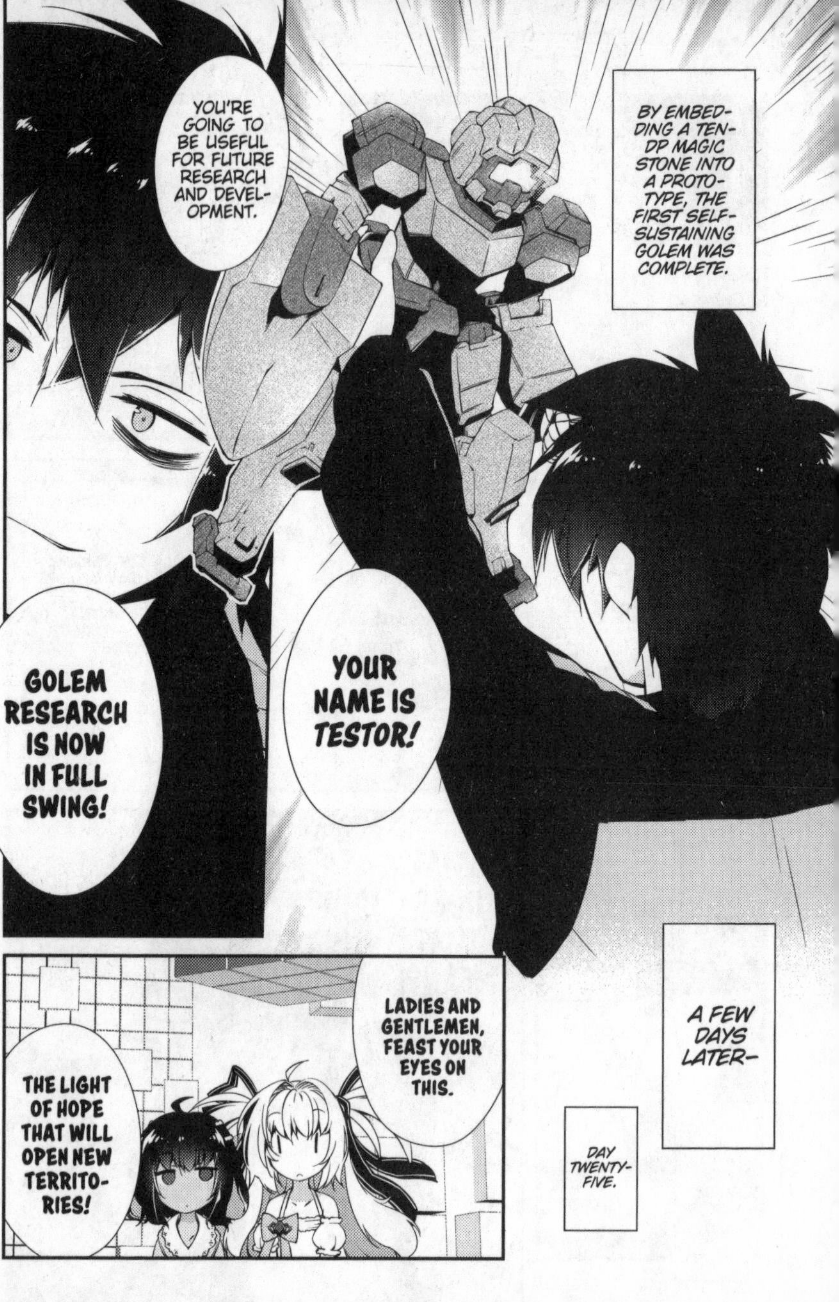
BY EMBEDDING A TEN-DP MAGIC STONE INTO A PROTOTYPE, THE FIRST SELF-SUSTAINING GOLEM WAS COMPLETE.
YOU'RE GOING TO BE USEFUL FOR FUTURE RESEARCH AND DEVELOPMENT.
YOUR NAME IS TESTOR!
GOLEM RESEARCH IS NOW IN FULL SWING!
A FEW DAYS LATER—
DAY TWENTY-FIVE.
LADIES AND GENTLEMEN, FEAST YOUR EYES ON THIS.
THE LIGHT OF HOPE THAT WILL OPEN NEW TERRITORIES!

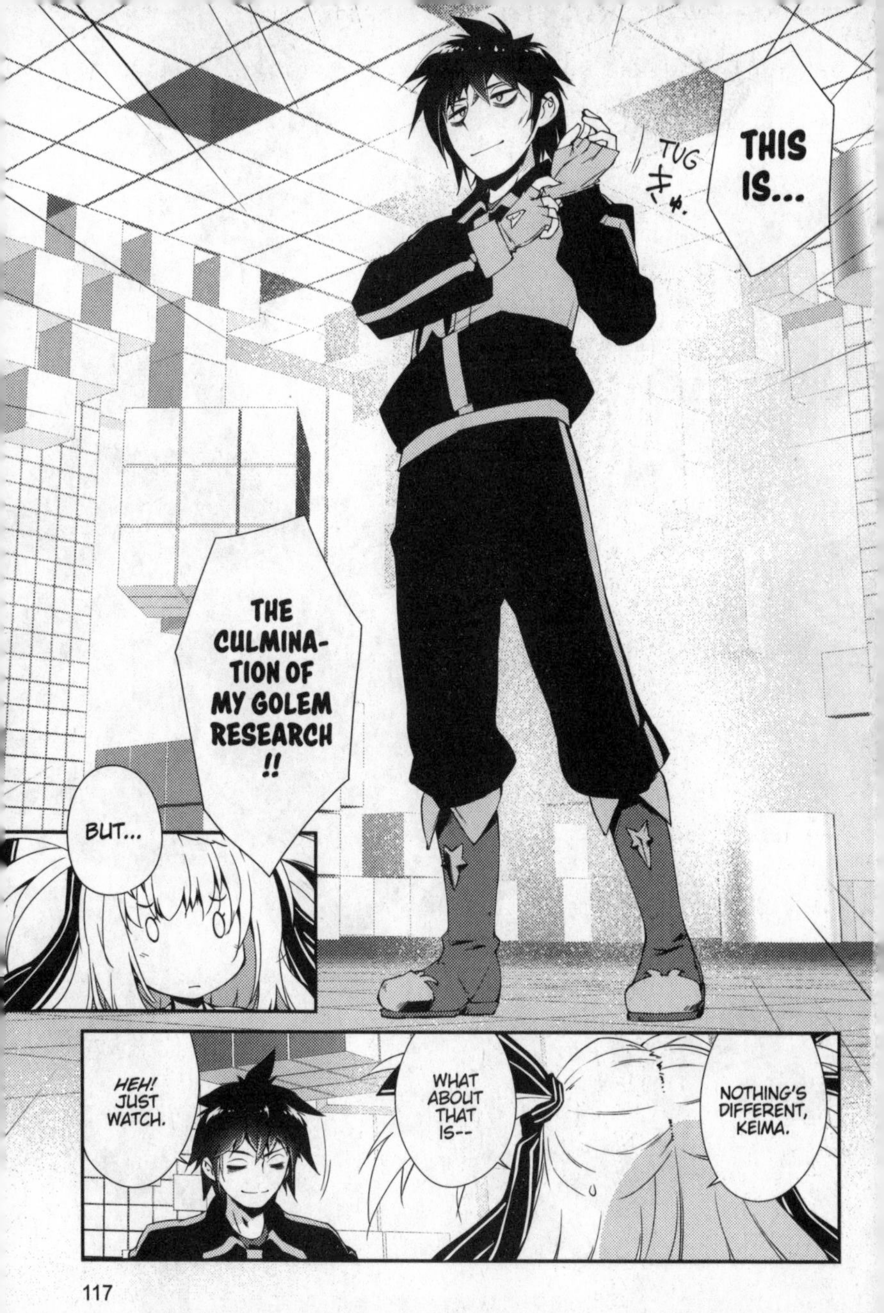
THIS IS...
TUG
THE CULMINATION OF MY GOLEM RESEARCH!!
BUT...
NOTHING'S DIFFERENT, KEIMA.
WHAT ABOUT THAT IS--
HEH! JUST WATCH.

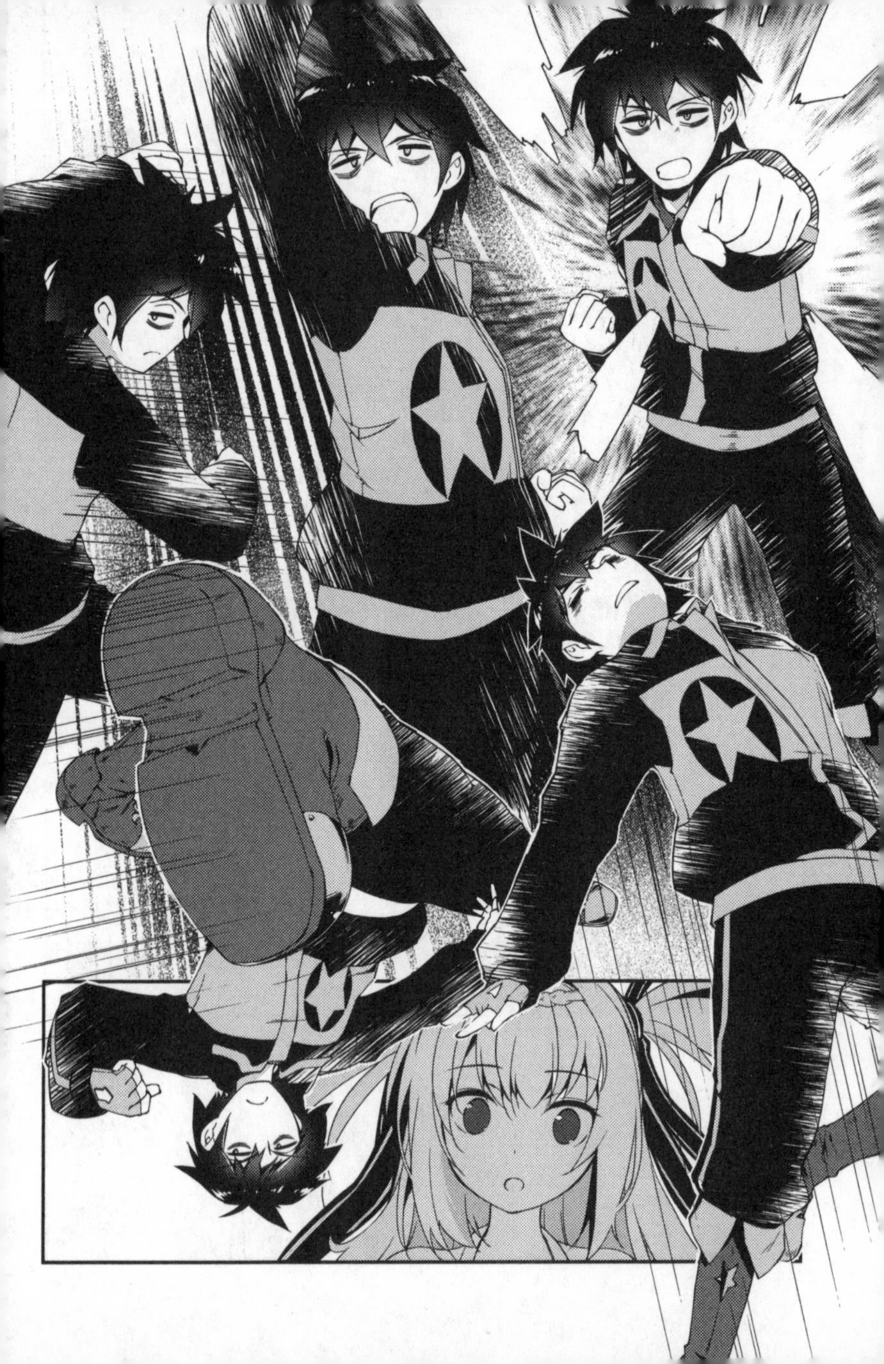

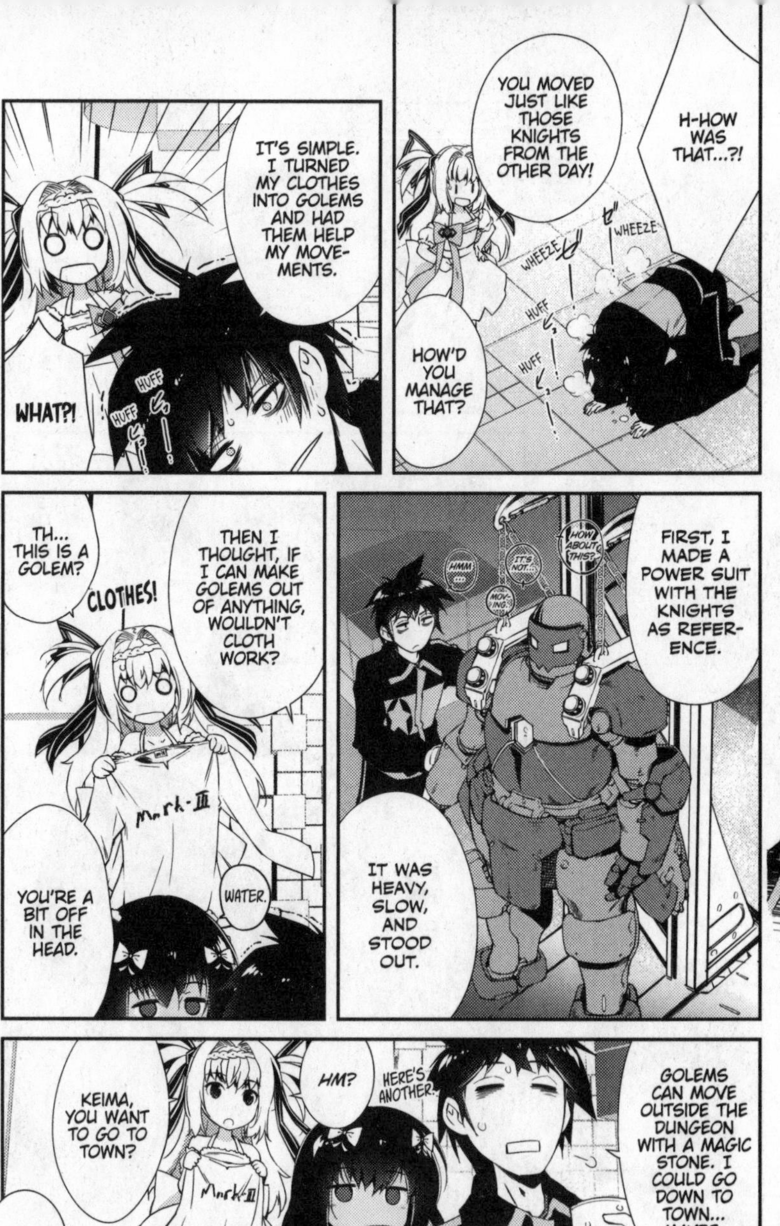
H-HOW WAS THAT...?!
YOU MOVED JUST LIKE THOSE KNIGHTS FROM THE OTHER DAY!
WHEEZE
WHEEZE
HUFF
HUFF
HOW'D YOU MANAGE THAT?
IT'S SIMPLE. I TURNED MY CLOTHES INTO GOLEMS AND HAD THEM HELP MY MOVEMENTS.
WHAT?!
HUFF
HUFF
FIRST, I MADE A POWER SUIT WITH THE KNIGHTS AS REFERENCE.
HOW ABOUT THIS?
IT'S NOT...
MOVING.
HMM...
IT WAS HEAVY, SLOW, AND STOOD OUT.
THEN I THOUGHT, IF I CAN MAKE GOLEMS OUT OF ANYTHING, WOULDN'T CLOTH WORK?
TH... THIS IS A GOLEM?
CLOTHES!
Mark-III
WATER.
YOU'RE A BIT OFF IN THE HEAD.
GOLEMS CAN MOVE OUTSIDE THE DUNGEON WITH A MAGIC STONE. I COULD GO DOWN TO TOWN... MAYBE.
HERE'S ANOTHER.
HM?
KEIMA, YOU WANT TO GO TO TOWN?
Mark-III
YEAH.

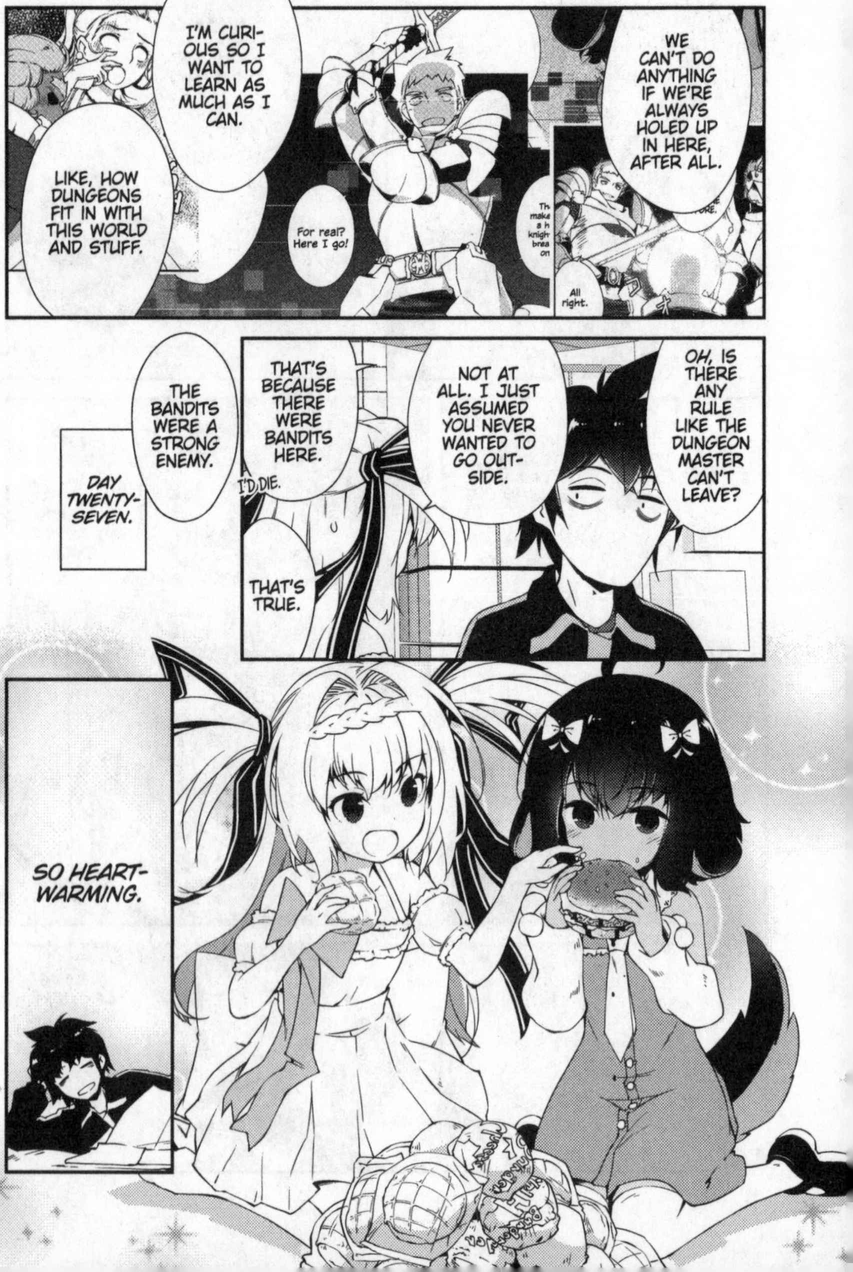
WE CAN'T DO ANYTHING IF WE'RE ALWAYS HOLED UP IN HERE, AFTER ALL.
All right.
I'M CURIOUS SO I WANT TO LEARN AS MUCH AS I CAN.
For real? Here I go!
LIKE, HOW DUNGEONS FIT IN WITH THIS WORLD AND STUFF.
OH, IS THERE ANY RULE LIKE THE DUNGEON MASTER CAN'T LEAVE?
NOT AT ALL. I JUST ASSUMED YOU NEVER WANTED TO GO OUTSIDE.
I'D DIE.
THAT'S BECAUSE THERE WERE BANDITS HERE.
THAT'S TRUE.
THE BANDITS WERE A STRONG ENEMY.
DAY TWENTY-SEVEN.
SO HEART-WARMING.

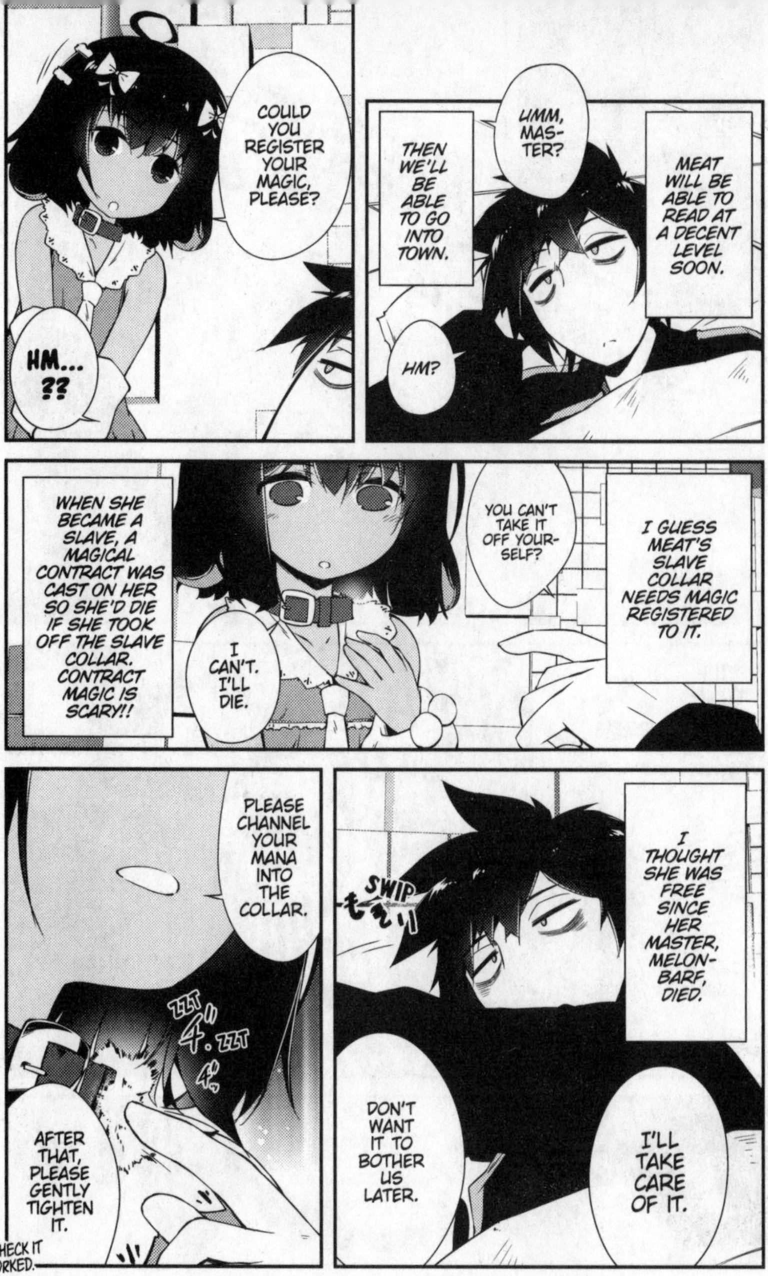
MEAT WILL BE ABLE TO READ AT A DECENT LEVEL SOON.
UMM, MAS-TER?
THEN WE'LL BE ABLE TO GO INTO TOWN.
HM?
COULD YOU REGISTER YOUR MAGIC, PLEASE?
HM... ??
I GUESS MEAT'S SLAVE COLLAR NEEDS MAGIC REGISTERED TO IT.
YOU CAN'T TAKE IT OFF YOUR-SELF?
I CAN'T. I'LL DIE.
WHEN SHE BECAME A SLAVE, A MAGICAL CONTRACT WAS CAST ON HER SO SHE'D DIE IF SHE TOOK OFF THE SLAVE COLLAR. CONTRACT MAGIC IS SCARY!!
I THOUGHT SHE WAS FREE SINCE HER MASTER, MELON-BARF, DIED.
SWIP
I'LL TAKE CARE OF IT.
DON'T WANT IT TO BOTHER US LATER.
PLEASE CHANNEL YOUR MANA INTO THE COLLAR.
ZZT
ZZT
AFTER THAT, PLEASE GENTLY TIGHTEN IT.
TO CHECK IT WORKED.

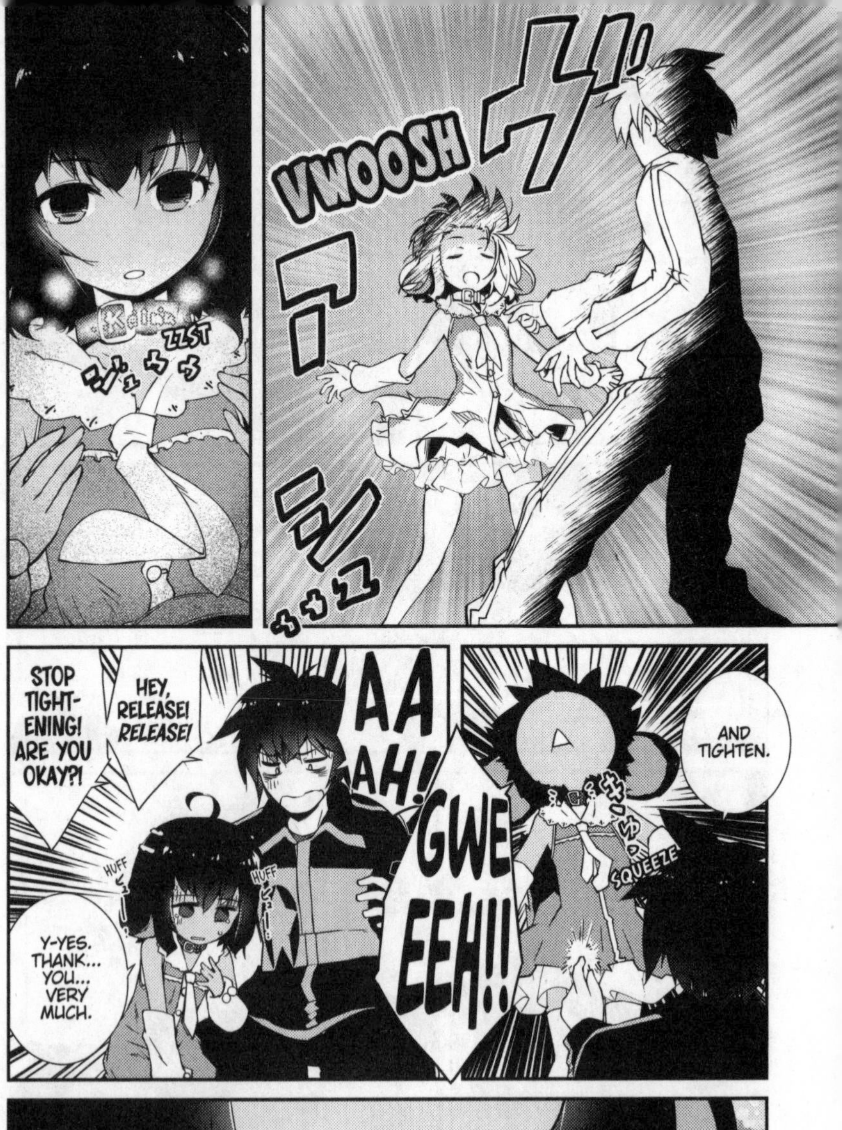
VWOOSH
ZZST
AND TIGHTEN.
SQUEEZE
AAAH!
HEY, RELEASE! RELEASE!
STOP TIGHTENING! ARE YOU OKAY?!
GWEEEH!!
HUFF
HUFF
Y-YES. THANK... YOU... VERY MUCH.
TEE HEE...

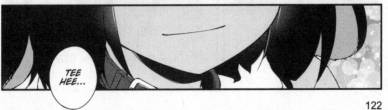

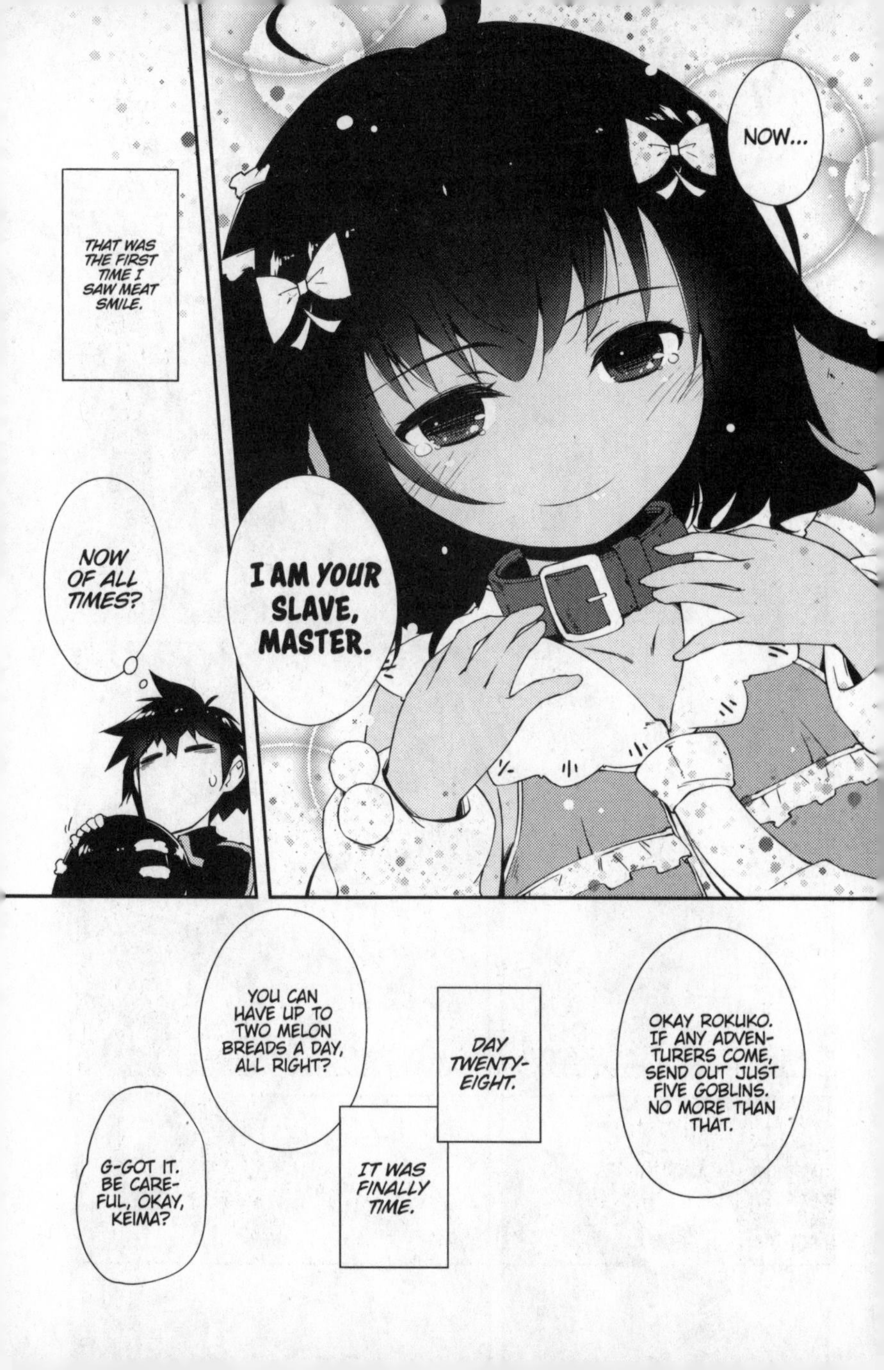
NOW...
I AM YOUR SLAVE, MASTER.
THAT WAS THE FIRST TIME I SAW MEAT SMILE.
NOW OF ALL TIMES?
OKAY ROKUKO. IF ANY ADVENTURERS COME, SEND OUT JUST FIVE GOBLINS. NO MORE THAN THAT.
DAY TWENTY-EIGHT.
YOU CAN HAVE UP TO TWO MELON BREADS A DAY, ALL RIGHT?
IT WAS FINALLY TIME.
G-GOT IT. BE CAREFUL, OKAY, KEIMA?

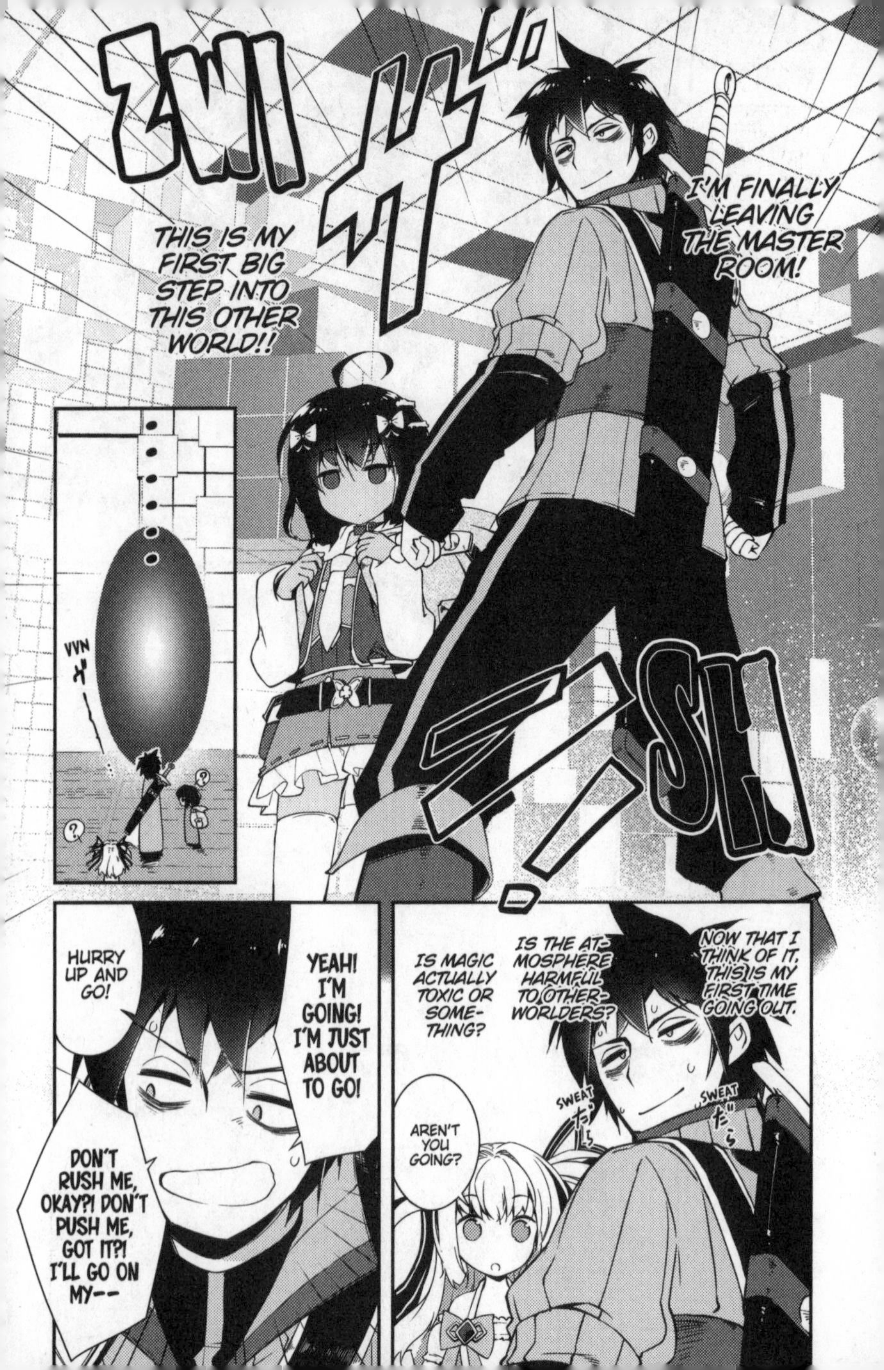

I'M FINALLY LEAVING THE MASTER ROOM!
THIS IS MY FIRST BIG STEP INTO THIS OTHER WORLD!!
ZWM
SH
VVN
NOW THAT I THINK OF IT, THIS IS MY FIRST TIME GOING OUT.
IS THE ATMOSPHERE HARMFUL TO OTHER-WORLDERS?
IS MAGIC ACTUALLY TOXIC OR SOME-THING?
SWEAT
SWEAT
AREN'T YOU GOING?
YEAH! I'M GOING! I'M JUST ABOUT TO GO!
HURRY UP AND GO!
DON'T RUSH ME, OKAY?! DON'T PUSH ME, GOT IT?! I'LL GO ON MY--

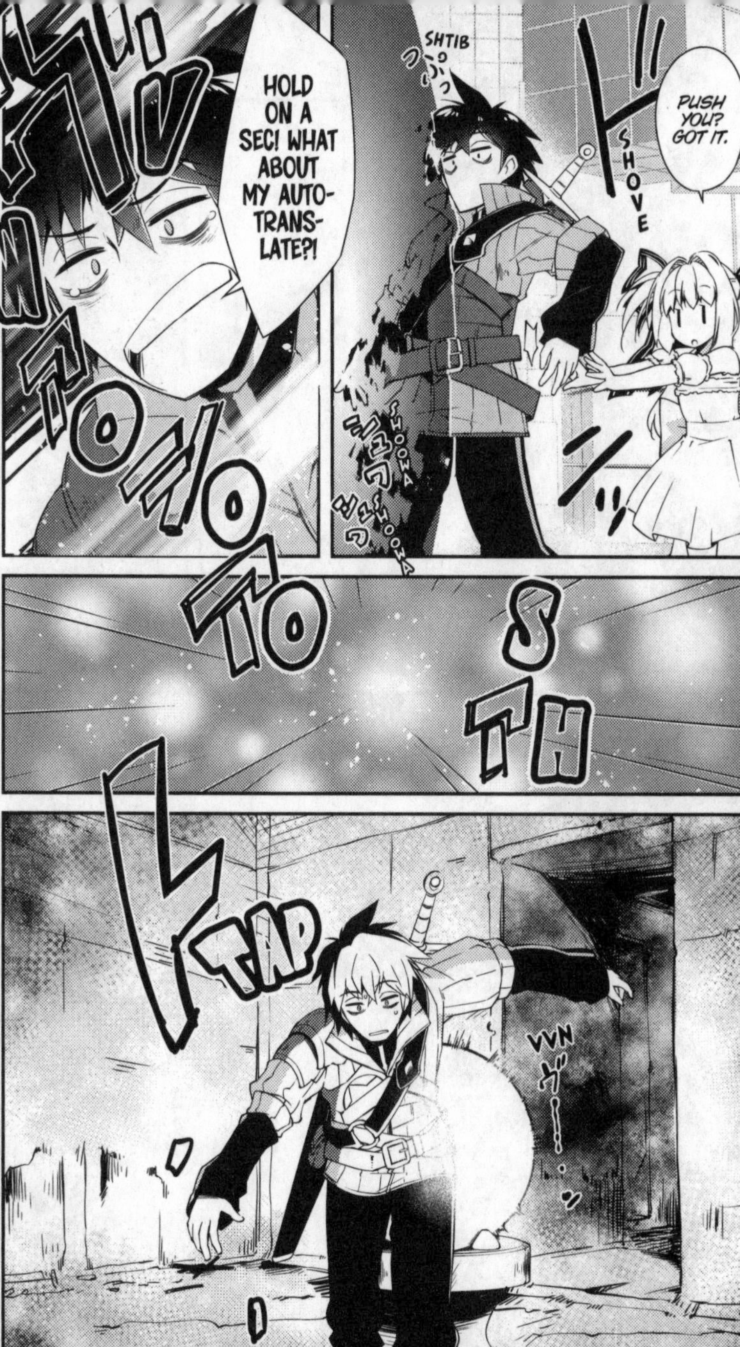
PUSH YOU? GOT IT.
SHOVE
SHTIB
SHOOWA
SHOOWA
HOLD ON A SEC! WHAT ABOUT MY AUTO-TRANSLATE?!
TAP
VVN

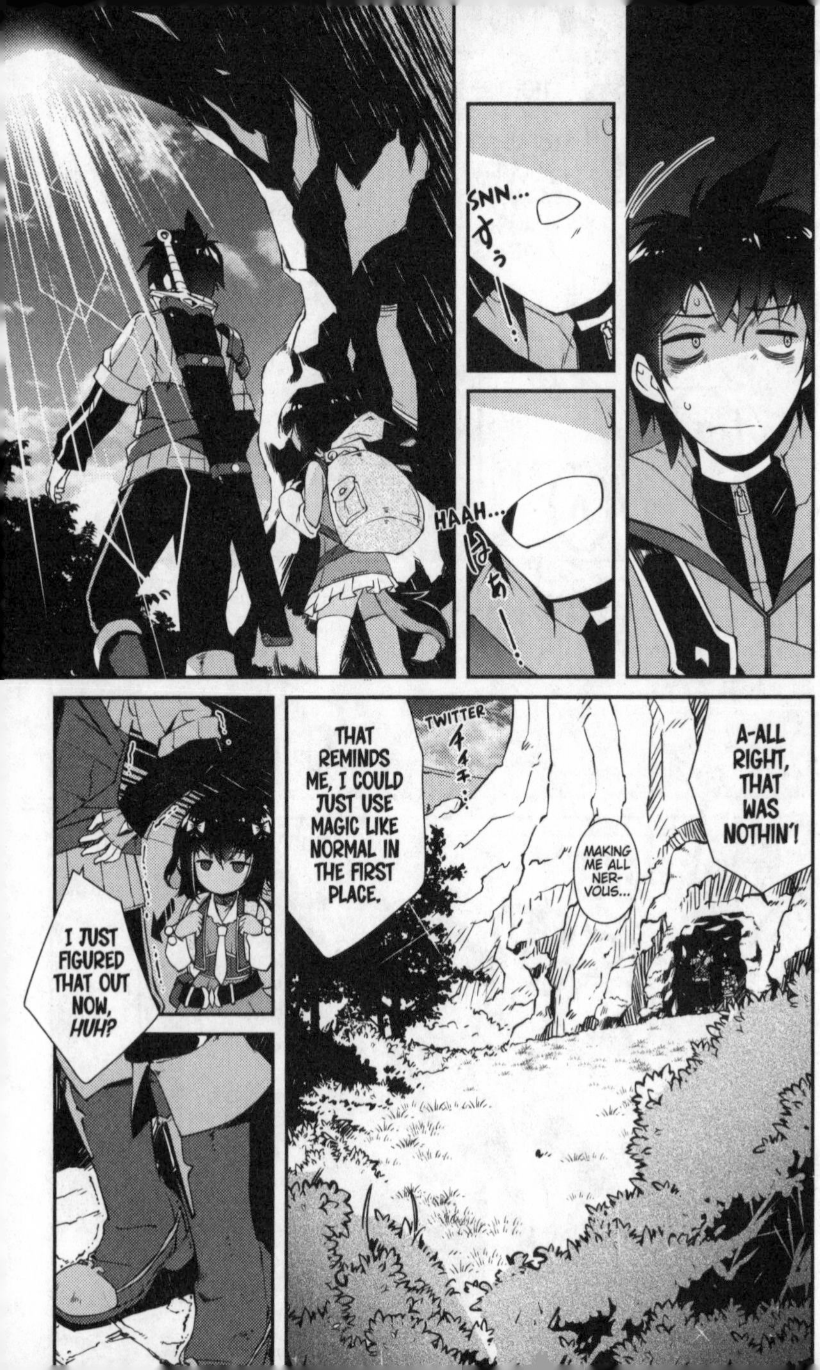
SNN...
すぅ
HAAH...
はぁ
A-ALL RIGHT, THAT WAS NOTHIN'!
MAKING ME ALL NER-VOUS...
TWITTER
THAT REMINDS ME, I COULD JUST USE MAGIC LIKE NORMAL IN THE FIRST PLACE.
I JUST FIGURED THAT OUT NOW, *HUH?*

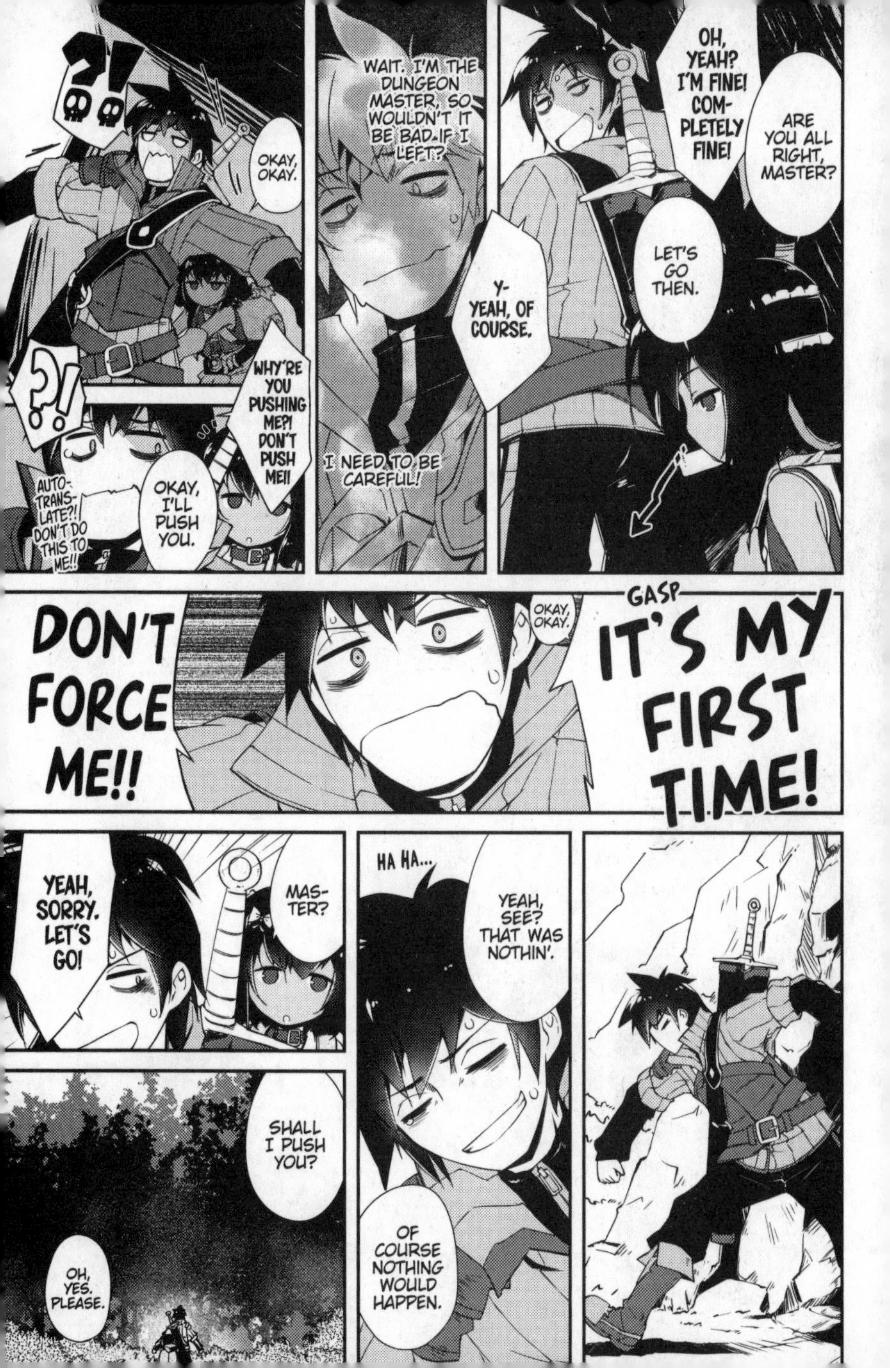
ARE YOU ALL RIGHT, MASTER?
OH, YEAH? I'M FINE! COM-PLETELY FINE!
LET'S GO THEN.
WAIT. I'M THE DUNGEON MASTER, SO WOULDN'T IT BE BAD IF I LEFT?
Y-YEAH, OF COURSE.
I NEED TO BE CAREFUL!
?!
OKAY, OKAY.
WHY'RE YOU PUSHING ME?! DON'T PUSH ME!!
OKAY, I'LL PUSH YOU.
AUTO-TRANS-LATE?! DON'T DO THIS TO ME!!
?!
GASP
IT'S MY FIRST TIME!
OKAY, OKAY.
DON'T FORCE ME!!
HA HA...
YEAH, SEE? THAT WAS NOTHIN'.
OF COURSE NOTHING WOULD HAPPEN.
MAS-TER?
YEAH, SORRY. LET'S GO!
SHALL I PUSH YOU?
OH, YES. PLEASE.

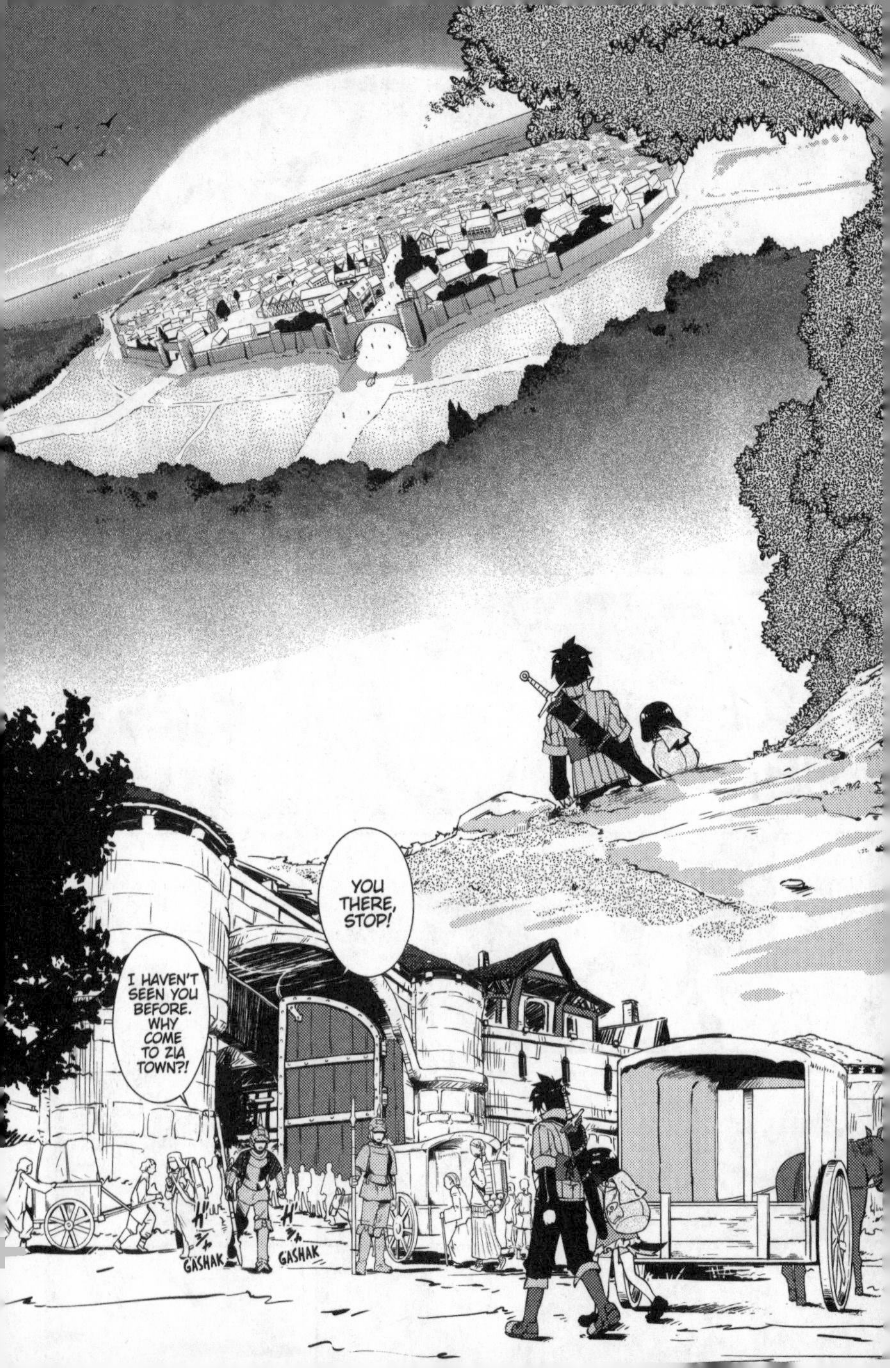
YOU THERE, STOP!
I HAVEN'T SEEN YOU BEFORE. WHY COME TO ZIA TOWN?!
GASHAK
GASHAK

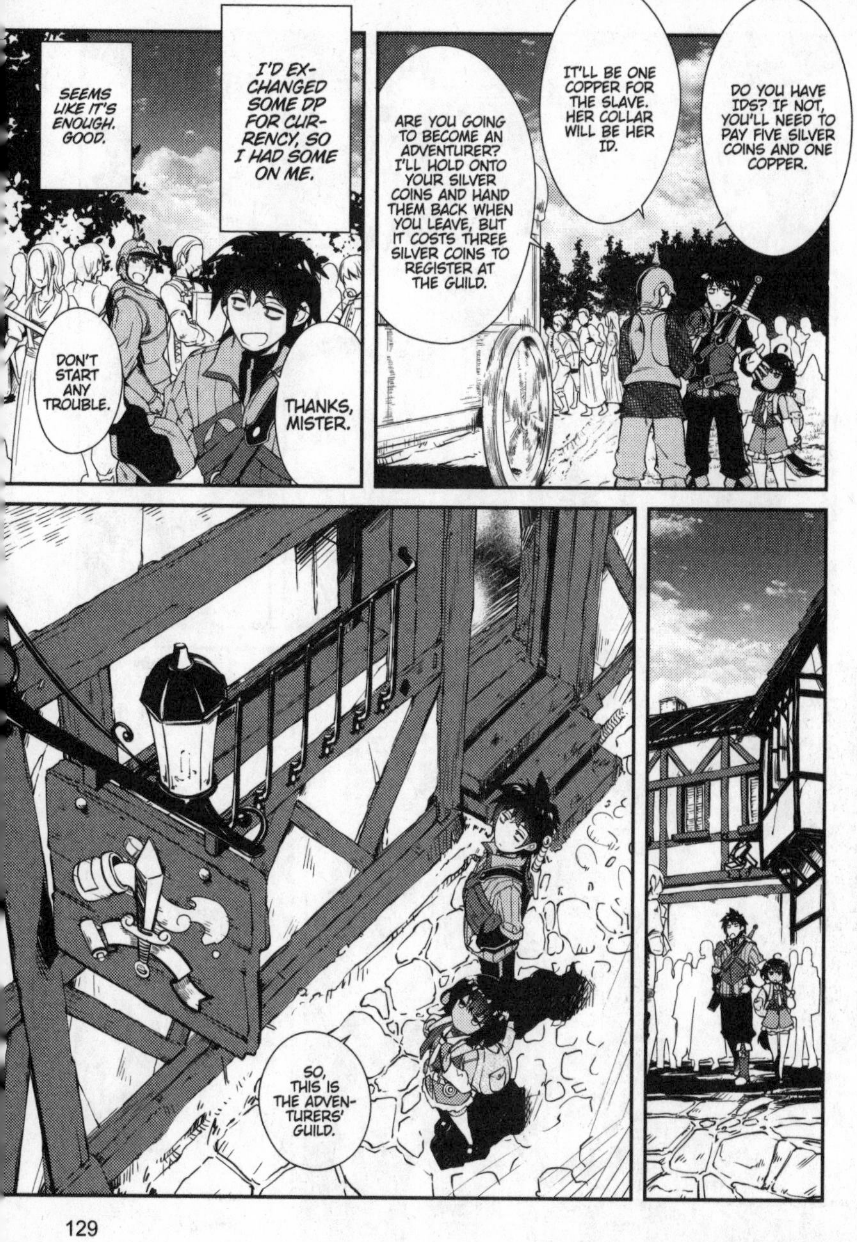
DO YOU HAVE IDS? IF NOT, YOU'LL NEED TO PAY FIVE SILVER COINS AND ONE COPPER.
IT'LL BE ONE COPPER FOR THE SLAVE. HER COLLAR WILL BE HER ID.
ARE YOU GOING TO BECOME AN ADVENTURER? I'LL HOLD ONTO YOUR SILVER COINS AND HAND THEM BACK WHEN YOU LEAVE, BUT IT COSTS THREE SILVER COINS TO REGISTER AT THE GUILD.
I'D EXCHANGED SOME DP FOR CURRENCY, SO I HAD SOME ON ME.
SEEMS LIKE IT'S ENOUGH. GOOD.
THANKS, MISTER.
DON'T START ANY TROUBLE.
SO, THIS IS THE ADVENTURERS' GUILD.

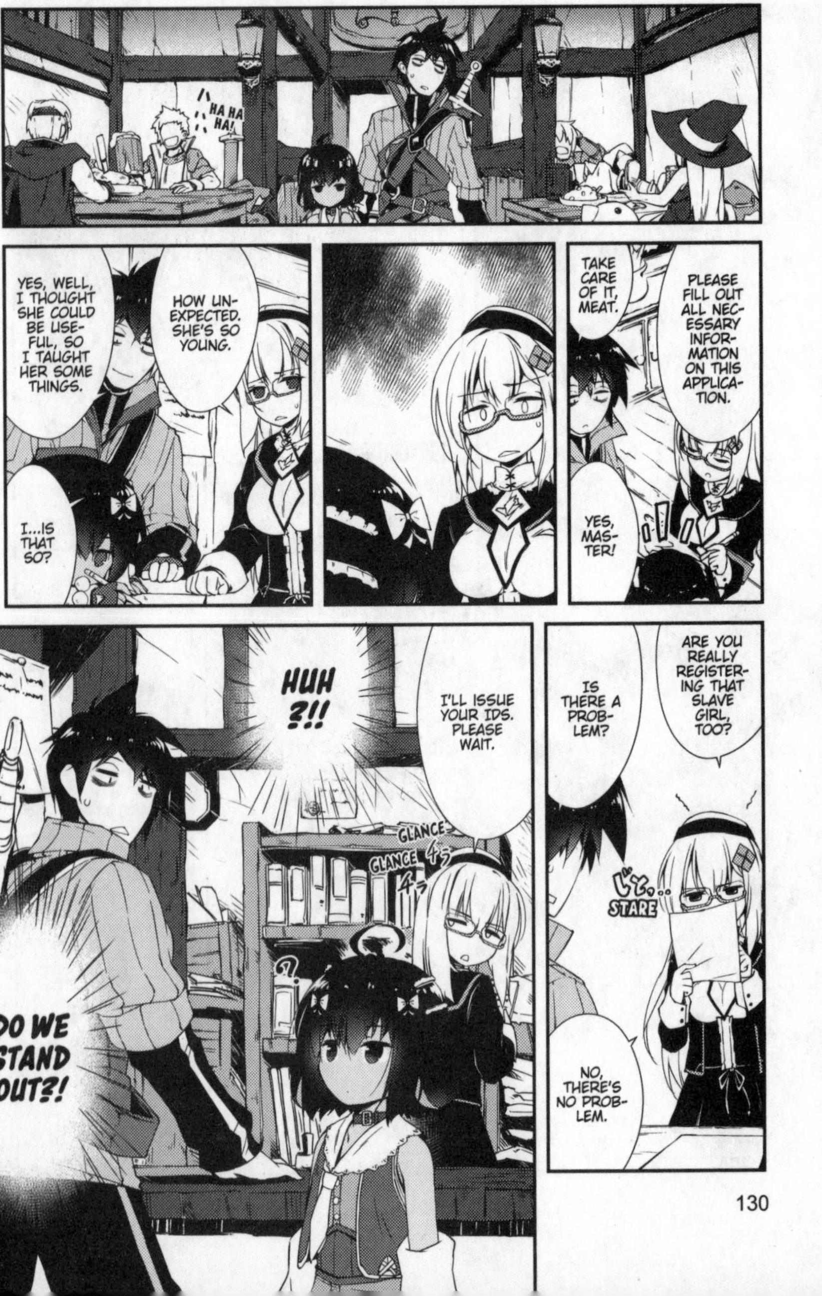
HA HA HA!
PLEASE FILL OUT ALL NECESSARY INFORMATION ON THIS APPLICATION.
TAKE CARE OF IT, MEAT.
YES, MASTER!
HOW UNEXPECTED. SHE'S SO YOUNG.
YES, WELL, I THOUGHT SHE COULD BE USEFUL, SO I TAUGHT HER SOME THINGS.
I...IS THAT SO?
ARE YOU REALLY REGISTERING THAT SLAVE GIRL, TOO?
IS THERE A PROBLEM?
STARE
NO, THERE'S NO PROBLEM.
I'LL ISSUE YOUR IDS. PLEASE WAIT.
HUH?!!
GLANCE
GLANCE
DO WE STAND OUT?!

LAZY DUNGEON MASTER

LAZY
DUNGEON
MASTER

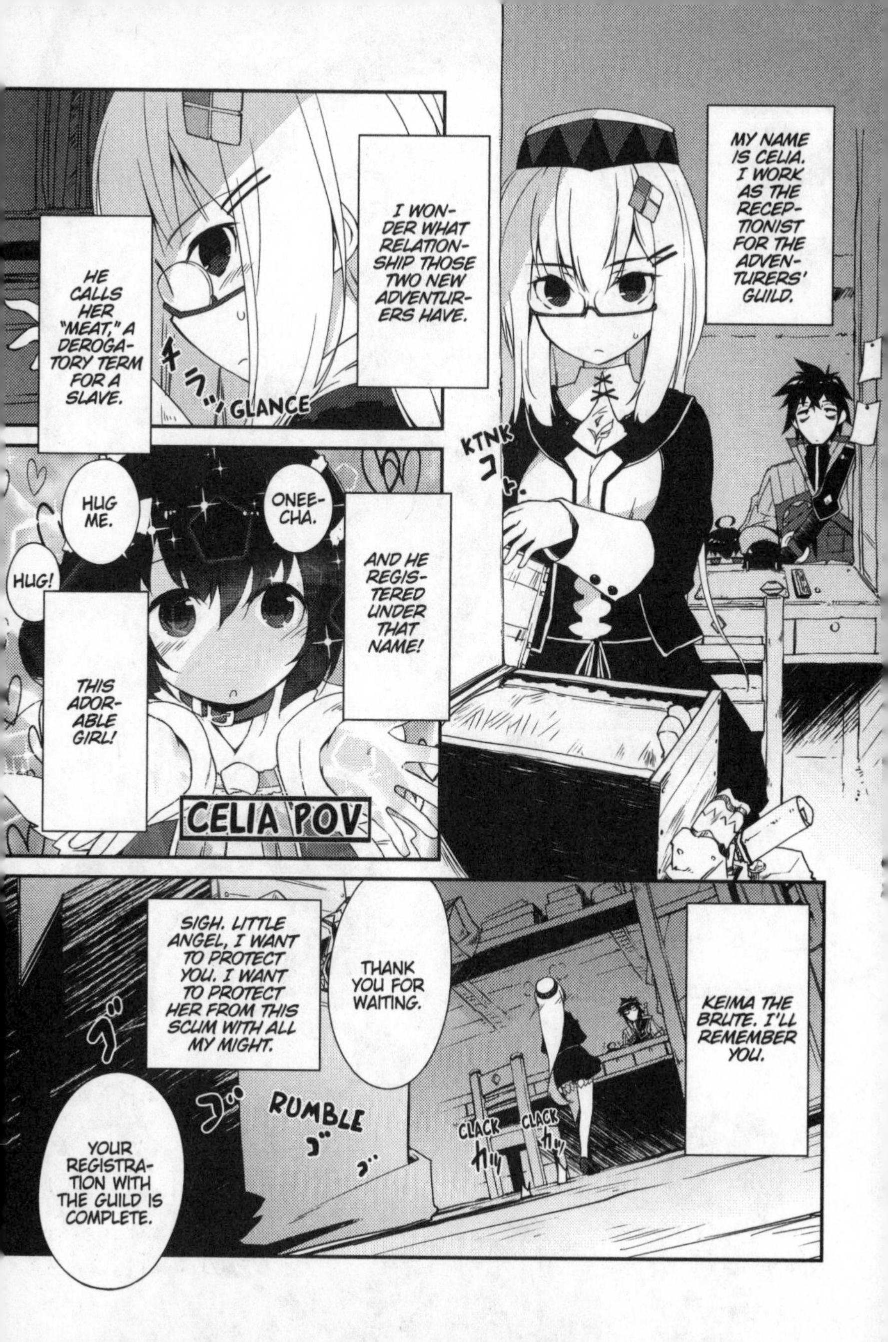
MY NAME IS CELIA. I WORK AS THE RECEPTIONIST FOR THE ADVENTURERS' GUILD.
KTNK
I WONDER WHAT RELATIONSHIP THOSE TWO NEW ADVENTURERS HAVE.
HE CALLS HER "MEAT," A DEROGATORY TERM FOR A SLAVE.
GLANCE
AND HE REGISTERED UNDER THAT NAME!
ONEE-CHA.
HUG ME.
HUG!
THIS ADORABLE GIRL!
CELIA POV
KEIMA THE BRUTE. I'LL REMEMBER YOU.
THANK YOU FOR WAITING.
SIGH. LITTLE ANGEL, I WANT TO PROTECT YOU. I WANT TO PROTECT HER FROM THIS SCUM WITH ALL MY MIGHT.
CLACK
CLACK
RUMBLE
YOUR REGISTRATION WITH THE GUILD IS COMPLETE.

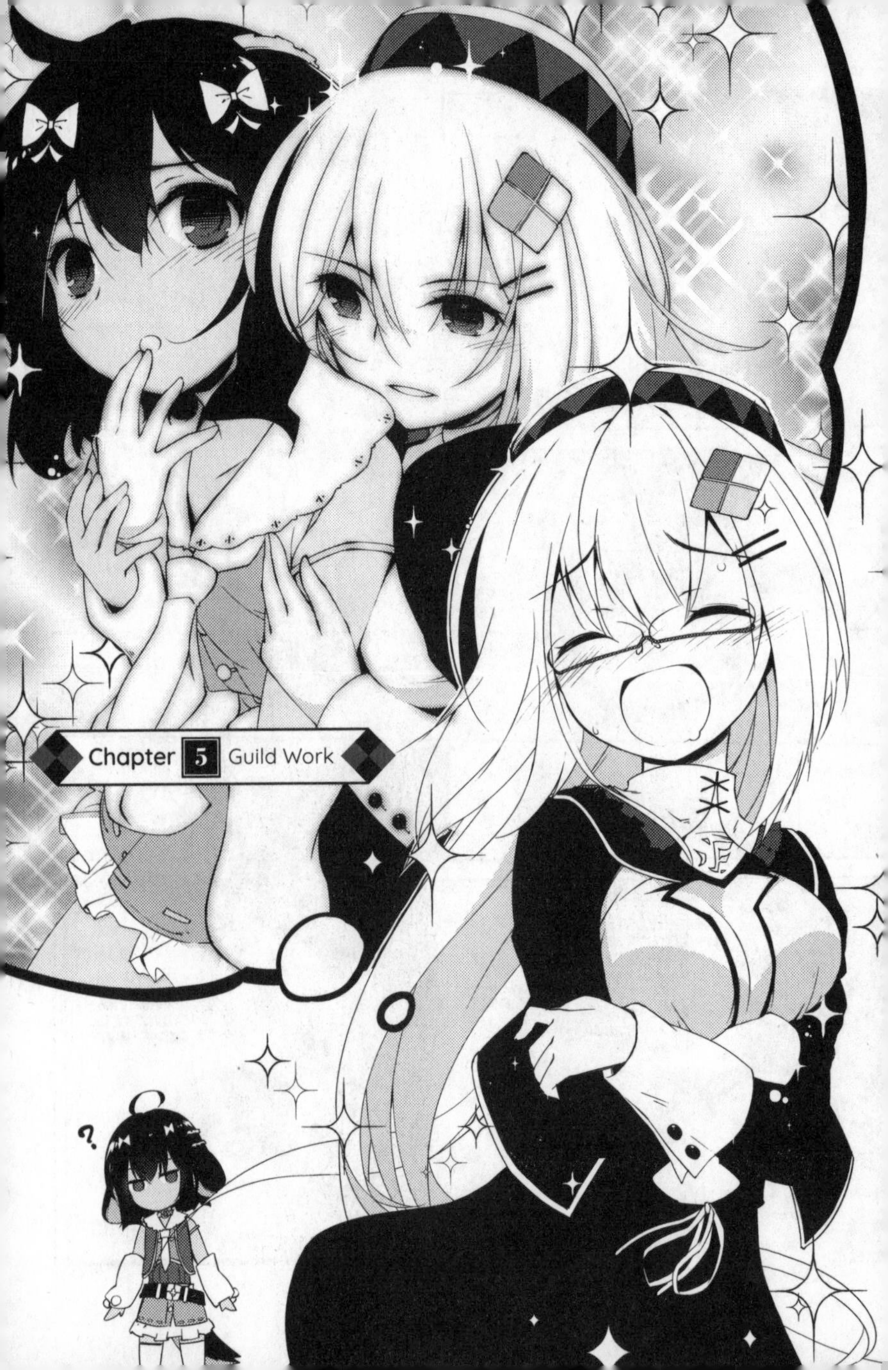
Chapter 5 Guild Work
?

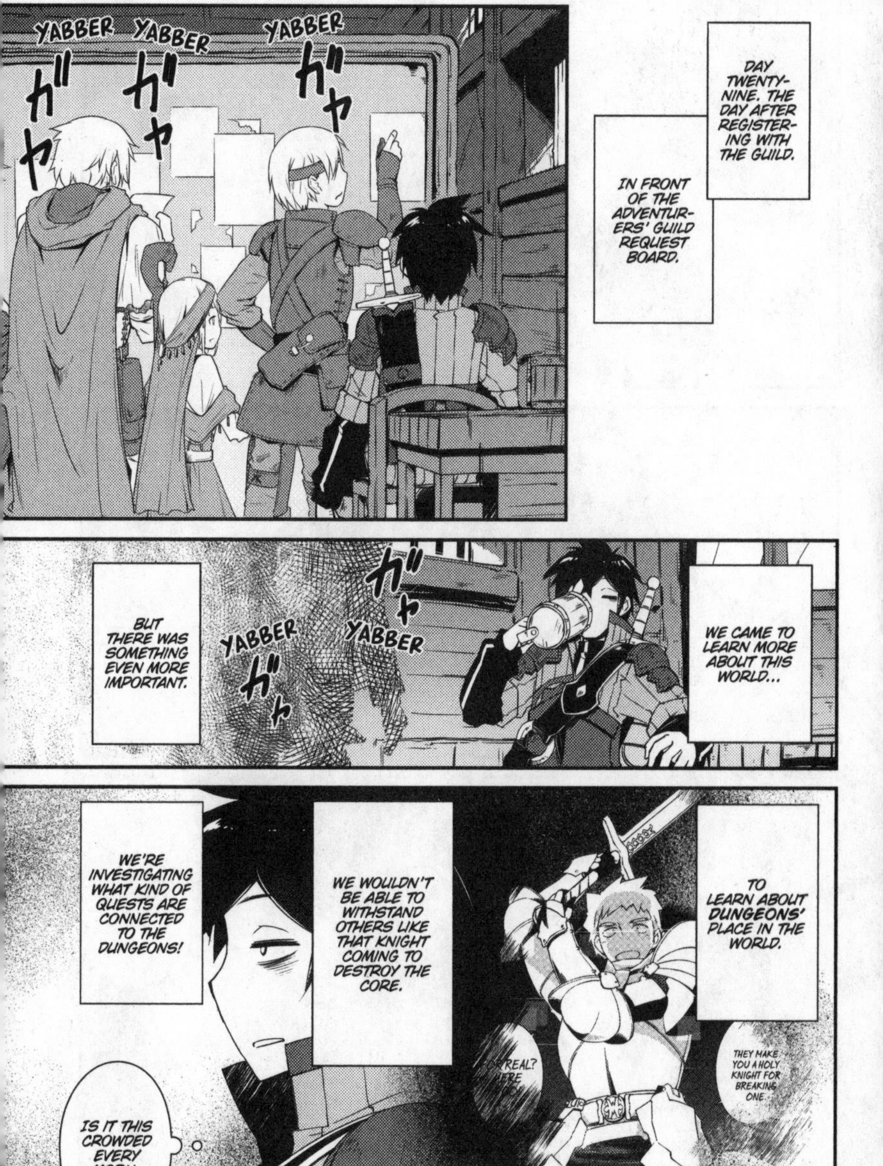
DAY TWENTY-NINE. THE DAY AFTER REGISTERING WITH THE GUILD.
IN FRONT OF THE ADVENTURERS' GUILD REQUEST BOARD.
YABBER
ガヤ
YABBER
ガヤ
YABBER
ガヤ
WE CAME TO LEARN MORE ABOUT THIS WORLD...
YABBER
ガヤ
YABBER
ガヤ
BUT THERE WAS SOMETHING EVEN MORE IMPORTANT.
TO LEARN ABOUT DUNGEONS' PLACE IN THE WORLD.
THEY MAKE YOU A HOLY KNIGHT FOR BREAKING ONE.
WE WOULDN'T BE ABLE TO WITHSTAND OTHERS LIKE THAT KNIGHT COMING TO DESTROY THE CORE.
WE'RE INVESTIGATING WHAT KIND OF QUESTS ARE CONNECTED TO THE DUNGEONS!
IS IT THIS CROWDED EVERY MORNING?

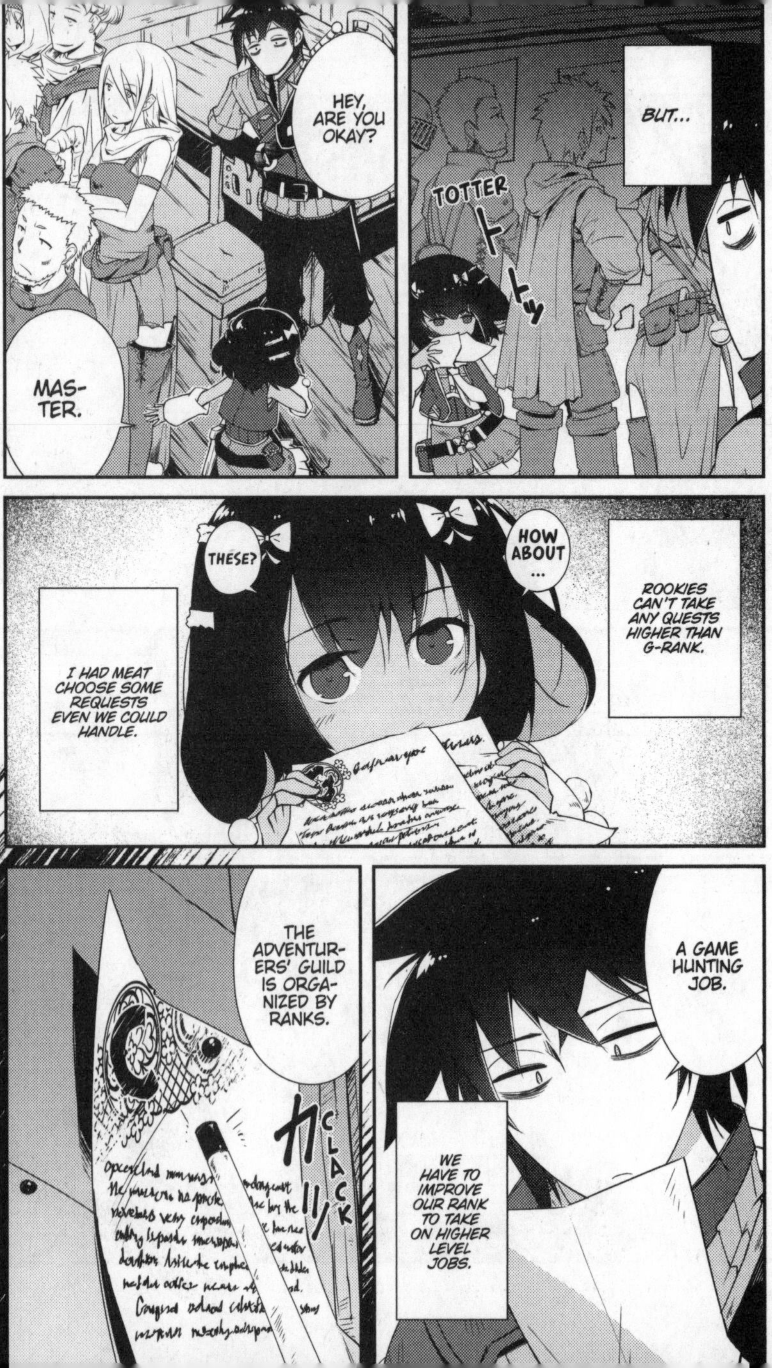
BUT...
TOTTER
トトッ
HEY, ARE YOU OKAY?
MAS-TER.
ROOKIES CAN'T TAKE ANY QUESTS HIGHER THAN G-RANK.
HOW ABOUT...
THESE?
I HAD MEAT CHOOSE SOME REQUESTS EVEN WE COULD HANDLE.
A GAME HUNTING JOB.
WE HAVE TO IMPROVE OUR RANK TO TAKE ON HIGHER LEVEL JOBS.
THE ADVENTURERS' GUILD IS ORGANIZED BY RANKS.
カッ
CLACK

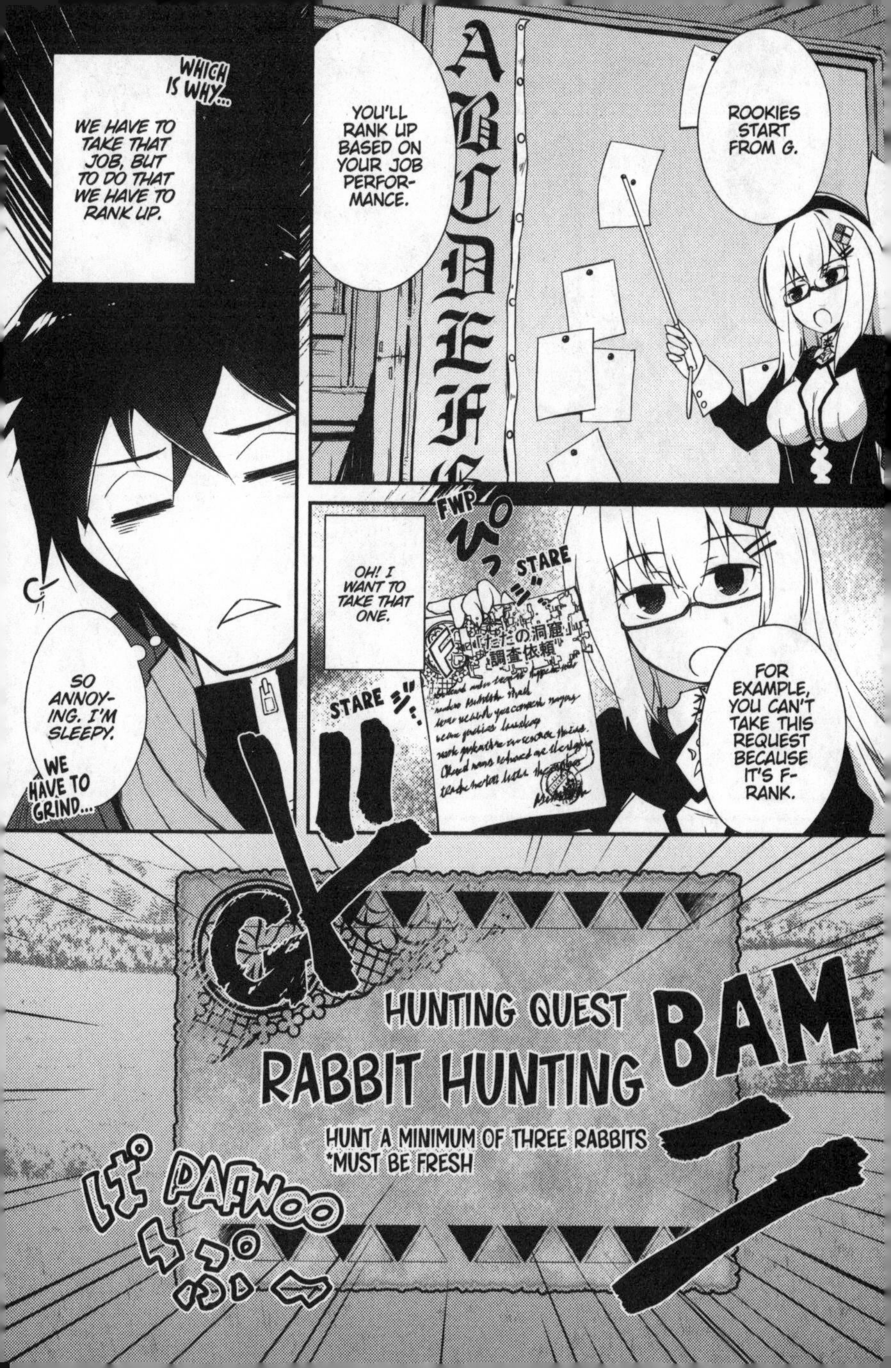
ROOKIES START FROM G.
YOU'LL RANK UP BASED ON YOUR JOB PERFORMANCE.
A B C D E F G
FOR EXAMPLE, YOU CAN'T TAKE THIS REQUEST BECAUSE IT'S F-RANK.
FWP
STARE
「ただの洞窟」調査依頼
STARE
OH! I WANT TO TAKE THAT ONE.
WHICH IS WHY...
WE HAVE TO TAKE THAT JOB, BUT TO DO THAT WE HAVE TO RANK UP.
SO ANNOYING. I'M SLEEPY.
WE HAVE TO GRIND...
BAM
G
HUNTING QUEST
RABBIT HUNTING
HUNT A MINIMUM OF THREE RABBITS
*MUST BE FRESH
PAFWOO

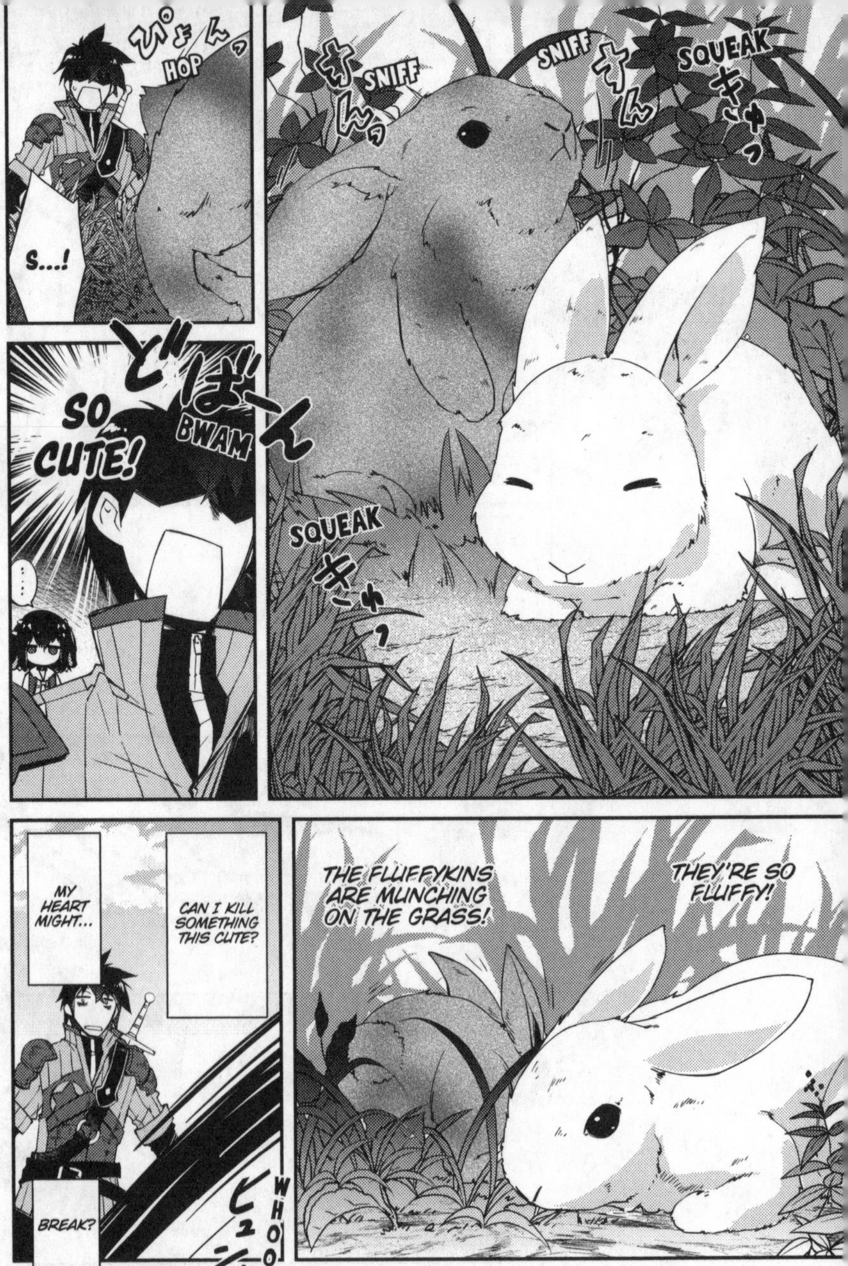
SNIFF
SNIFF
SQUEAK
SQUEAK
HOP
S...!
SO CUTE!
BWAM
...
THEY'RE SO FLUFFY!
THE FLUFFYKINS ARE MUNCHING ON THE GRASS!
CAN I KILL SOMETHING THIS CUTE?
MY HEART MIGHT...
BREAK?
WHOOSH

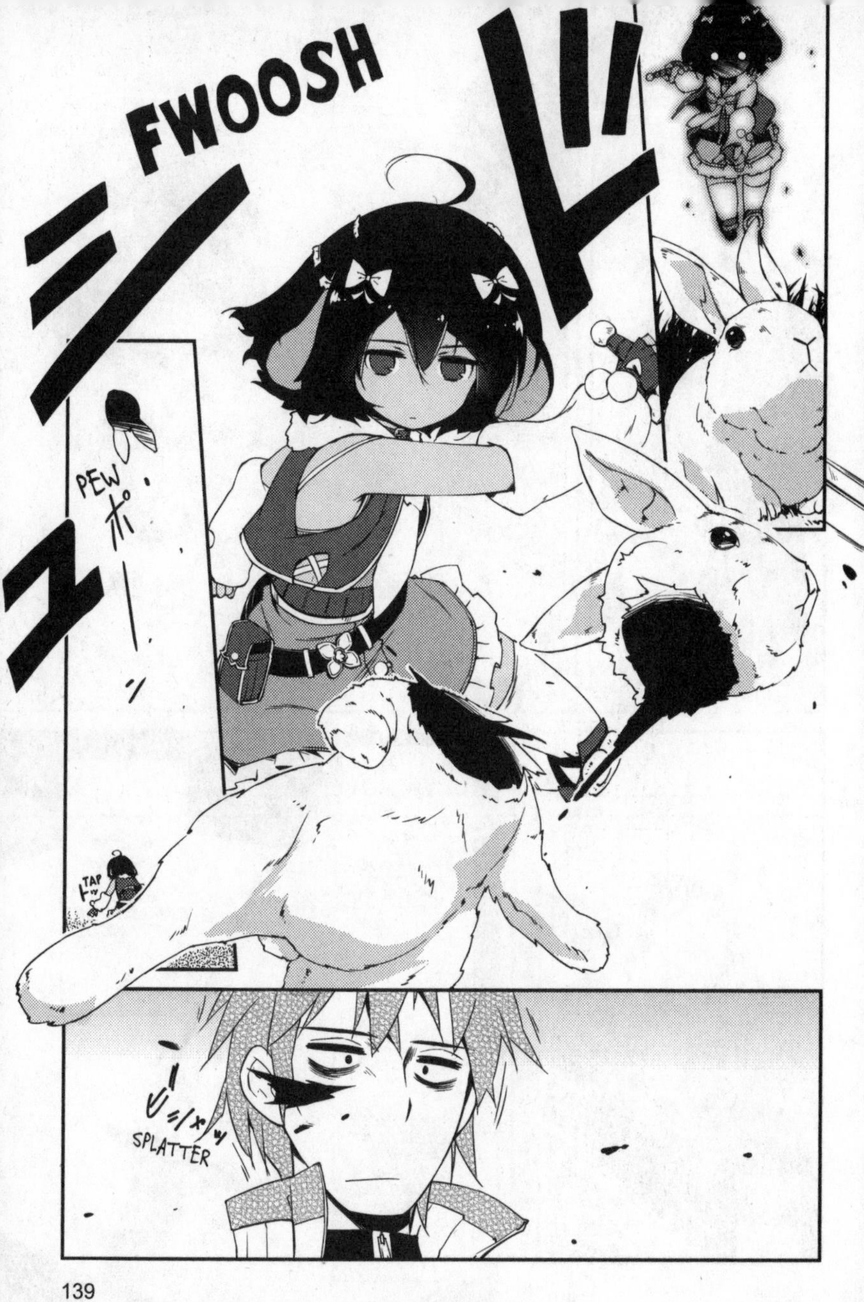
FWOOSH
ズドド
PEW
ポ
TAP
SPLATTER

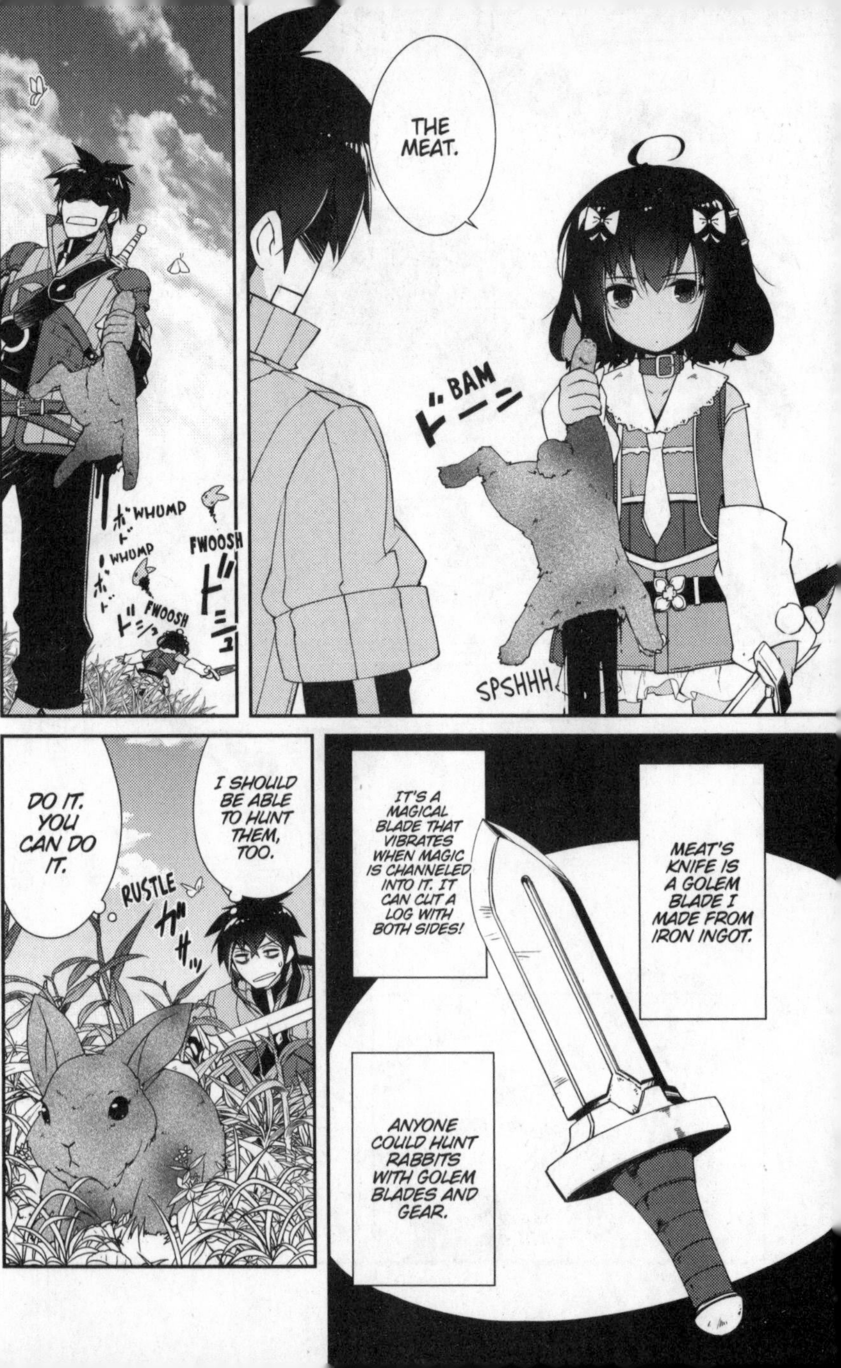
THE MEAT.
BAM
SPSHHH
WHUMP
WHUMP
FWOOSH
FWOOSH
MEAT'S KNIFE IS A GOLEM BLADE I MADE FROM IRON INGOT.
IT'S A MAGICAL BLADE THAT VIBRATES WHEN MAGIC IS CHANNELED INTO IT. IT CAN CUT A LOG WITH BOTH SIDES!
ANYONE COULD HUNT RABBITS WITH GOLEM BLADES AND GEAR.
I SHOULD BE ABLE TO HUNT THEM, TOO.
DO IT. YOU CAN DO IT.
RUSTLE

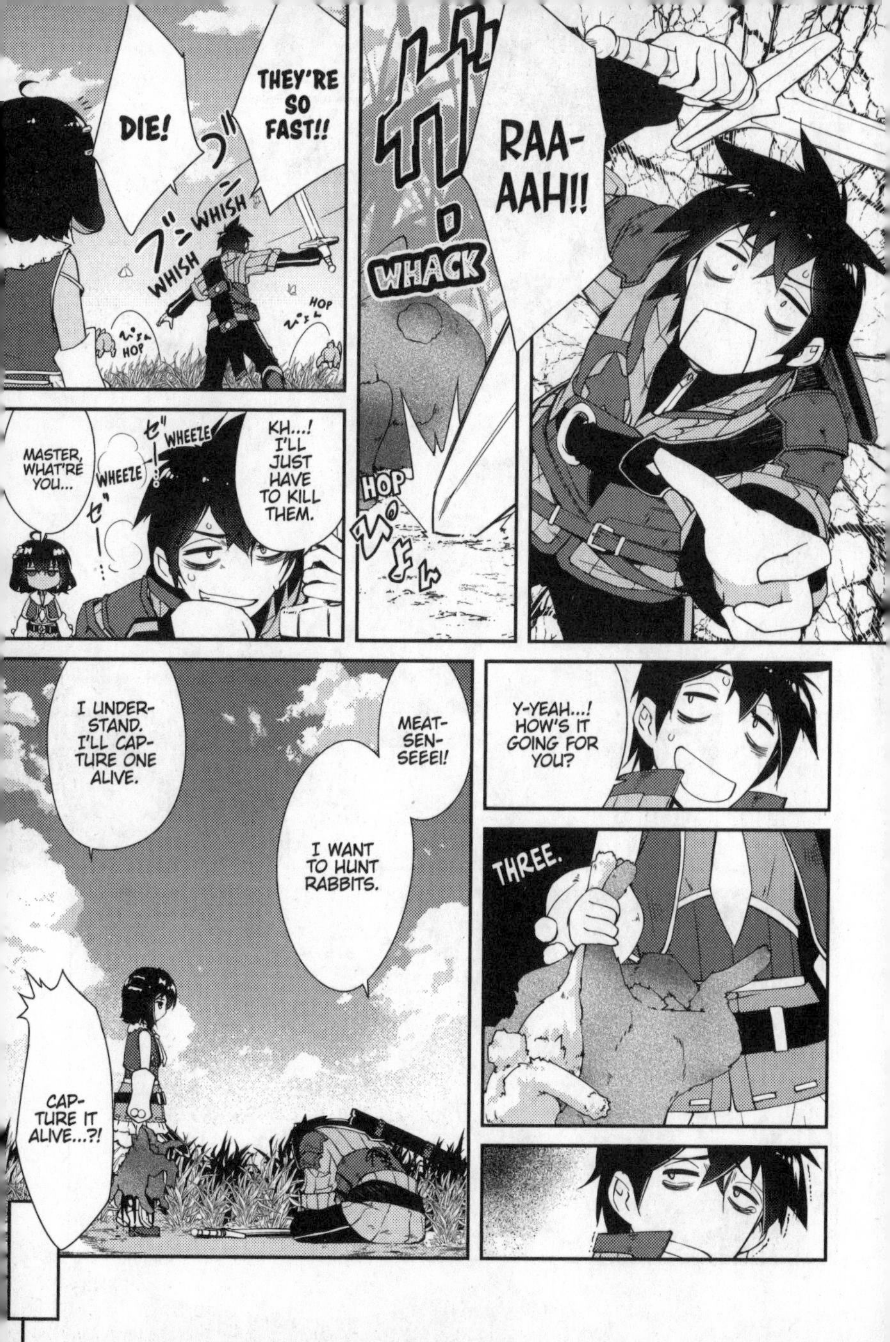
RAA-AAH!!
WHACK
HOP
THEY'RE SO FAST!!
DIE!
WHISH
WHISH
HOP
HOP
KH...! I'LL JUST HAVE TO KILL THEM.
WHEEZE
WHEEZE
MASTER, WHAT'RE YOU...
Y-YEAH...! HOW'S IT GOING FOR YOU?
THREE.
MEAT-SEN-SEEEI!
I WANT TO HUNT RABBITS.
I UNDER-STAND. I'LL CAP-TURE ONE ALIVE.
CAP-TURE IT ALIVE...?!

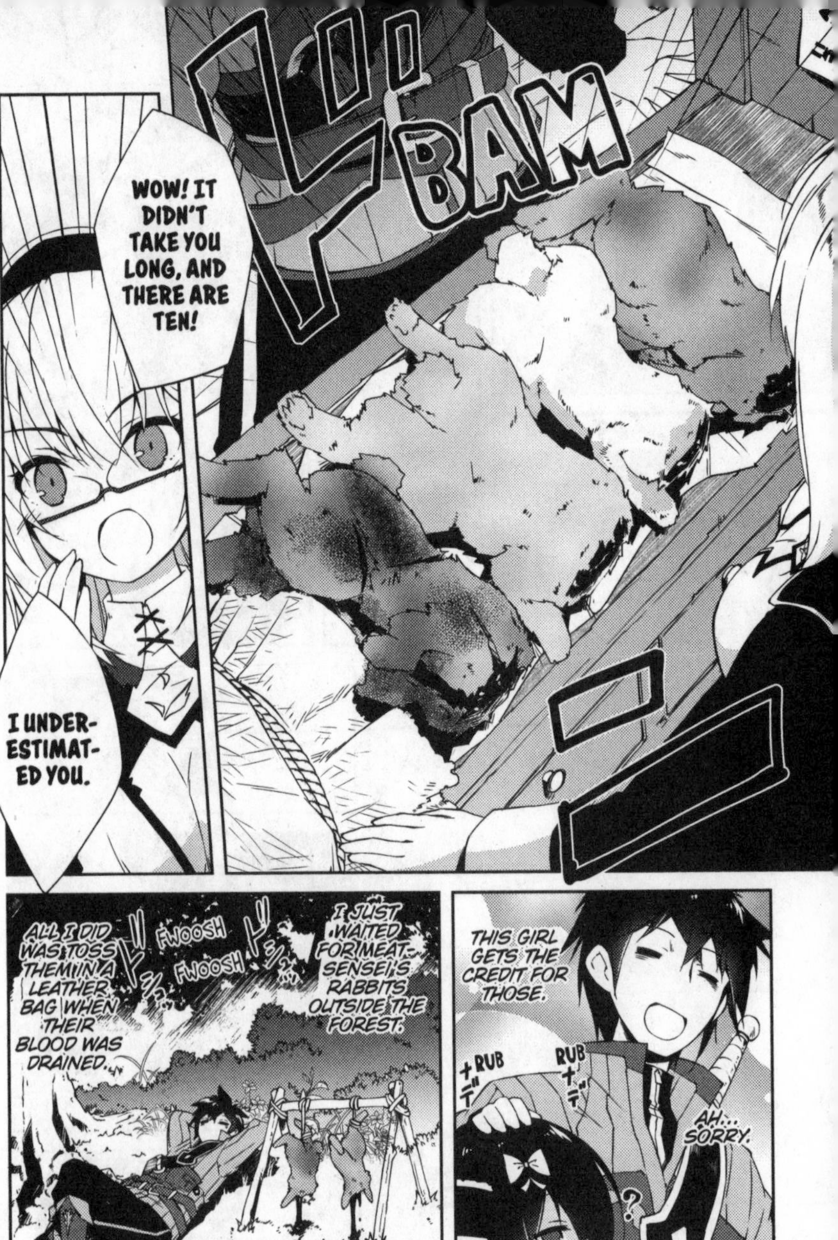
BAM
WOW! IT DIDN'T TAKE YOU LONG, AND THERE ARE TEN!
I UNDER-ESTIMAT-ED YOU.
THIS GIRL GETS THE CREDIT FOR THOSE.
RUB
RUB
AH... SORRY.
I JUST WAITED FOR MEAT-SENSEI'S RABBITS OUTSIDE THE FOREST.
FWOOSH
FWOOSH
ALL I DID WAS TOSS THEM IN A LEATHER BAG WHEN THEIR BLOOD WAS DRAINED.

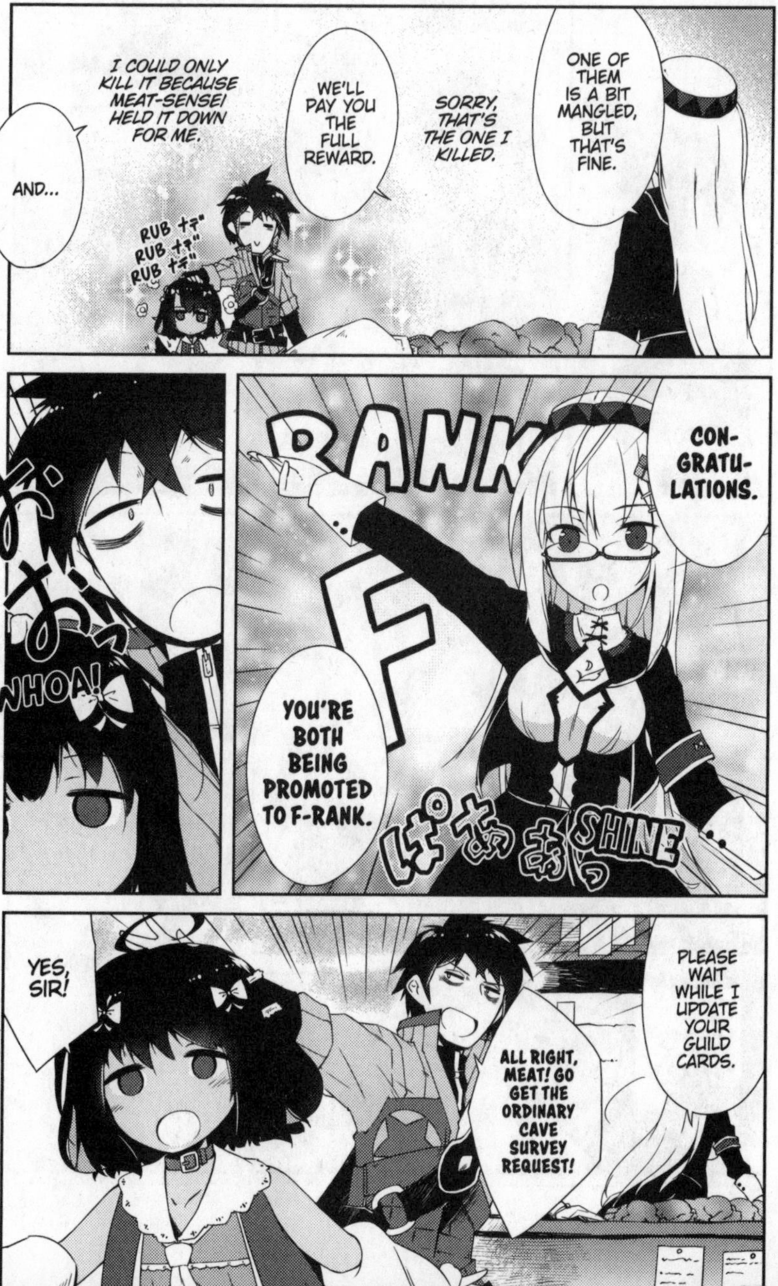
ONE OF THEM IS A BIT MANGLED, BUT THAT'S FINE.
SORRY, THAT'S THE ONE I KILLED.
WE'LL PAY YOU THE FULL REWARD.
I COULD ONLY KILL IT BECAUSE MEAT-SENSEI HELD IT DOWN FOR ME.
AND...
RUB RUB RUB
RANK F
CONGRATULATIONS.
YOU'RE BOTH BEING PROMOTED TO F-RANK.
SHINE
WHOA!
PLEASE WAIT WHILE I UPDATE YOUR GUILD CARDS.
ALL RIGHT, MEAT! GO GET THE ORDINARY CAVE SURVEY REQUEST!
YES, SIR!

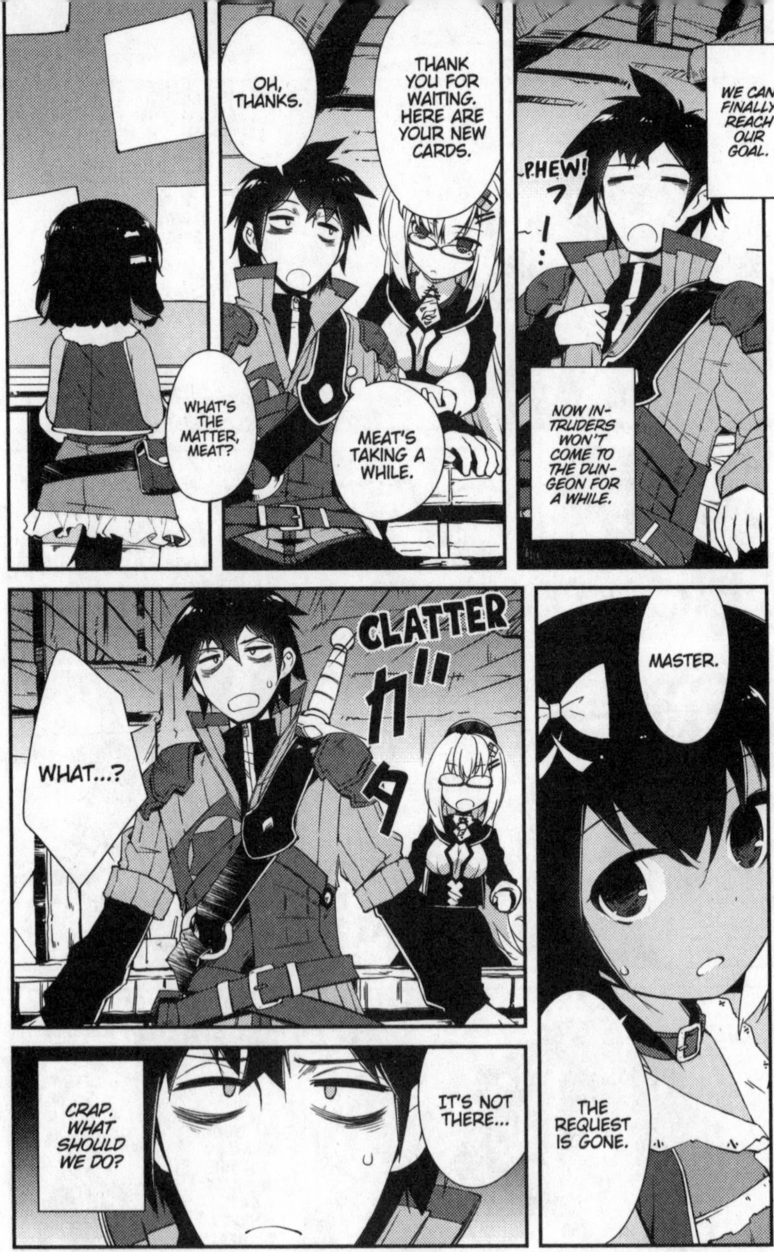
~PHEW!
WE CAN FINALLY REACH OUR GOAL.
NOW INTRUDERS WON'T COME TO THE DUNGEON FOR A WHILE.
THANK YOU FOR WAITING. HERE ARE YOUR NEW CARDS.
OH, THANKS.
MEAT'S TAKING A WHILE.
WHAT'S THE MATTER, MEAT?
MASTER.
THE REQUEST IS GONE.
CLATTER
ガタ
WHAT...?
IT'S NOT THERE...
CRAP. WHAT SHOULD WE DO?

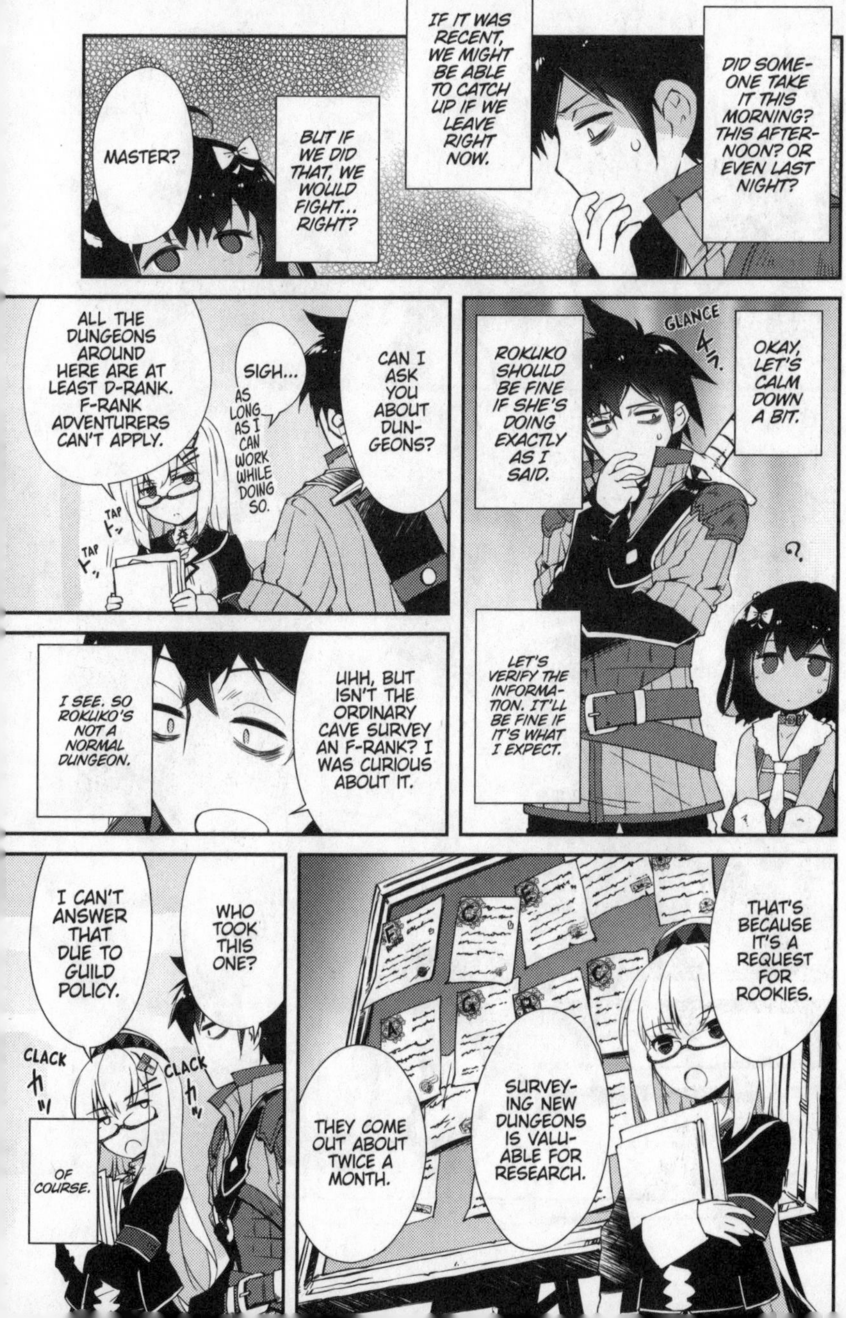
DID SOME-ONE TAKE IT THIS MORNING? THIS AFTER-NOON? OR EVEN LAST NIGHT?
IF IT WAS RECENT, WE MIGHT BE ABLE TO CATCH UP IF WE LEAVE RIGHT NOW.
BUT IF WE DID THAT, WE WOULD FIGHT... RIGHT?
MASTER?
OKAY, LET'S CALM DOWN A BIT.
GLANCE
ROKUKO SHOULD BE FINE IF SHE'S DOING EXACTLY AS I SAID.
LET'S VERIFY THE INFORMA-TION. IT'LL BE FINE IF IT'S WHAT I EXPECT.
CAN I ASK YOU ABOUT DUN-GEONS?
SIGH...
AS LONG AS I CAN WORK WHILE DOING SO.
TAP
TAP
ALL THE DUNGEONS AROUND HERE ARE AT LEAST D-RANK. F-RANK ADVENTURERS CAN'T APPLY.
UHH, BUT ISN'T THE ORDINARY CAVE SURVEY AN F-RANK? I WAS CURIOUS ABOUT IT.
I SEE. SO ROKUKO'S NOT A NORMAL DUNGEON.
THAT'S BECAUSE IT'S A REQUEST FOR ROOKIES.
SURVEY-ING NEW DUNGEONS IS VALU-ABLE FOR RESEARCH.
THEY COME OUT ABOUT TWICE A MONTH.
WHO TOOK THIS ONE?
I CAN'T ANSWER THAT DUE TO GUILD POLICY.
CLACK
CLACK
OF COURSE.

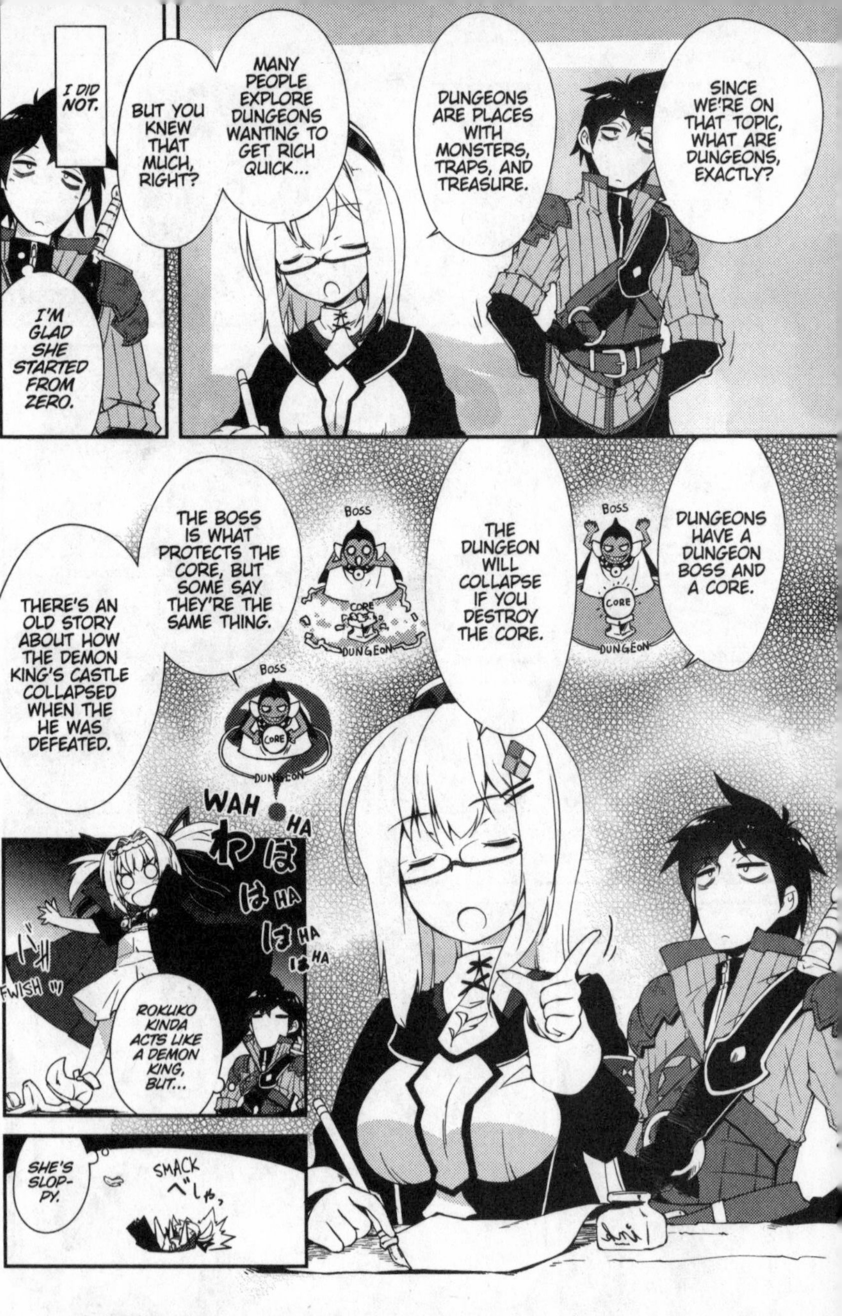

SINCE WE'RE ON THAT TOPIC, WHAT ARE DUNGEONS, EXACTLY?
DUNGEONS ARE PLACES WITH MONSTERS, TRAPS, AND TREASURE.
MANY PEOPLE EXPLORE DUNGEONS WANTING TO GET RICH QUICK...
BUT YOU KNEW THAT MUCH, RIGHT?
I DID NOT.
I'M GLAD SHE STARTED FROM ZERO.
DUNGEONS HAVE A DUNGEON BOSS AND A CORE.
BOSS
CORE
DUNGEON
THE DUNGEON WILL COLLAPSE IF YOU DESTROY THE CORE.
BOSS
CORE
DUNGEON
THE BOSS IS WHAT PROTECTS THE CORE, BUT SOME SAY THEY'RE THE SAME THING.
BOSS
CORE
DUNGEON
THERE'S AN OLD STORY ABOUT HOW THE DEMON KING'S CASTLE COLLAPSED WHEN THE HE WAS DEFEATED.
WAH HA HA HA HA
わははははは
FWISH
ROKUKO KINDA ACTS LIKE A DEMON KING, BUT...
SHE'S SLOP-PY.
SMACK
べしゃ

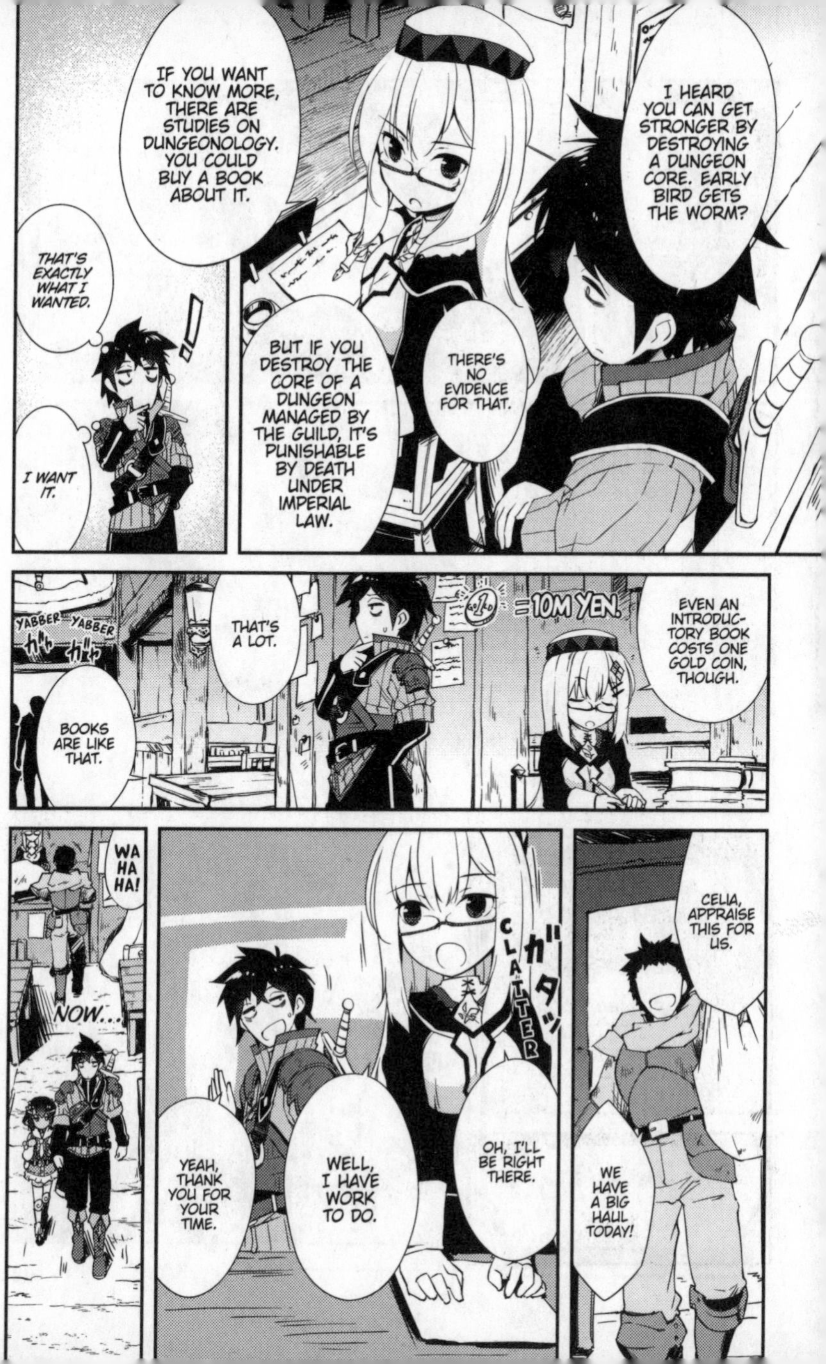

I HEARD YOU CAN GET STRONGER BY DESTROYING A DUNGEON CORE. EARLY BIRD GETS THE WORM?
THERE'S NO EVIDENCE FOR THAT.
BUT IF YOU DESTROY THE CORE OF A DUNGEON MANAGED BY THE GUILD, IT'S PUNISHABLE BY DEATH UNDER IMPERIAL LAW.
IF YOU WANT TO KNOW MORE, THERE ARE STUDIES ON DUNGEONOLOGY. YOU COULD BUY A BOOK ABOUT IT.
THAT'S EXACTLY WHAT I WANTED.
!
I WANT IT.
EVEN AN INTRODUCTORY BOOK COSTS ONE GOLD COIN, THOUGH.
=10M YEN.
THAT'S A LOT.
BOOKS ARE LIKE THAT.
YABBER YABBER
CELIA, APPRAISE THIS FOR US.
WE HAVE A BIG HAUL TODAY!
CLATTER
OH, I'LL BE RIGHT THERE.
WELL, I HAVE WORK TO DO.
YEAH, THANK YOU FOR YOUR TIME.
WA HA HA!
NOW...

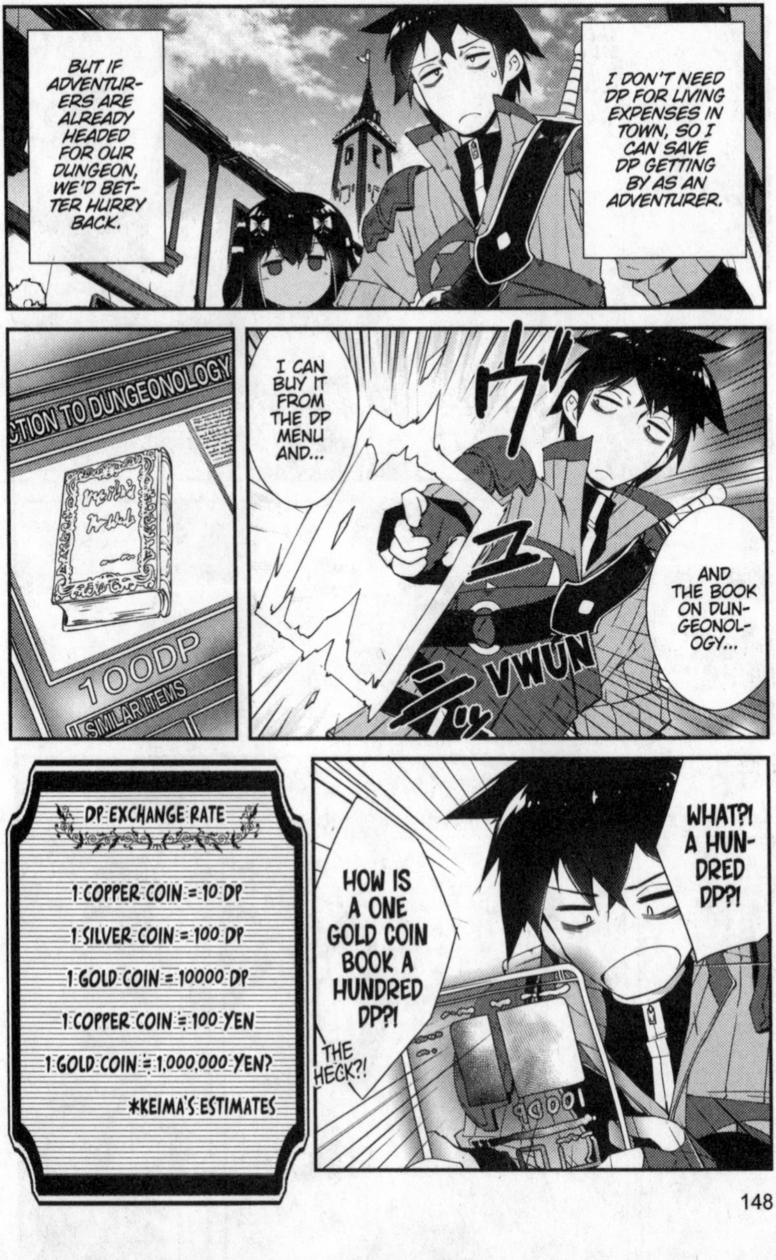
I DON'T NEED DP FOR LIVING EXPENSES IN TOWN, SO I CAN SAVE DP GETTING BY AS AN ADVENTURER.
BUT IF ADVENTURERS ARE ALREADY HEADED FOR OUR DUNGEON, WE'D BETTER HURRY BACK.
I CAN BUY IT FROM THE DP MENU AND...
AND THE BOOK ON DUNGEONOLOGY...
VWUN
CTION TO DUNGEONOLOGY
100DP
SIMILAR ITEMS
WHAT?! A HUNDRED DP?!
HOW IS A ONE GOLD COIN BOOK A HUNDRED DP?!
THE HECK?!
DP EXCHANGE RATE
1 COPPER COIN = 10 DP
1 SILVER COIN = 100 DP
1 GOLD COIN = 10000 DP
1 COPPER COIN ≒ 100 YEN
1 GOLD COIN ≒ 1,000,000 YEN?
*KEIMA'S ESTIMATES

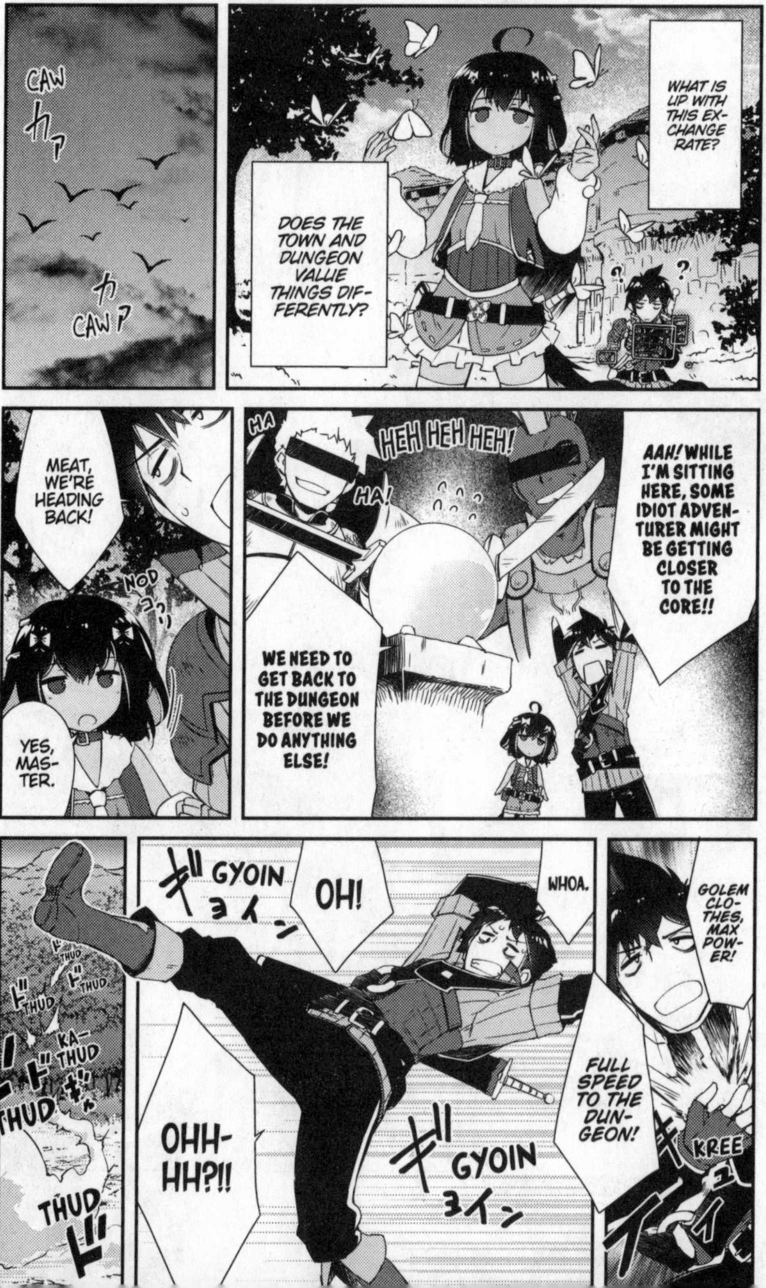
WHAT IS UP WITH THIS EX-CHANGE RATE?
DOES THE TOWN AND DUNGEON VALUE THINGS DIF-FERENTLY?
? ?
CAW カァ
カァ CAW
HA
HEH HEH HEH!
HA!
AAH! WHILE I'M SITTING HERE, SOME IDIOT ADVEN-TURER MIGHT BE GETTING CLOSER TO THE CORE!!
WE NEED TO GET BACK TO THE DUNGEON BEFORE WE DO ANYTHING ELSE!
MEAT, WE'RE HEADING BACK!
NOD コク
YES, MASTER.
GOLEM CLO-THES, MAX POW-ER!
FULL SPEED TO THE DUN-GEON!
KREE
WHOA.
GYOIN
OH!
OHH-HH?!!
GYOIN
THUD
THUD
THUD
THUD
KA-THUD
THUD
THUD

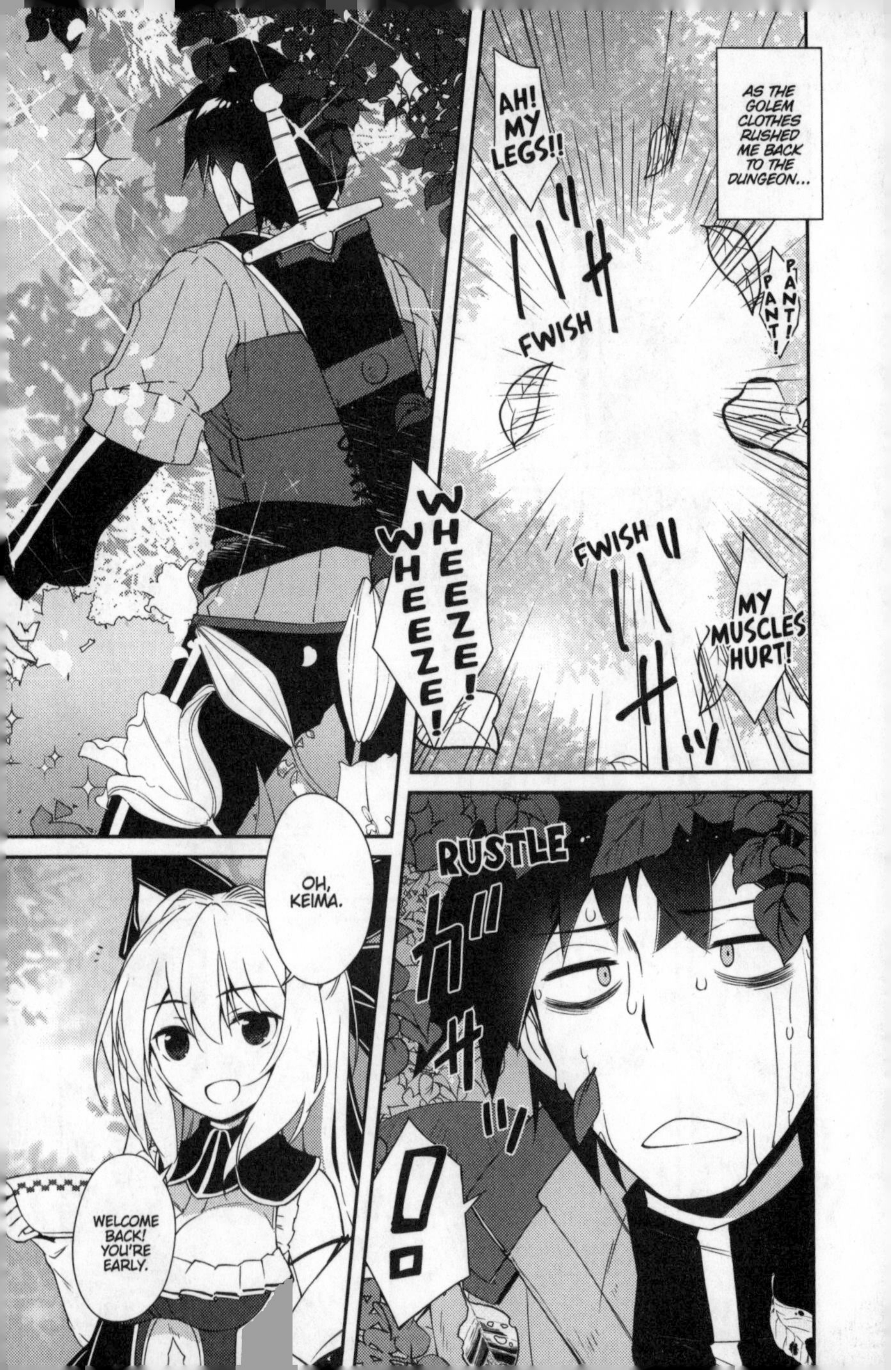

AS THE GOLEM CLOTHES RUSHED ME BACK TO THE DUNGEON...
AH! MY LEGS!!
FWISH
PANT! PANT!
FWISH
MY MUSCLES HURT!
WHEEZE! WHEEZE!
RUSTLE
ガサッ
OH, KEIMA.
WELCOME BACK! YOU'RE EARLY.

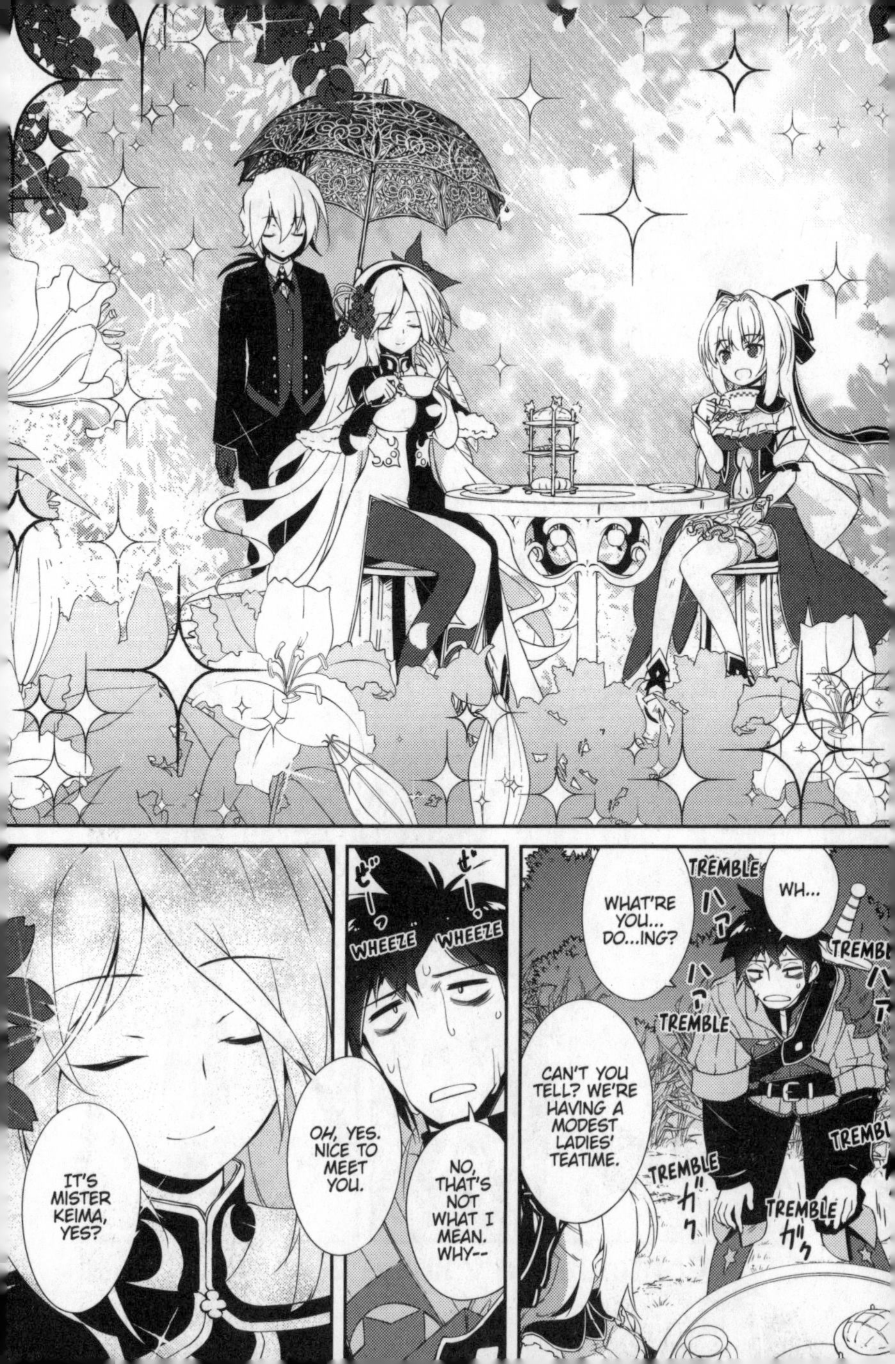
TREMBLE
WH...
WHAT'RE YOU... DO...ING?
TREMBLE
TREMBLE
CAN'T YOU TELL? WE'RE HAVING A MODEST LADIES' TEATIME.
TREMBLE
TREMBLE
TREMBLE
WHEEZE
WHEEZE
NO, THAT'S NOT WHAT I MEAN. WHY--
OH, YES. NICE TO MEET YOU.
IT'S MISTER KEIMA, YES?

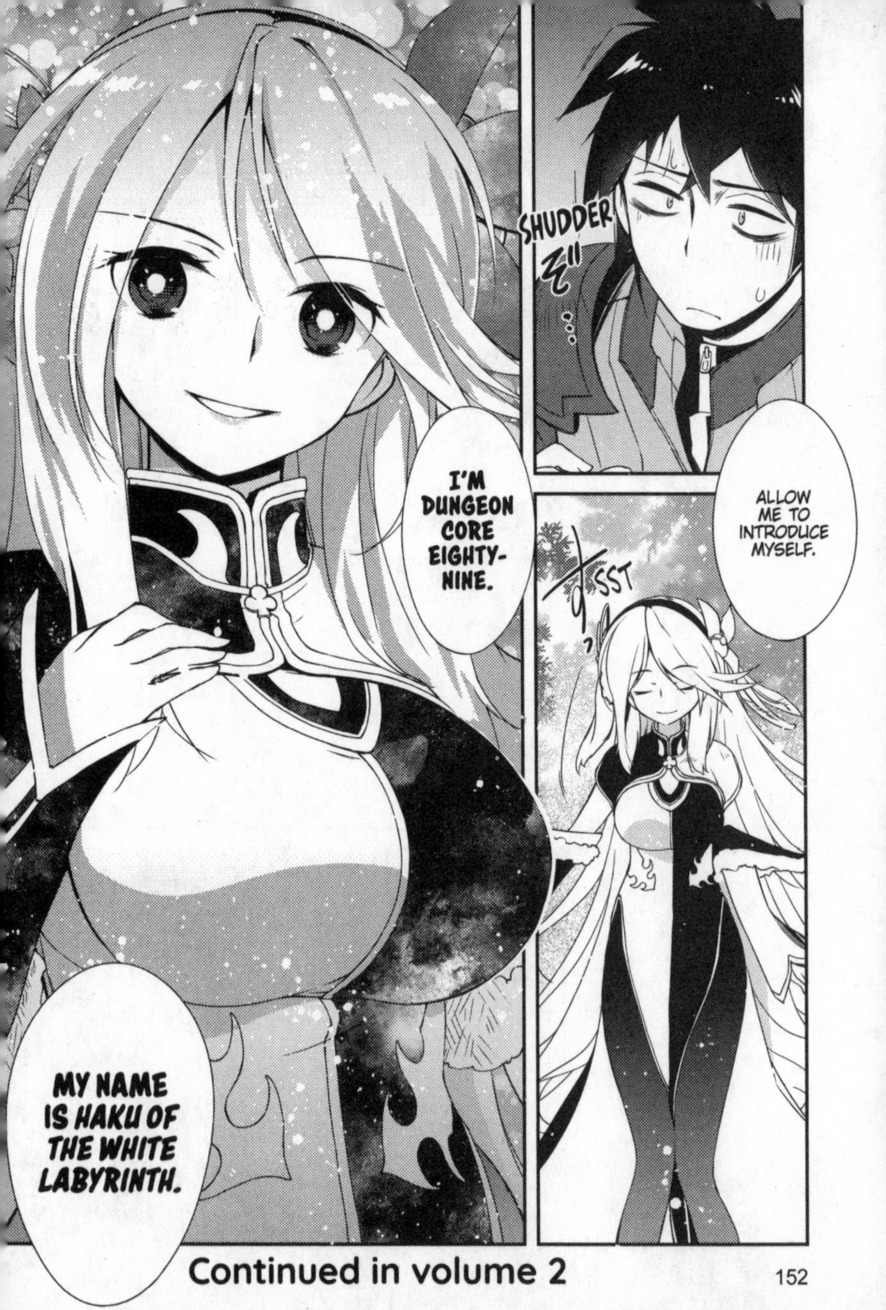
SHUDDER
ALLOW ME TO INTRODUCE MYSELF.
SST
I'M DUNGEON CORE EIGHTY-NINE.
MY NAME IS HAKU OF THE WHITE LABYRINTH.

Continued in volume 2

LAZY DUNGEON MASTER

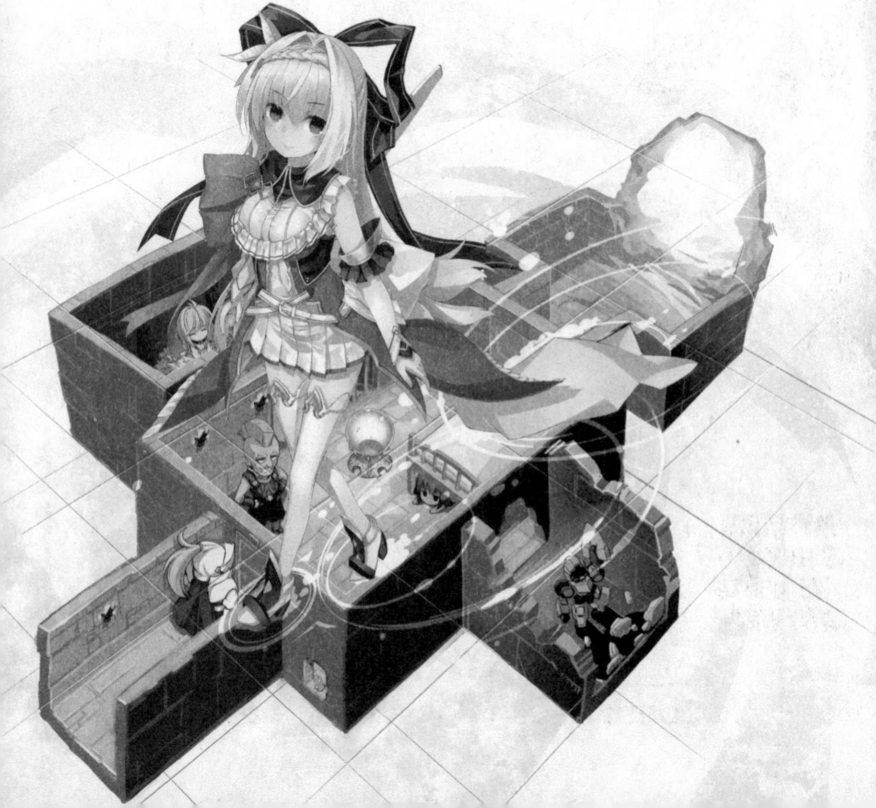

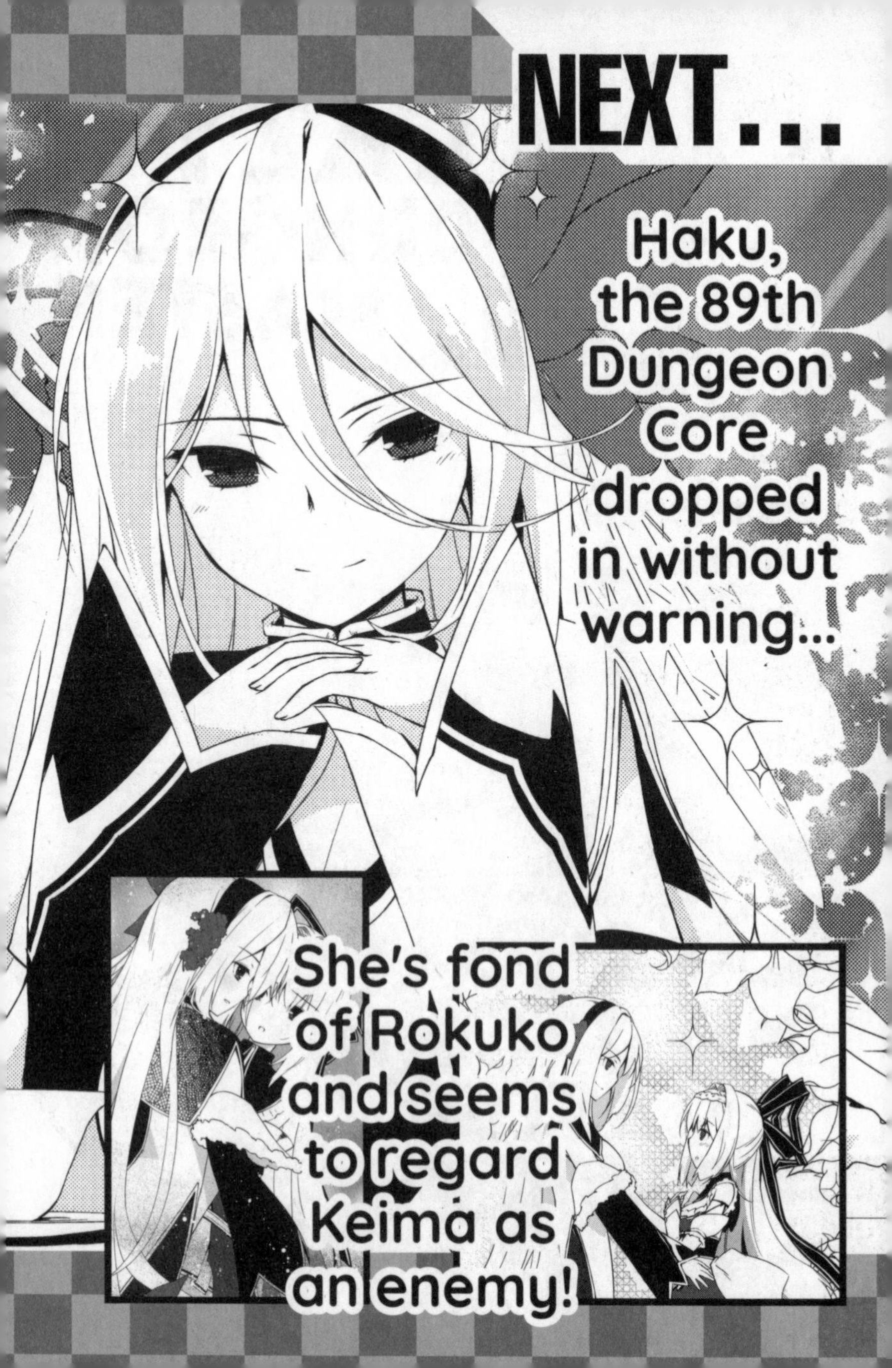
NEXT...
Haku, the 89th Dungeon Core dropped in without warning...
She's fond of Rokuko and seems to regard Keima as an enemy!

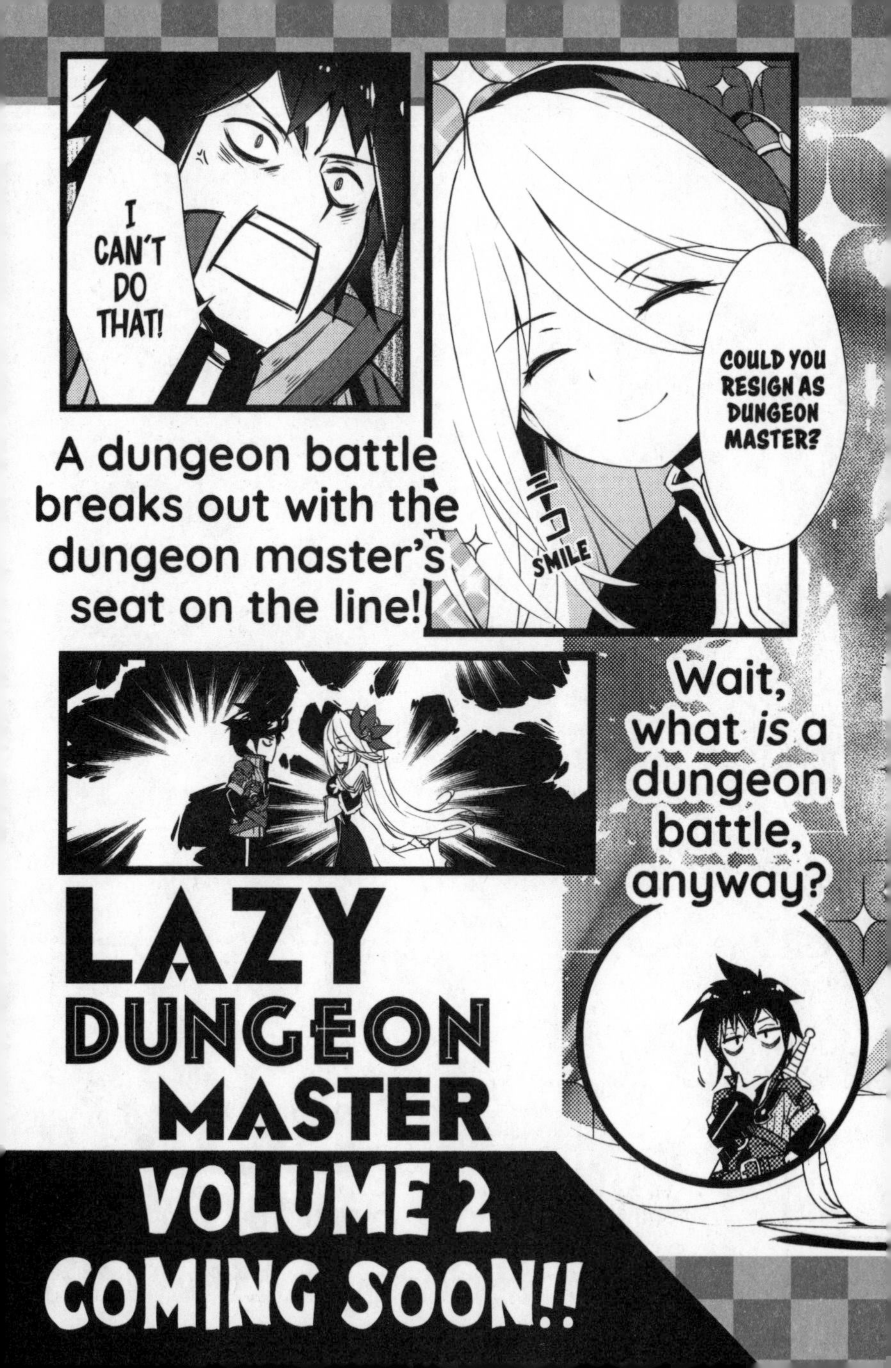
COULD YOU RESIGN AS DUNGEON MASTER?
SMILE
I CAN'T DO THAT!
A dungeon battle breaks out with the dungeon master's seat on the line!
Wait, what *is* a dungeon battle, anyway?
LAZY DUNGEON MASTER
VOLUME 2 COMING SOON!!

LAZY
DUNGEON
MASTER

Rabbit Meat Delivery from the Guild to the Butcher

Rabbit meat was delivered to the adventurers' guild and Celia, the guild receptionist, put it together and sold it to the butcher.

"Here's the rabbit meat you requested."

"Oh, Celia. Thanks again."

"And thank you for always putting in requests through the guild."

The man accepted the rabbit meat immediately and evaluated it.

"This is some good product! I can see the blood has been drained."

"The blood was drained? Um, that's when you hang the animal after chopping off its head, right?"

"Yes. I typically do it when I make meat from cattle and other livestock, but I don't usually drain the blood from rabbits. I didn't realize it right away. It's pretty unusual."

"Is it really that unusual? I thought people wouldn't bother to prep a rabbit like that."

By draining the blood, the unpleasant animal odor wouldn't be so strong. It improved the quality of the meat and made it easier to eat. That made sense for a large animal like cows, but Celia didn't think most people would bother with a tiny rabbit.

"Hm. I thought that you'd have some insight, but perhaps not."

"I'm sorry?"

Celia was a little angry at the butcher's words.

"That's right. It's usually G-rank adventurers—or at best E-rank rookies—hunt rabbits, right? Most of them don't know about draining blood unless they've worked here. And even if they do know, goblins are attracted to the smell of blood. You couldn't safely finish."

"Oh. Yes, I understand."

Celia was relieved. It'd be a catastrophe if a rookie was surrounded by goblins. But…it would take too long to bring the rabbits back and then drain the blood. It would be incredibly rare for there to be rabbit meat with the blood drained.

"It's easy to see no ordinary rookie took the job. Just look at the cuts on their necks. They lopped off their heads with one swing. No hesitation. Except on this one."

Glancing down, he looked at the single beat-up rabbit.

"You're right. This one looks like it was reluctantly killed by a timid kid. Probably a little girl who never hurt anything before but tried her best."

Celia nodded as she imagined a young, dog-eared girl who wielded a sword. This one rabbit made her want to praise the girl and say, "You did your best." She considered purchasing that rabbit for herself.

"Anyway, the rest are good quality. I'll throw in this one as a bonus and pay the full amount."

"Sure. Actually, they're so good even I'd like to throw in a bonus reward."

"That's true. I'll have to request a skilled adventurer if I wanted to obtain some blood-drained rabbits, after all. If the guy who hunted these brings more rabbits like this, tell him I'll buy them from him in batches of twenty, anytime. If you look at 'em and think they're good quality, then you can give them a bonus reward, too, Celia-chan."

"Understood. Shall I tell him he can bring them here directly?"

"Sure, I'll buy 'em here. As long as it's a proper guild request."

If an adventurer took their spoils directly to the butcher, the butcher and adventurer's share could split the profit without the adventurers' guild as a middle man. But the owner of the butcher shop decided to continue giving requests to the guild till the end.

Fulfilling a guild's request would earn an adventurer trust and achievement on top of money.

"Wouldn't it be better for you to continue asking for the lowest rank possible?"

"Gimme a break. An adventurer who decapitates a rabbit like this will surely rise above D-rank. I can't interfere with that."

"Well, that's certainly true. While it's frustrating, that man seems to have some ability, if nothing else."

In fact, on the day he registered as an adventurer, he was able to do chores like delivery requests smoothly. For an outsider to the town, he was able to navigate without getting lost.

Maybe he had a secret. Regardless, there was no doubt that he was an excellent adventurer, secret included.

"Do you know how delicious blood-drained rabbit meat is? Considering how long it takes to age, I'm looking forward to next week."

You shouldn't eat the meat you hunted right away. The meat should mature over time it become more flavorful. Depending on how the meat tasted, he might consider making a special request for it.

"I'll grill them on some skewers and sell them at a food stall I run for fun, so please come and eat some, Celia."

"Sure. I'll go when I have some time. While I'm here, I'd like that beat-up rabbit meat."

"The taste won't be that much different since it was also drained of blood, but are you sure you want it?"

"I do. It looks like it'll taste like the hard work of an adventurer. Hee hee hee! I'm looking forward to eating it."

"Ha ha ha. As expected of the guild's receptionist. I'll set it aside for you."

Celia imagined the flavor of next week's rabbit. "What will rabbit meat hunted by an angelic girl taste like?" She wondered.

Afterword

Heyo! The manga version has finally been made into a book! I started the web series about four years ago, so it feels like, "I've finally come this far." I'd like to make this into an anime one day. And I want someone to make a fanfic doujinshi. That's what I feel like right now.

Okay, that brings us to my manga artist Nanaroku-san. Thank you for your continued support. I have them fill in the parts where the novel lacks description when I need it. They all fit Rokuko, Keima, and Meat nicely. Oh, but about the goblin's nose. I'm sorry. I missed that when checking it over. In the novel, I wrote that their noses are smashed. I think I'm going to have them use this nose going forward. Yes, Gobby's nose is splendid. But, in comparison with Rokuko's sudden growth between the web version → book version, it's a very small difference. The development has changed a little too, so it's an error. Just an error, but also for a bit of drama.

In addition, although it's a new story for this book, the side story is based on the manga version, but it's formatted so that you can enjoy it separately from the comic. Please note that it may not be enough for some of you if you were expecting a bonus like something from the novel (post-approval).

Well, I'll leave it at that since there's no more space for my afterword. Volume 10 of the novel will be going on sale at the same time. I hope you read it as well!

Supana Onikage

Afterword

When I obtained a sample of *The Lazy Dungeon Master*, I was taken in by it and read all the volumes in one go. There's something interesting going on in each spread, so it's difficult to create a storyboard. But, as a comedy-lover, I thought, "I want to put all the interesting parts in there," so I did my best. This will be my first manga with an original story, but I hope you like it.

By the way, my favorite bedding that I've been using lately is a mattress that's said to give you support with these bumpy hard sponge points. It's so nice. When I'm drowsy and half-awake, it's a bedding of the gods that allows me to keep sleeping for twelve hours. It's too bad I can't get work done. But, it also has its weaknesses. I can't use it like how I've drawn in the illustration at the bottom of the page. Anyway, please go to the store, find one, and try it out. It's an amazing thing.

Supana Onikage-sensei, Youta-sensei.
The Lazy Dungeon Master is so interesting.
Keep up the good work!

Nanaroku

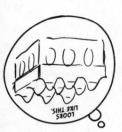

LOOKS LIKE THIS.

Assistants:　Ren Otsuki　Raku Gaki

I'M HUMAN. IT'S NICE TO LEAN ON IT AND BE LAZY.

LAZY DUNGEON MASTER

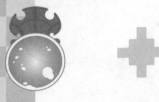

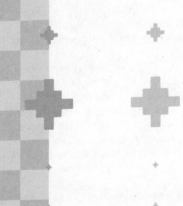

SEVEN SEAS ENTERTAINMENT PRESENTS

LAZY DUNGEON MASTER

story by **SUPANA ONIKAGE** art by **NANAROKU** character designs by **YOUTA** **VOLUME ONE**

TRANSLATION
Jessica Latherow

LETTERING
Jamil Stewart

COVER DESIGN
H. Qi

PROOFREADER
James Rhoden

SENIOR COPY EDITOR
Dawn Davis

EDITOR
Drew Taenaye

PRODUCTION DESIGNER
Christina McKenzie

PRODUCTION MANAGER
Lissa Pattillo

PREPRESS TECHNICIAN
Jules Valera

PRINT MANAGER
Rhiannon Rasmussen-Silverstein

EDITOR-IN-CHIEF
Julie Davis

ASSOCIATE PUBLISHER
Adam Arnold

PUBLISHER
Jason DeAngelis

Lazy Dungeon Master (Manga) Vol. 1

Seven Seas press and purchase enquiries can be sent to Marketing Manager Lianne Sentar at press@gomanga.com. Information regarding the distribution and purchase of digital editions is available from Digital Manager CK Russell at digital@gomanga.com.

ISBN: 978-1-63858-586-2
Printed in Canada
First Printing: September 2022
10 9 8 7 6 5 4 3 2 1

READING DIRECTIONS

This book reads from ***right to left***, Japanese style. If this is your first time reading manga, you start reading from the top right panel on each page and take it from there. If you get lost, just follow the numbered diagram here. It may seem backwards at first, but you'll get the hang of it! Have fun!!

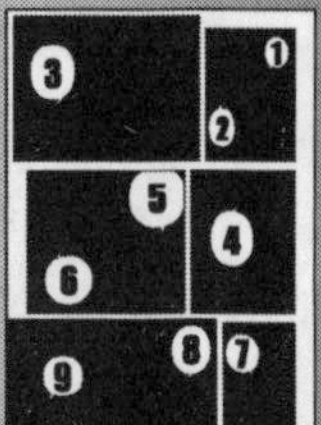

Follow us online: www.SevenSeasEntertainment.com